AF808678

LAW LIBRARY
GOLDEN GATE UNIVERSITY

LAW, CRIME AND LAW ENFORCEMENT

ILLEGAL ALIENS

ENFORCEMENT AND RESTRICTIONS BY STATE AND LOCALITIES

LAW, CRIME AND LAW ENFORCEMENT

Additional books in this series can be found on Nova's website under the Series tab.

Additional e-books in this series can be found on Nova's website under the e-book tab.

AMERICAN POLITICAL, ECONOMIC, AND SECURITY ISSUES

Additional books in this series can be found on Nova's website under the Series tab.

Additional e-books in this series can be found on Nova's website under the e-book tab.

LAW, CRIME AND LAW ENFORCEMENT

Illegal Aliens

Enforcement and Restrictions by State and Localities

Kelly Downs
and
Delmer Rasmussen
Editors

Nova Science Publishers, Inc.
New York

LAW LIBRARY
OCT 16 2012
GOLDEN GATE UNIVERSITY

Copyright © 2012 by Nova Science Publishers, Inc.

All rights reserved. No part of this book may be reproduced, stored in a retrieval system or transmitted in any form or by any means: electronic, electrostatic, magnetic, tape, mechanical photocopying, recording or otherwise without the written permission of the Publisher.

For permission to use material from this book please contact us:
Telephone 631-231-7269; Fax 631-231-8175
Web Site: http://www.novapublishers.com

NOTICE TO THE READER

The Publisher has taken reasonable care in the preparation of this book, but makes no expressed or implied warranty of any kind and assumes no responsibility for any errors or omissions. No liability is assumed for incidental or consequential damages in connection with or arising out of information contained in this book. The Publisher shall not be liable for any special, consequential, or exemplary damages resulting, in whole or in part, from the readers' use of, or reliance upon, this material. Any parts of this book based on government reports are so indicated and copyright is claimed for those parts to the extent applicable to compilations of such works.

Independent verification should be sought for any data, advice or recommendations contained in this book. In addition, no responsibility is assumed by the publisher for any injury and/or damage to persons or property arising from any methods, products, instructions, ideas or otherwise contained in this publication.

This publication is designed to provide accurate and authoritative information with regard to the subject matter covered herein. It is sold with the clear understanding that the Publisher is not engaged in rendering legal or any other professional services. If legal or any other expert assistance is required, the services of a competent person should be sought. FROM A DECLARATION OF PARTICIPANTS JOINTLY ADOPTED BY A COMMITTEE OF THE AMERICAN BAR ASSOCIATION AND A COMMITTEE OF PUBLISHERS.

Additional color graphics may be available in the e-book version of this book.

Library of Congress Cataloging-in-Publication Data

ISBN: 978-1-61942-631-3

Published by Nova Science Publishers, Inc. † New York

CONTENTS

PREFACE

This report discusses the power and ability of state and local authorities to assist in the enforcement of federal immigration law through the investigation and arrest of persons believed to have violated such laws. It describes federal statutes that expressly permit state and local police to enforce immigration law directly, and analyzes major cases concerning the ability of states and localities to assist in immigration enforcement.

Chapter 1 - The power to prescribe rules as to which aliens may enter the United States and which aliens may be removed resides solely with the federal government, and in particular with Congress. Concomitant to its exclusive power to determine which aliens may enter and which may stay in the country, the federal government also has the power to sanction activities that subvert this system. Congress has defined our nation's immigration laws in the Immigration and Nationality Act (INA), a comprehensive set of laws governing legal immigration, naturalization, work authorization, and the entry and removal of aliens. These requirements are bolstered by an enforcement regime containing both civil and criminal provisions. Deportation and associated administrative processes related to the removal of aliens are civil in nature, while certain violations of federal immigration law, such as smuggling unauthorized aliens into the country, carry criminal penalties. Congressional authority to prescribe rules on immigration does not necessarily imply exclusive authority to enforce those rules. In certain circumstances, Congress has expressly authorized states and localities to assist in enforcing federal immigration law. Moreover, there is a notion that has been articulated in some federal courts and by the executive branch that states may possess "inherent" authority to assist in the enforcement of federal immigration law, even in the absence of clear authorization by federal statute. Nonetheless, states may be precluded from taking actions if federal law would thereby be thwarted.

Chapter 2 - In May 2011, the Supreme Court ruled in Chamber of Commerce of the United States of America v. Whiting that federal immigration law did not preempt an Arizona statute that authorized or required the suspension or termination of the licenses of businesses that knowingly or intentionally hire unauthorized aliens, and also required that employers within Arizona use the federal government's E-Verify database to check employees' work authorization.

The doctrine of preemption derives from the Supremacy Clause of the U.S. Constitution, which establishes that federal law, treaties, and the Constitution itself are "the supreme Law of the Land." Thus, one essential aspect of the federal structure of government is that states can be precluded from taking actions that are otherwise within their authority if federal law is thereby thwarted. An act of Congress may preempt state or local action in a given area in any one of three ways: (1) the statute expressly states preemptive intent (express preemption); (2) a court concludes that Congress intended to occupy the regulatory field, thereby implicitly precluding state or local action in that area (field preemption); or (3) state or local action directly conflicts with or otherwise frustrates the purpose of the federal scheme (conflict preemption).

Chapter 3 - An estimated 37 million foreign-born persons currently reside in the United States, almost a third of whom may be present without legal authorization. The reaction of state and local jurisdictions to unauthorized immigration has varied. In some cases, states and localities have adopted measures intended to deter unlawfully present aliens from arriving and settling within their jurisdictions, including by restricting such aliens' access to work, housing, and benefits. Typically, such measures have sought to (1) limit the hiring and employment of unauthorized aliens, including through the denial of permits to persons that employ unauthorized aliens and the regulation of day labor centers; (2) restrict the ability of unlawfully present aliens to rent or occupy dwellings within the state or locality; and/or (3) deny unlawfully present aliens access to state or local services or benefits.

Chapter 4 - On April 23, 2010, Arizona enacted S.B. 1070, which is designed to discourage and deter the entry or presence of aliens who lack lawful status under federal immigration law. Potentially sweeping in effect, the measure requires state and local law enforcement officials to facilitate the detection of unauthorized aliens in their daily enforcement activities. The measure also establishes criminal penalties under state law, in addition to those already imposed under federal law, for alien smuggling offenses and failure to carry or complete alien registration documents. Further, it makes it a crime under Arizona law for an unauthorized alien to apply for or perform work in the state, either as an employee or an independent contractor.

In: Illegal Aliens
Editor: K. Downs and D. Rasmussen
ISBN: 978-1-61942-631-3
© 2012 Nova Science Publishers, Inc.

Chapter 1

AUTHORITY OF STATE AND LOCAL POLICE TO ENFORCE FEDERAL IMMIGRATION LAW*

Michael John Garcia and Kate M. Manuel

SUMMARY

The power to prescribe rules as to which aliens may enter the United States and which aliens may be removed resides solely with the federal government, and in particular with Congress. Concomitant to its exclusive power to determine which aliens may enter and which may stay in the country, the federal government also has the power to sanction activities that subvert this system. Congress has defined our nation's immigration laws in the Immigration and Nationality Act (INA), a comprehensive set of laws governing legal immigration, naturalization, work authorization, and the entry and removal of aliens. These requirements are bolstered by an enforcement regime containing both civil and criminal provisions. Deportation and associated administrative processes related to the removal of aliens are civil in nature, while certain violations of federal immigration law, such as smuggling unauthorized aliens into the country, carry criminal penalties. Congressional authority to prescribe rules on immigration does not necessarily imply exclusive authority to enforce those rules. In certain circumstances, Congress has expressly authorized states and localities to assist in enforcing federal

---

* This is an edited, reformatted and augmented version of a Congressional Research Service publication, CRS Report for Congress RL32292, from www.crs.gov, dated August 17, 2011.

immigration law. Moreover, there is a notion that has been articulated in some federal courts and by the executive branch that states may possess "inherent" authority to assist in the enforcement of federal immigration law, even in the absence of clear authorization by federal statute. Nonetheless, states may be precluded from taking actions if federal law would thereby be thwarted.

Recently, several states have enacted measures to facilitate the detection of unlawfully present aliens by state and local law enforcement officials. Some of these measures have been subject to legal challenge. The ability of state and local police to make arrests for federal immigration violations is a subject of ongoing legal debate and conflicting jurisprudence. Traditionally, the prevailing view has been that state and local police are permitted, to the extent allowed under state and local law, to enforce the criminal provisions of the INA. By contrast, the enforcement of the civil provisions, including the apprehension of deportable aliens, was viewed as a federal responsibility, with state and local police playing, at most, a supporting role. This view may be changing, however, as some courts have concluded that, at least in some instances, state and local police are not preempted from arresting persons on the grounds that they are deportable, even in the absence of express authorization by federal statute. The Department of Justice (DOJ) currently takes the view that state and local police are not always preempted from arresting persons for immigration violations. However, in legal challenges brought against Arizona and Alabama, it has argued that federal immigration law and policy impose some limitations upon the exercise of this authority by state and local officers.

This report discusses the authority of state and local law enforcement to assist in the enforcement of federal immigration law through the investigation and arrest of persons believed to have violated such laws. It describes federal statutes that expressly permit state and local police to enforce immigration law directly, analyzes major cases concerning the ability of states and localities to assist in immigration enforcement, and briefly examines opinions on the issue by the DOJ's Office of Legal Counsel. This report does not directly address legal issues raised by states and localities enacting their own immigration-related laws, including measures intended to supplement federal law through the imposition of additional criminal or civil penalties.

INTRODUCTION

The power to prescribe rules as to which aliens may enter the United States and which aliens may be removed resides solely with the federal government, and in particular with Congress.[1] Concomitant to its exclusive power to establish rules which determine which aliens may enter and which may stay in the country, the federal government also has the power to proscribe activities that subvert this system and establish penalties for those who undertake prohibited activities. These powers have primarily been implemented through the Immigration and Nationality Act of 1952, as amended (INA).[2] The INA establishes a comprehensive set of requirements for legal immigration, naturalization, and the removal of aliens, as well as rules governing aliens' continued presence in the United States. The INA also establishes an enforcement regime to deter violations of federal immigration law, including through the imposition of penalties upon persons who violate INA requirements.

In examining the INA, it is crucial to distinguish between its civil and criminal provisions. For example, the INA generally makes it a criminal offense for an alien to enter the United States without authorization,[3] with heightened penalties available in cases where an alien unlawfully reenters after having previously been ordered removed from the country.[4] Moreover, persons who transport unauthorized aliens into or within the United States, or harbor such aliens within the country, are generally subject to criminal penalty.[5]

On the other hand, some violations of the INA are subject to civil penalties.[6] For example, an entity that knowingly hires an alien who is not authorized to work in the United States may be subject to a civil monetary penalty.[7] Moreover, deportation and associated administrative processes related to the removal of aliens are civil in nature.[8] For example, an alien's unauthorized immigration status makes him removable, but absent additional factors (e.g., having reentered the United States after being formally removed), unlawful presence does not constitute a criminal offense.[9] In some cases, conduct may potentially be subject to both civil and criminal sanction under the INA. For instance, an alien who unlawfully enters the United States may be subject to criminal penalty as well as deportation. However, the fact that an alien may be subject to both criminal sanction and removal for an immigration violation does not mean that each tool shall be employed.[10]

Congressional authority to prescribe rules on immigration does not necessarily imply exclusive authority to enforce those rules.[11] Congress may expressly authorize states and localities to assist in enforcing federal law. Moreover, there is a notion that has been articulated in some federal courts and by the executive branch that states may possess "inherent" authority to assist in the enforcement of federal immigration law, even in the absence of express authorization by federal statute.

Nonetheless, state enforcement of federal immigration law must always be consistent with federal authority. The Supremacy Clause of the Constitution establishes that federal law, treaties, and the Constitution itself are "the supreme Law of the Land."[12] States can therefore be precluded from taking actions that are otherwise within their authority if federal law would thereby be thwarted. Congressional intent is paramount in the analysis as to whether federal law preempts state or local activity; accordingly, a court must determine whether Congress expressly or implicitly intended to preempt state or local action.[13] Generally, a court will determine that Congress intended to preempt a state regulation or activity when (1) Congress expresses preemptive intent in "explicit statutory language," (2) a state entity regulates "in a field that Congress intended the Federal Government to occupy exclusively," or (3) a state entity's activity "actually conflicts with federal law."[14] A question of ongoing legal dispute concerns whether state and local law enforcement may directly enforce federal immigration law, even in the absence of express authorization by federal statute, or whether they are generally preempted from such activity.

Recently, several states have enacted measures to facilitate the detection of unlawfully present aliens by state and local law enforcement officials. Many of these measures are the subject of ongoing litigation. The U.S. Department of Justice, in particular, has challenged measures enacted by Arizona and Alabama which are intended to deter the presence of unlawfully present aliens within their jurisdictions.

EXPRESS AUTHORIZATION FOR STATE AND LOCAL LAW ENFORCEMENT OFFICERS TO ENFORCE FEDERAL IMMIGRATION LAW

The enforcement of federal immigration law by state and local police is most clearly permissible when Congress has evidenced intent to authorize such activity.[15] In exercising its power to regulate immigration, Congress is free to delegate to the states, among other things, the authority to arrest, hold, and transport aliens into federal custody. Indeed, Congress has created several avenues for states and localities to assist in the enforcement of the federal immigration laws. The following sections discuss notable provisions in federal statutes that expressly authorize state and local law enforcement to directly engage in immigration enforcement activities, including arresting persons who have violated federal immigration law. This section does not discuss those provisions of federal law that, while contemplating participation by state and local authorities in immigration enforcement matters, do not directly authorize state and local police to perform immigration enforcement duties.[16]

Delegation of Immigration Enforcement Authority via Cooperative Agreement under INA Section 287(g)

One of the broadest grants of authority for state and local immigration enforcement activity stems from Section 133 of the Illegal Immigration Reform and Immigrant Responsibility Act of 1996 (IIRIRA), which amended INA Section 287 to permit the delegation of certain immigration enforcement functions to state and local officers. Pursuant to INA Section 287(g), the Attorney General (now the Secretary of Homeland Security[17]) is authorized

> to enter into a written agreement with a State, or any political subdivision of a State, pursuant to which an officer or employee of the State or subdivision, who is determined by the [Secretary of Homeland Security] to be qualified to perform a function of an immigration officer in relation to the investigation, apprehension, or detention of aliens in the United States (including the transportation of such aliens across State lines to detention centers), may carry out such function at the expense of the State or political subdivision and to the extent consistent with State and local law.[18]

Agreements entered pursuant to INA Section 287(g) (commonly referred to as "287(g) agreements") enable specially trained state or local officers to perform specific functions relative to the investigation, apprehension, or detention of aliens, during a predetermined time frame and under federal supervision.[19] In order for state or local officers to perform functions pursuant to a 287(g) agreement, they must "have knowledge of and adhere to" federal law governing immigration officers and be certified as having received "adequate training" regarding the enforcement of immigration laws.[20] State or local officers performing functions pursuant to 287(g) agreements are not considered federal employees, except for purposes relating to certain tort claims and compensation matters, but are considered to be acting under color of federal law for purposes of liability and immunity from suit in any civil actions brought under federal or state law.[21]

INA Section 287(g)(10) specifies that a written agreement is not required for state or local officials to engage in certain cooperative functions with federal immigration authorities (though these officials would not be entitled to the same rights and immunities as persons operating under a 287(g) agreement[22]). Specifically, no agreement is necessary for a state or local officer to communicate with federal authorities concerning the immigration status of any person, including persons believed to be unlawfully present in the United States.[23] More broadly, no agreement is necessary in order for a state or local officer "otherwise to cooperate ... in the identification, apprehension, detention, or removal of aliens not lawfully present in the United States."[24] An unsettled issue concerning state efforts to enforce federal immigration law is whether the "cooperation" contemplated under INA Section 287(g)(10) requires states and localities to consult and coordinate their immigration enforcement efforts with federal authorities, or whether the provision may also be interpreted to permit states and localities to independently pursue measures that are consistent with, and arguably further, federal policies related to the detection and removal of unauthorized aliens.

The 287(g) agreements follow two different models. Under the jail enforcement model (also referred to as the "detention model"), designated officers within state or local detention facilities are authorized to identify and process criminal aliens in preparation for removal by federal immigration authorities.[25] Under the task force model, designated officers may, during the course of their regular law enforcement duties within the community or under the direction of a supervising federal immigration officer, identify and arrest certain removable aliens.[26] Some 287(g) agreements singularly employ a task force or detention model, whereas others use both.[27] In 2009, U.S. Immigration and Customs Enforcement (ICE), the agency within the Department of Homeland Security which administers the 287(g) program, renegotiated agreements with participating jurisdictions in an effort to bolster federal oversight, training, and communication within the 287(g) program, and to prioritize the arrest and detention of aliens involved in serious criminal activity.[28] As of October 29, 2010, agreements pursuant to INA Section 287(g) were in place with 69 law enforcement agencies within 24 states.[29]

It should be noted that federal immigration authorities have entered cooperative arrangements with states pursuant to statutory authorities other than INA Section 287(g).[30] For example, under the Criminal Alien Program (CAP), ICE officers assigned to federal, state, and local prisons are tasked with identifying criminal aliens in order to facilitate their removal, including through the placement of detainers upon such aliens so that federal immigration authorities may take them into custody upon completion of their criminal sentences.[31] A separate program, Secure Communities, is also used to identify criminal aliens in local law enforcement custody. When a person is booked by a law enforcement agency participating in the Secure Communities program, his fingerprints are checked against FBI and DHS records. If fingerprints match DHS immigration records, ICE is immediately made aware and determines whether to pursue the removal of the identified alien.[32] Unlike 287(g) agreements, neither CAP nor the Secure Communities initiative involves direct enforcement of federal immigration law by state or local law enforcement officers or agencies.[33] Moreover, federal immigration authorities sometimes have informal cooperative arrangements with state or local law enforcement, particularly along the northern and southern border, in which officers will provide support to one another in the performance of their law enforcement duties.

Delegation of Immigration Enforcement Authority to Respond to Mass Influx of Aliens

Section 372 of IIRIRA amended INA Section 103(a) to authorize the Attorney General (now the Secretary of Homeland Security[34]) to call upon state and local police to perform immigration enforcement functions in response to an actual or imminent mass influx of aliens. Specifically, INA Section 103(a) provides:

> In the event that the [Secretary of Homeland Security] determines that an actual or imminent mass influx of aliens arriving off the coast of the United States or near a land border presents urgent circumstances requiring an immediate Federal response, the [Secretary] may authorize any State or local law enforcement officer, with the consent of the head of the department, agency or establishment under whose jurisdiction the individual is serving, to perform or exercise any of the power, privileges or duties conferred or imposed by the Act or regulations issued thereunder upon officers or employees of the service.[35]

Thus, state and local officers may exercise the civil or criminal arrest powers of federal immigration officers when certain criteria are met: (1) the designated state and local officers are expressly authorized by the Secretary of Homeland Security to exercise such authority; (2) the head of the relevant state or local law enforcement agency has given its consent to the performance of federal immigration functions by the agency's officers; and (3) the Secretary has made a determination that an imminent or ongoing mass influx of aliens requires an immediate response. Any authority delegated to state or local law enforcement officers under this provision can only be exercised for the duration of the emergency.

In 2002, the Department of Justice (DOJ) issued a final rule that implemented INA Section 103(a)(10) and described the cooperative process by which state or local governments could agree to place authorized state and local law enforcement officers under the direction of the INS in exercising federal immigration enforcement authority.[36] The following year the DOJ found it necessary to amend the previous regulations, determining that the regulations did not provide the Attorney General with sufficient flexibility to address unanticipated situations that might occur during a mass influx of aliens. When such action is deemed necessary to protect public safety, public health, or national security, the new rules also allow the abbreviation or waiver of training requirements for state and local law enforcement.[37]

Although one preemptory agreement was entered with Florida pursuant to INA Section 103(a)(1) in 1998, which could go into effect in the event that a mass influx of aliens is declared,[38] it does not appear that any other agreements have been entered pursuant to this authority.

Authorization to Arrest and Detain Previously Removed Criminal Aliens

Section 439 of the Antiterrorism and Effective Death Penalty Act of 1996 (AEDPA, P.L. 104-132) authorizes state and local law enforcement officers to arrest unlawfully present criminal aliens who have presumably violated INA Section 276 (concerning the reentry of previously removed aliens). Section 439 states in part:

> [T]o the extent permitted by relevant State and local law, State and local law enforcement officials are authorized to arrest and detain an individual who—(1) is an alien illegally present in the United States; and (2) has previously been convicted of a felony in the United States and deported or left the United States after such conviction, but only after the State or local law enforcement officials obtain appropriate confirmation from the Immigration and Naturalization Service of the status of such

> individual and only for such period of time as may be required for the Service to take the individual into Federal custody for purposes of deporting or removing the alien from the United States.[39]

This provision originated as a floor amendment during congressional consideration of AEDPA, and its author intended it to overcome a perceived federal limitation on state or local officers' ability to arrest and detain criminal aliens so that they could be transferred to the custody of federal immigration authorities.[40] There is some debate as to whether such a limitation actually existed prior to the enactment of AEDPA, and whether states and localities are now only permitted to arrest and detain aliens on account of their unlawful reentry pursuant to the procedure established under AEDPA Section 439 (i.e., when state or local officers have obtained prior confirmation by federal immigration authorities of a suspect's unauthorized immigration status). As discussed *infra*, the U.S. Court of Appeals for the Ninth Circuit (Ninth Circuit) appears to have construed AEDPA Section 439 in this manner,[41] while the U.S. Court of Appeals for the Tenth Circuit (Tenth Circuit) has recognized that federal law pre-AEDPA did not preclude states and localities from enforcing federal immigration law.[42]

Authorization to Enforce the Federal Alien Smuggling Statute

Congress appears to have authorized state and local police to enforce INA Section 274, which criminalizes activities relating to the smuggling, transport, or harboring of unauthorized aliens.[43] INA Section 274(c), entitled "Authority to Arrest," states that:

> No officer or person shall have authority to make any arrest for a violation of any provision of this section except officers and employees of the Service designated by the Attorney General, either individually or as a member of a class, and all other officers whose duty it is to enforce criminal laws.[44]

The plain language in this subsection seems to indicate that state and local law enforcement officers are permitted to make arrests for violations of the federal alien smuggling statute, as they are "officers whose duty it is to enforce criminal laws." The legislative history of INA Section 274 seems to confirm this understanding. The Senate-passed version of this provision stated that arrests for violations could only be made by federal immigration agents and "other officers *of the United States* whose duty it is to enforce criminal laws."[45] The House, however, struck the words "of the United States," so that state and local officials could enforce this provision as well.[46]

Although the federal alien smuggling provision appears to permit state and local law enforcement to directly enforce its provisions, other INA provisions which criminalize immigration-related conduct do not contain similar authorizing language. Nonetheless, as discussed *infra*, reviewing courts have recognized that state and local law enforcement may arrest persons for criminal violations of the INA, regardless of whether the applicable INA provision expressly authorizes such arrests.[47]

APPELLATE COURT DECISIONS CONCERNING IMMIGRATION ENFORCEMENT

The degree to which state and local police officers may, in the absence of express authorization by federal law, act to enforce federal immigration law is a subject of ongoing legal dispute and conflicting judicial opinion. Thus far, reviewing federal courts have recognized that state and local law enforcement officers may make arrests for *criminal* violations of the INA, at least so long as such arrests are permitted under state law. However, courts have disagreed as to whether state and local officers may, in the absence of express federal statutory authorization, arrest a person on account of his commission of a *civil* violation of the INA that renders him removable.

It should be noted that inquiries by state and local law enforcement that touch upon the immigration status of stopped individuals do not always constitute attempts to enforce federal immigration law. Such inquiries might arise in the normal course of an investigation unrelated to immigration enforcement. For example, an officer investigating an offense under state or local law might question a person regarding his identity, and such questioning might possibly touch upon that person's immigration status (e.g., requesting the production of any documents that may verify the person's purported identify, including perhaps any federal immigration documents in the person's possession).[48] These situations might not raise the same legal issues as situations where questioning regarding immigration status either serves as the legal justification for a person's initial stop, detention, or arrest,[49] or constitutes a basis for detaining a person beyond the period necessary to resolve any non-immigration related matters that justified the person's stop or detention.[50]

This section discusses notable appellate court decisions addressing the ability of state and local law enforcement to detain or arrest persons for violations of the INA in the absence of clear federal authorization.[51] The U.S. Court of Appeals for the Ninth Circuit (Ninth Circuit) and the U.S. Court of Appeals for the Sixth Circuit (Sixth Circuit) have issued opinions which recognize that state and local law enforcement are generally preempted from making arrests for civil violations of the INA in the absence of clear authorization under federal law. On the other hand, the Tenth Circuit has issued a series of rulings which appear to support the position that state and local law enforcement have implicit authority to investigate and arrest persons for *either* criminal or civil violations of federal immigration law.

It seems likely that this body of jurisprudence will develop noticeably in the near future, though it remains to be seen whether any consensus will be reached by reviewing courts. In recent years, several states have enacted measures designed to discourage the presence of unlawfully present aliens within their jurisdictions, including by authorizing state and local police to investigate the status of persons within their custody who are suspected of being in the United States illegally. Many of these state laws have been challenged on preemption grounds and are the subject of ongoing litigation in different federal circuits.[52] As of the date of this report, only one federal appellate court has rendered an opinion on the legality of a state measure requiring state and local police to investigate the immigration status of a person suspected of being unlawfully present. In that case (*United States v. Arizona*, discussed *infra*), the Ninth Circuit held that state and local police are generally preempted from arresting persons solely on account of being unlawfully present. It remains to be seen whether the Ninth Circuit's analysis will be endorsed by other circuits in their consideration of legal challenges to state laws targeting unlawfully present aliens. Moreover, it remains to be seen whether any of these lawsuits will ultimately be reviewed by the Supreme Court, potentially leading to a more definitive pronouncement as to the degree to which state and local police may enforce federal immigration law.[53]

Ninth Circuit Jurisprudence

The issue of whether state and local law enforcement agencies are precluded from enforcing provisions of the INA was analyzed by the Ninth Circuit in the 1983 case of *Gonzales* v. *City of Peoria*[54] and the 2011 case of

United States v. Arizona.[55] In *Gonzales*, a three-judge panel examined a Peoria policy that authorized local officers to arrest aliens who violated INA Section 275, which makes it a criminal offense for an alien to enter the United States unlawfully.[56] The petitioners, who had been questioned and detained pursuant to the city's policy, claimed that enforcement of federal immigration laws was the exclusive responsibility of the federal government, precluding any concurrent enforcement activities by states or localities.

The appellate court disagreed. As an initial matter, the *Gonzales* court noted that the "general rule is that local police are not precluded from enforcing federal statutes,"[57] and that federal regulation of a particular field "should not be presumed to preempt state enforcement activity 'in the absence of persuasive reasons—either that the nature of the regulated subject matter permits no other conclusion, or that the Congress has unmistakably so ordained.'"[58] The court concluded that the enforcement of the criminal provisions of the INA by states and localities did not inherently conflict with federal interests. Moreover, the court found that neither the structure nor legislative history of the INA manifested an intent by Congress to preclude state or local enforcement of the INA's criminal provisions.[59] Accordingly, the *Gonzales* court declared that local police officers may, subject to state law, constitutionally stop or detain individuals when there is reasonable suspicion or, in the case of arrest, probable cause that such persons have violated, or are in the process of violating, the *criminal* provisions of the INA.[60]

In the course of its analysis of the preemptive effect of federal immigration law, the *Gonzales* court appeared to distinguish the preemptive effect of the INA's civil and criminal provisions, and assumed that the former constituted a pervasive and preemptive regulatory scheme, whereas the latter did not. The court stated:

> We assume that the civil provisions of the [INA], regulating authorized entry, length of stay, residence status, and deportation, constitute such a pervasive regulatory scheme, as would be consistent with the exclusive federal power over immigration. However, this case does not concern that broad scheme, but only a narrow and distinct element of it—the regulation of criminal immigration activity by aliens. The statutes relating to that element are few in number and relatively simple in their terms. They are not, and could not be, supported by a complex administrative structure. It therefore cannot be inferred that the federal government has occupied the field of criminal immigration enforcement.[61]

Whereas the Ninth Circuit had "assumed" in *Gonzales* that state and local law enforcement were precluded from directly enforcing the civil provisions of federal immigration law, a more definitive pronouncement to that effect was made by the circuit court in *Arizona*. The case centered on legislation enacted by Arizona in 2010, commonly referred to as S.B. 1070, which is intended to deter the entry or presence of aliens within the state who lack lawful status under federal immigration law.[62] S.B. 1070 generally (1) requires state and local police to investigate the immigration status of persons in their custody who are reasonably believed to be unlawfully present aliens; (2) authorizes the police to make warrantless arrests of aliens when there is probable cause to believe they have committed a criminal offense making them deportable; and (3) establishes criminal penalties for certain conduct that may facilitate the presence of unlawfully present aliens within the state. The Department of Justice and a number of private entities filed separate lawsuits to prevent aspects of the Arizona statute from going into effect. The reviewing federal district court granted the federal government's request to preliminarily enjoin most of the challenged provisions of the Arizona law from going into effect, after it found that the DOJ was likely to prevail in its argument that these provisions were preempted by federal immigration law and policy.[63]

On appeal, a three-judge panel of the Ninth Circuit affirmed the lower court's ruling. While unanimous on some aspects of its decision, the panel split on the permissibility of those provisions of S.B. 1070 concerning immigration status verifications and warrantless arrests of deportable aliens by state and local police. By a 2-1 decision, the panel held that state and local police officers generally lacked the authority to enforce the non-criminal provisions of the INA, and also held that states may not mandate that police investigate the immigration status of persons suspected of being unlawfully present aliens.

In reaching this conclusion, the panel majority construed those provisions of INA Section 287(g) permitting state and local officers to perform immigration enforcement functions pursuant to a written agreement with the Secretary of DHS as indicative of congressional intent for state involvement in immigration enforcement to generally occur under federal supervision.[64] The majority further found that INA Section 287(g)(10), which refers to state and local "cooperation" in immigration enforcement in the absence of a 287(g) agreement, encompasses only assistance on "an incidental and as needed basis" when requested by the Secretary or otherwise necessary.[65] The majority also viewed the Arizona statute as being inconsistent with congressional intent, on the ground that it permits state and local police to arrest aliens for civil deportation violations in a broader set of circumstances than had been authorized under AEDPA Section 439.

The panel majority further found that the government was likely to prevail in its preemption challenge because of the Arizona measure's "deleterious effect" on foreign relations, as well as "the threat of 50 states layering their own immigration enforcement rules on top of the INA."[66]

In a partial dissent from the majority's ruling, one member of the panel criticized the majority for holding that states and localities are generally preempted from enforcing the civil provisions of the INA or investigating the immigration status of persons suspected of being deportable aliens. He characterized most jurisprudence as supporting the proposition that state and local officers are generally not preempted from making arrests for violations of federal law, including arrests for immigration violations.[67] The dissent also construed INA Section 287(g)(10) as reflecting congressional recognition that state police may assist in the enforcement of both the civil and criminal provisions of the INA, even in the absence of a 287(g) agreement. The dissent further claimed that AEDPA Section 439 was not intended to define the parameters of state authority to arrest aliens for civil immigration violations.[68] The dissenting judge also construed 8 U.S.C. Section 1373(c), which requires federal authorities to respond to immigration status requests by state and local authorities, as being indicative of congressional support for state and local participation in immigration enforcement activities.[69]

It should be noted that while the circuit panel majority found that state and local police are generally preempted from making arrests for civil violations of the INA, its related ruling that S.B. 1070's immigration verification requirements were preempted appeared to be based on the "mandatory" nature of these requirements. Thus, the court's decision would not necessarily bar Arizona law enforcement from attempting to verify the immigration status of persons on a more limited, case-by-case basis. The panel majority's opinion apparently contemplates such attempts at verification in limited circumstances.[70] The DOJ also seemed to suggest in its argument before the district court that it did not view discretionary attempts by state or local law enforcement to verify the immigration status of individuals as raising the same preemption concerns as Arizona's "mandatory" requirements relating to status verification.[71]

Arizona has submitted a petition for certiorari to the Supreme Court. If the Supreme Court decides to review the case, it could potentially set the stage for a definitive pronouncement as to the degree to which state and local police may enforce federal immigration law.

United States v. Urrieta (Sixth Circuit)

In the 2008 case of *United States v. Urrieta,*[72] a three-judge circuit panel similarly appeared to construe federal immigration law as generally precluding states and localities from arresting or detaining persons for civil immigration violations. The case concerned the lawfulness of the petitioner's extended detention following the issuance of a traffic citation by local law enforcement, during which time the officer attempted to determine whether the petitioner was an unlawfully present alien. During the extended detention, the petitioner consented to a search of his vehicle, which resulted in the discovery of firearms and fraudulent documents. In his subsequent criminal trial for unlawful possession of these items, the petitioner sought to have the evidence discovered during his extended detention suppressed, arguing that his extended detention beyond the period necessary to issue a traffic citation was unlawful.

The circuit panel concluded that the petitioner's extended detention could not be justified solely on account of the police officer's reasonable suspicion that the petitioner was an unlawfully present alien. In so doing, the panel characterized INA Section 287(g) as "stating that local law enforcement officers cannot enforce completed violations of civil immigration law (i.e., illegal presence) unless specifically authorized to do so by the Attorney General under special conditions that are not applicable in the present case."[73] Although the majority opinion in *Urrieta* appeared to recognize that state or local law enforcement could detain a person on account of a *criminal* violation of the INA,[74] it indicated that an alien could not be detained solely on account of unauthorized immigration status in the absence of a 287(g) agreement or other express federal authority.[75] Because the local officer did not have "reasonable suspicion that [the petitioner] was engaged in some nonimmigration-related illegal activity" that could justify his extended detention,[76] the court ruled that the petitioner was unlawfully detained and ordered the evidence discovered during this detention to be suppressed in subsequent criminal proceedings.[77]

Tenth Circuit Jurisprudence

In contrast to the approach taken by the Sixth and Ninth Circuits, the Tenth Circuit Court of Appeals has issued a series of rulings that arguably supports the view that state and local officers are not preempted from investigating and arresting persons who have violated *either* the criminal or civil provisions of the INA. Although these cases arose in the context of criminal investigations, they concerned activities undertaken by state or local officers involving the enforcement of the civil provisions of federal immigration law—namely, the arrest or extended detention of persons in order to determine whether they were unlawfully present aliens.

In the 1984 case of *United States* v. *Salinas-Calderon,*[78] a three-judge circuit panel considered a case involving a state trooper who had pulled over the criminal defendant for driving erratically, and who had subsequently found six individuals in the back of the defendant's truck. Because neither the driver nor the six individuals spoke English or carried identification documentation, and another passenger (the driver's wife) stated that they were from Mexico, the state trooper arrested them and attempted to verify their immigration status. The driver was subsequently charged with the criminal offense of unlawfully transporting unauthorized aliens, but moved to suppress statements made by himself and the six passengers in which they admitted their unauthorized immigration status.

Examining the record, the circuit panel found that, based on the observable facts that had been available, the trooper had probable cause to detain and arrest all of the individuals. Moreover, the court rejected the defendant's argument that the state trooper lacked authority to detain the passengers in order to inquire into their immigration status. The court determined that a "state trooper has general investigatory authority to inquire into possible immigration violations,"[79] and that based on his questioning of the defendant and passengers, the trooper had "probable cause to make a warrantless arrest for violation of the immigration laws."[80]

In 1999, the Tenth Circuit Court of Appeals once again considered state and local authority to enforce federal immigration laws in the case of *United States v. Vasquez-Alvarez.*[81] The case concerned an Oklahoma police officer's arrest of an individual, who was being monitored by the officer partially due to suspicion of drug trafficking, following the individual's admission that he was an "illegal alien."[82] Subsequently, the alien admitted that he had a felony record and had previously been deported from the United States, and was charged by federal authorities with the criminal offense of unlawfully reentering the United States.[83] As discussed previously,[84] Section 439 of AEDPA expressly permits state and local law enforcement to arrest previously deported aliens who have been convicted of criminal activity and thereafter unlawfully reenter the United States, but requires that law enforcement acting pursuant to this authority first obtain confirmation of the alien's immigration status prior to making an arrest. In the instant case, however, the law enforcement officer did not act pursuant to the authority conferred under AEDPA Section 439. Instead, the arrest was premised upon Oklahoma state law, which permitted state and local law enforcement to make arrests for any violation of federal law.[85]

The *Vasquez-Alvarez* court rejected the defendant's argument that because his arrest was not in accordance with the procedure detailed in AEDPA Section 439, it was therefore unlawful. Citing *Salinas-Calderon*, the circuit court noted that it had previously "held that state law-enforcement officers have the general authority to investigate and make arrests for violations of federal immigration laws."[86] Examining the language and legislative history of AEDPA Section 439, the court determined that the provision neither expressly nor implicitly limited or displaced "the preexisting general authority of state or local police officers to investigate and make arrests for violations of federal law, including immigration law."[87] Instead, the circuit panel held that AEDPA Section 439 "merely creates an additional vehicle for the enforcement of federal immigration law,"[88] besides any independent authority to make such arrests under state law.

In the 2001 case of *United States* v. *Santana-Garcia*,[89] the Tenth Circuit once again addressed the role of state and local law enforcement in immigration matters, reaffirming and expanding upon its prior rulings in *Salinas-Calderon* and *Vasquez-Alvarez*. The case concerned a traffic stop by a Utah state trooper. The driver of the car did not possess a driver's license, a misdemeanor under Utah law, and did not speak English. The passenger in the car spoke limited English and explained that he and the driver were traveling from Mexico to Colorado, which prompted the officer to ask if they were "legal." The passenger and the driver appeared to understand the question and answered "no."[90] Following further inquiry, the driver and passenger consented to a search of their vehicle, which revealed illegal drugs. In subsequent criminal proceedings, the driver and passenger moved to suppress this evidence on the grounds that the police lacked reasonable suspicion to detain them beyond the purpose of the initial stop.

The circuit panel upheld the admission of the evidence, finding that the state trooper had probable cause to arrest the defendants for violations of state criminal law (i.e., driving without a valid driver's license) and federal law at the time they consented to a search of the vehicle. With respect to federal law, the court held that the defendants' admission of unlawful status provided the state officer with probable cause to arrest them for suspected violations of federal immigration law. The *Santana-Garcia* panel also seemed to dismiss the suggestion that state law must explicitly authorize state and local officials to make such arrests.[91] The court relied upon a number of inferences from earlier decisions that recognized the "implicit authority" or "general investigatory authority" of state officers to inquire into possible immigration violations.[92] The court also seemed to rely upon a broad understanding of a Utah state law that empowers officers to make warrantless arrests for any public offense committed in the officer's presence to include violations of federal law.[93]

Although the defendants in *Santana-Garcia* were apparently in violation of a *civil* provision of the INA (i.e., unauthorized presence), the *Santana-Garcia* court made no distinction between state and local police officers' ability to enforce either the civil or criminal provisions of federal immigration law, although the supporting cases which the court cited generally involved arrests for criminal matters. Moreover, it remains unclear how the court, pursuant to its broad understanding of Utah state law, would have ruled if there had not been an independent legal basis supporting the state officer's stop (i.e., a traffic violation) unrelated to the investigation as to whether a civil violation of federal immigration laws had occurred. Accordingly, it can be argued that this decision still leaves unresolved the precise circumstances in which state and local police officers may enforce the civil provisions of the INA.[94]

Office of Legal Counsel Opinions

In recent decades, the executive branch has repeatedly opined on the scope of potential state and local involvement in the enforcement of federal immigration law. Over the years, it has modified its views as to whether state and local officials may enforce the civil provisions of the INA. In a 1978 press release, the Department of Justice (DOJ) "reaffirmed ... that the enforcement of the immigration laws rests with [federal immigration authorities], and not with state and local police."[95] The DOJ further urged state and local police not to "stop and question, detain, arrest, or place an 'immigration hold' on any persons not suspected of crime, solely on the ground that they may be deportable aliens."[96] In 1983, the DOJ announced revisions to this policy to encourage greater involvement by state and local police in the enforcement of immigration laws, but emphasized that federal authorities "remain responsible for all arrests for [civil] immigration violations."[97] In 1989, the DOJ's Office of Legal Counsel (OLC) opined that while state and local law enforcement could enforce the provisions of the INA concerning criminal offenses, it was "unclear" whether they could enforce non-criminal federal statutes.[98]

In 1996, the OLC reached a more definitive conclusion on the question, issuing an opinion which found that while state and local police are not preempted from making arrests for criminal violations of the INA, they "lack recognized legal authority" to enforce the INA's civil provisions.[99] The opinion acknowledged that "[i]t is well-settled that state law enforcement officers are permitted to enforce federal statutes where such enforcement activities do not impair federal regulatory interests."[100] Such enforcement is "subject to the provisions and limitations of state law."[101] However, the OLC concluded, based upon an examination of jurisprudence, that "state and local police lack recognized legal authority to stop and detain an alien solely on suspicion of civil deportability, as opposed to a criminal violation of the immigration laws or other laws."[102] In particular, the OLC construed the Ninth Circuit's ruling in *Gonzales v. City of Peoria* as holding that state and local authority to enforce the INA "is limited to criminal violations."[103]

2002 OLC Opinion

In 2002, the OLC issued a memorandum which concluded that "federal law did not preempt state police from arresting aliens on the basis of civil deportability," and it withdrew the advice of the 1996 opinion which had suggested otherwise.[104] The 2002 OLC Opinion described the states, like the federal government, as possessing the status of "sovereign entities."[105] Because of this status, states do not require affirmative delegation of federal authority in order to make arrests for violations of federal law—"[i]nstead, the power to make arrests inheres in the ability of one sovereign to accommodate the interests of the other."[106]

The 2002 OLC Opinion recognized that the exercise of states' inherent authority to arrest persons for federal violations may be subject to federal preemption. However, it concluded that "federal law should be presumed not to preempt this arrest authority," because "it is ordinarily unreasonable to assume that Congress intended to deprive the federal government of whatever assistance States may provide in identifying and detaining those who have violated federal law."[107] The 2002 OLC Opinion explicitly rejected the 1996 opinion's conclusion that federal law preempts state or local enforcement of the civil provisions of the INA, because "[o]n reexamination, we believe that the authorities we cited in the 1996 OLC opinion provide no support for our conclusion that state police lack the authority to arrest aliens solely on the basis of civil deportability."[108] In particular, it construed the Ninth Circuit's statements in *Gonzales v. City of Peoria* regarding the preemptive nature of the INA's civil provisions as "mere *assumption in dictum*,"[109] and instead emphasized Tenth Circuit jurisprudence supporting the inherent authority of state and local police to enforce both the criminal and civil provisions of federal immigration law.[110]

Some critics of the 2002 OLC Opinion have characterized it as "deeply flawed" and unsupported by judicial precedent or historical practice in the field of immigration.[111] For example, it has been argued that immigration has long been understood to be a distinctly federal concern, and that Congress would not have provided express statutory authorization for state and local enforcement of civil immigration laws in limited circumstances (e.g., pursuant to INA Section 287(g)) unless it was understood that state and local police were otherwise preempted from making arrests for civil immigration violations.[112]

It should be noted that the 2002 OLC Opinion concerned whether states are preempted from arresting persons for violations of federal immigration law. The opinion characterized this as "an extremely limited ... preemption question," which does not, "[u]nlike the typical preemption scenario," involve a state enacting its own immigration-related measures, which might "arguably conflict with federal law or intrude into a field that is reserved to Congress or that federal law has occupied."[113]

OLC opinions are generally viewed as providing binding interpretive guidance for executive agencies and reflecting the legal position of the executive branch,[114] but they cannot compel state action and do not have the same weight as an act of Congress. Generally, courts will consider opinion letters by executive agencies on legal matters to the extent that they "have the power to persuade."[115]

Department of Justice Legal Challenges to State Immigration Laws

Although the 2002 OLC Opinion remains in effect, some of the arguments raised by the DOJ in legal challenges brought against Arizona and Alabama indicate that the Justice Department believes there are limitations on the ability of state and local police to investigate and arrest persons for suspected violations of federal immigration law. These lawsuits center on measures enacted by Arizona and Alabama which are intended to deter the entry or presence of aliens who lack lawful status under federal immigration law.[116] Both statutes impose sanctions upon certain activity that may facilitate the presence of unlawfully present aliens within the states' jurisdictions. Each statute also contains provisions which involve the direct enforcement of federal immigration law by state and local police. Specifically, both the Arizona and Alabama statutes generally require state and local police to investigate the immigration status of persons who come within their custody when they have reason to believe those individuals are unlawfully present aliens. In addition, the Arizona statute authorizes state and local police to make warrantless arrests of persons who have committed certain kinds of deportable offenses.

The DOJ claims that aspects of the Arizona and Alabama statutes, including those provisions involving the direct enforcement of federal immigration law by state and local police, are preempted by federal immigration law and policy. As previously discussed, most of the challenged provisions of the Arizona statute were preliminarily enjoined by the reviewing district court pending a final ruling on the merits of the DOJ's challenge. The district court's injunction was affirmed by the Ninth Circuit, and Arizona is now seeking Supreme Court review. The DOJ's legal challenge against Alabama, which was filed in August 2011, raises many of the same arguments that were brought against the Arizona statute. As of the date of this report, the reviewing court has yet to issue a ruling.

In its legal challenge against Arizona's S.B. 1070, the DOJ has argued that the measure's grant of authority to state and local police to make warrantless arrests of aliens believed to be deportable on criminal grounds is preempted because of the burdens it would impose on lawfully present aliens. The DOJ claims that the measure would likely lead to the harassment and arrest of lawfully present aliens who were mistakenly believed by state or local authorities to have committed a criminal offense that made them deportable. The DOJ argued that determining whether an alien is deportable on account of criminal activity falls under the exclusive authority of the federal government, and state and local police are ill-equipped to determine whether a particular crime makes an alien removable. The DOJ has further argued that law enforcement officers acting pursuant to S.B. 1070 would "undoubtedly erroneously arrest many aliens who could not legitimately be subject to removal," and thereby impose "distinct and extraordinary" burdens upon aliens authorized to remain in the United States.[117]

With respect to the Arizona and Alabama laws' requirements concerning immigration status determinations, the DOJ argued that the "mandatory" nature of these requirements would unduly burden lawfully present aliens and also lead to a significant increase in immigration status verification requests being received by federal authorities, causing those authorities to divert resources away from other federal immigration enforcement priorities.[118] Accordingly, the DOJ alleges that these provisions are preempted because they conflict or otherwise interfere with the objectives of federal immigration law and policy.

The DOJ also appears to argue (at least in the Alabama challenge) that while federal immigration law permits state and local "cooperation" in matters of immigration enforcement, state and local participation in immigration enforcement must generally be responsive to federal immigration enforcement priorities. According to the DOJ, a "mandatory and systematic" immigration verification scheme would, by its nature, be "non-cooperative," on the ground that it would not take into account the enforcement priorities or preferences of the federal immigration authorities. In its legal challenge to the Alabama statute, the DOJ claims that:

> Because DHS is charged with administering the immigration laws, and therefore with setting a direction for enforcement, the INA's "cooperation" requirement means that a state may not adopt its own mandatory set of directives to implement the state's own enforcement policies because such a mandate would serve as an obstacle in every instance to the ability of individual state and local officers to cooperate with federal officers administering federal policies and discretion as the circumstances in the particular case require. Thus, for example, a state may systematically involve itself ... in immigration enforcement only if state and local officers remain in a position to respond to the judgment and discretion of appropriate federal officers, and only if the state acts consistently with the policies and any applicable direction set by federal officials. Accordingly, a state is not acting "cooperatively" if it disregards express federal direction; attempts to force the federal government to routinely deploy scarce enforcement resources in accordance with an immigration enforcement regime of a state's choosing; or if it attempts to deny its officers (who are assisting federal officers in enforcing the INA) the opportunity to exercise their discretion on a case-by-case basis so that they can be responsive to the direction and priorities of the federal officials charged with implementing and enforcing the immigration laws.[119]

At the same time, however, the DOJ has suggested that such activities would not raise the same preemption issues if they were done on a more limited, discretionary basis,[120] or if they were performed consistently with the priorities of federal immigration authorities. In its legal suit against Alabama, the DOJ noted that it was not challenging a state's "power to *authorize* its officers to assist federal officers in their enforcement of the immigration laws."[121] However, the DOJ claims that any such authorization must allow state and local officers to be responsive to the direction and priorities of federal immigration authorities.[122]

It remains to be seen whether the OLC will modify or supplement any of the conclusions reached in its 2002 opinion. In its decision in *United States v. Arizona*, a majority of the Ninth Circuit panel explicitly rejected the reasoning of the OLC opinion,[123] but it is possible that other courts will be more receptive to its arguments.

End Notes

[1] *See, e.g.,* Chinese Exclusion Case, 180 U.S. 581, 609 (1889). Federal authority to regulate immigration derives from multiple sources. The Constitution provides Congress with the authority "[t]o regulate Commerce with foreign Nations," and "[t]o establish an uniform Rule of Naturalization." U.S. CONST., Art. I, §8, cl. 3-4. Federal authority to regulate the admission and presence of aliens also derives from its authority over foreign affairs. Toll v. Moreno, 458 U.S. 1, 10 (1982) (discussing various constitutional provisions, as well as authority over foreign affairs, which may serve as a source for immigration regulation by the federal government). *See also* Kleindienst v. Mandel, 408 U.S. 753, 765-67 (1972) (discussing Congress's plenary authority over admission of aliens); Jean v. Nelson, 711 F.2d 1455, 1465-67 (11th Cir. 1983) (discussing sources of federal authority over immigration). For much of the nineteenth century, federal regulation of immigration was quite limited in scope, and state legislation concerning the rights and privileges of certain categories of aliens was common, including, for example, laws barring the admission of alien convicts arriving at state ports of entry. *See generally* Gerald L. Neuman, *The Lost Century of American Immigration Law (1776-1875)*, 93 COLUM. L. REV. 1833 (1993). Subsequent developments in jurisprudence, along with a significant expansion in federal legislation concerning aliens, has greatly circumscribed the ability of states to regulate immigration-related matters.

[2] 8 U.S.C. §§1101 *et seq.*

[3] INA §275, 8 U.S.C. §1325.

[4] INA §276, 8 U.S.C. §1326.

[5] INA §274, 8 U.S.C. §1324.

[6] *See, e.g.,* INA §274A(e)(4), 8 U.S.C. §1324A(e)(4) (civil penalties for knowingly hiring aliens who are not authorized to work in the United States); INA §274D, 8 U.S.C. §1324d (civil penalties for aliens ordered removed who willfully fail to depart).

[7] INA §274A(e)(4), 8 U.S.C. §1324A(e)(4). Such violations can also carry criminal penalties if the employer has engaged in a pattern or practice of hiring unauthorized aliens. INA §274A(f), 8 U.S.C. §1324A(f).

[8] Padilla v. Kentucky,—U.S.—, 130 S. Ct. 1473, 1481 (2010) ("We have long recognized that deportation is a particularly severe 'penalty,' but it is not, in a strict sense, a criminal sanction.") (internal citations omitted); INS v. Lopez-Mendoza, 468 U.S. 1032, 1038-39 (1984) ("A deportation proceeding is a purely civil action to determine eligibility to remain in this country, not to punish an unlawful entry. ... The purpose of deportation is not to punish past transgressions but rather to put an end to a continuing violation of the immigration laws.").

[9] Although unlawful entry by an alien into the United States constitutes a criminal offense, not every alien who is unlawfully present in the United States entered the country without authorization. Notably, an alien who overstayed his visa would be unlawfully present, despite having legally entered the country. The only situation where unlawful presence is itself a crime is when an alien is found in the country after having been formally removed or after voluntarily departing the country while a removal order was outstanding. INA §276, 8 U.S.C. §1326.

[10] The vast majority of aliens apprehended by Border Patrol unlawfully entering the United States are not prosecuted for the criminal offense of unlawful entry, but are instead either formally removed or permitted to depart voluntarily in lieu of removal. This is largely because pursuing criminal charges in all cases would place a heavy burden upon prosecutorial resources and detention facilities. In recent years, the percentage of persons prosecuted for unlawful entry or reentry has grown considerably, but most aliens apprehended by Border Patrol who are attempting to enter the country unlawfully are removed from the United States without criminal sanction. *See* Transactional Records Access Clearinghouse, Syracuse University, "Illegal Reentry Becomes Top Criminal Charge," *available at* http://trac.syr.edu/immigration/reports/251 (providing data regarding criminal prosecutions for unlawful entry or reentry in comparison to total apprehensions by Border Patrol).

[11] Moreover, federal authority to set rules on the entry of aliens and the conditions of their stay still leaves some room for state laws directed towards non-citizens. *See* De Canas v. Bica, 424 U.S. 351, 355 (1976) ("[T]he Court has never held that every state enactment which in any way deals with aliens is a regulation of immigration and thus *per se* preempted by this constitutional power, whether latent or exercised."). *See also* Chamber of Commerce of the United States v. Whiting,—U.S.—, 131 S. Ct. 1968 (2011) (holding that federal law did not preempt state measure which revoked the business licenses of businesses that knowingly employed aliens who were not authorized by the federal government to work in the United States).

[12] U.S. CONST., art. VI, cl. 2.

[13] *See, e.g.,* Altria Group, Inc. v. Good, 555 U.S. 70, 76-77 (2008); Medtronic, Inc. v. Lohr, 518 U.S. 470, 485-86 (1996); Jones v. Rath Packing Co., 430 U.S. 519, 525 (1977).

[14] English v. General Elec. Co., 496 U.S. 72, 78-79 (1990). *See also* Crosby v. Nat'l Foreign Trade Council, 530 U.S. 363, 373 (2000); Silkwood v. Kerr-McGee Corp., 464 U.S. 238, 248-49 (1984); Pac. Gas & Elec. Co. v. State Energy Res. Conservation & Dev. Comm'n, 461 U.S. 190, 203-04 (1983). Congressional intent to "occupy the field" to the exclusion of state law can be inferred when "[1] the pervasiveness of the federal regulation precludes supplementation by the States, [2] where the federal interest in the field is sufficiently dominant, or [3] where the object sought to be obtained by the federal law and the character

of obligations imposed by it ... reveal the same purpose." Schneidewind v. ANR Pipeline Co., 485 U.S. 293, 300 (1988) (internal quotations omitted).

[15] Conversely, state action may be preempted where Congress explicitly manifests its intent in law. *See* INA §274A(h)(2), 8 U.S.C. §1324A(h)(2) (explicitly prohibiting states from imposing criminal or civil sanctions [other than through licensing or similar laws] upon those who hire or employ unauthorized aliens).

[16] *See, e.g.*, INA §287(d), 8 U.S.C. §1357(d) (authorizing federal immigration authorities, when informed by state or local law enforcement that an alien is within its custody on account of a controlled substance violation, to place a detainer on the alien authorizing his detention until federal authorities may assume custody); 8.U.S.C. §1373 (requiring federal immigration authorities to respond from requests by federal, state, and local government agencies, seeking to verify the immigration status of an individual within their jurisdiction for any purpose authorized by law); District of Columbia Appropriations Act, 2001, P.L. 106-553, App'x B, Title I, §119, 114 Stat. 2762A-69 (Dec. 21, 2000) (providing the Department of Justice with permanent authority, later transferred to the Department of Homeland Security, to lease state and local facilities for the purpose of detaining deportable aliens pending their removal from the United States).

[17] For several decades, the primary authority to interpret, implement, and enforce the provisions of the INA was vested with the Attorney General. The Attorney General, in turn, delegated authority over immigration enforcement and service functions to the Immigration and Naturalization Service within the DOJ. Following the establishment of the Department of Homeland Security pursuant to the Homeland Security Act of 2002 (P.L. 107-296), the INS was abolished and its enforcement functions were transferred to DHS. *See* 6 U.S.C. §251. Although the INA still refers to the Attorney General as having authority over 287(g) agreements, this authority is now exercised by the Secretary of Homeland Security.

[18] INA §287(g)(1), 8 U.S.C. §1357(g)(1).

[19] INA §287(g)(5), 8 U.S.C. §1357(g)(5).

[20] INA §287(g)(2), 8 U.S.C. §1357(g)(2).

[21] INA §287(g)(7)-(8), 8 U.S.C. §1357(g)(7)-(8).

[22] *See id.* (providing that state and local authorities acting under a 287(g) agreement shall be treated as federal employees for purposes of compensation by the federal government for injuries occurring during the performance of their duties, and also stating that such persons shall be considered to be acting under color of federal law in any civil suit arising from their immigration enforcement activities).

[23] INA §287(g)(10), 8 U.S.C. §1357(g)(10).

[24] *Id.*

[25] Office of Inspector General, *The Performance of 287(g) Agreements*, Department of Homeland Security, Mar. 2010, at 3, *available at* http://www.dhs.gov/xoig/assets/ mgmtrpts/OIG_10-63_Mar10.pdf.

[26] *Id.*

[27] *Id.*

[28] *See* U.S. Immigration and Customs Enforcement, Office of State and Local Coordination, Updated Facts on ICE's 287(g) Program, Apr. 12, 2010, *available at* http://www.ice.gov/pi/news/factsheets/section287_g-reform.htm.

[29] *See* U.S. Immigration and Customs Enforcement, *Delegation of Immigration Authority Section 287(g) Immigration and Nationality Act*, *available at* http://www.ice.gov/news/ library/factsheets/287g.htm (discussing 287(g) program and providing links to copies of agreements in force) (last updated Oct. 29, 2010).

[30] Indeed, the 287(g) program is only one of several cooperative arrangements with state and local law enforcement that is administered by ICE, under the umbrella of the Agreements of Cooperation in Communities to Enhance Safety and Security (ACCESS) program. *See generally* U.S. Immigration and Customs Enforcement, ICE Agreements of Cooperation in Communities to Enhance Safety and Security (ACCESS) , *available at* http://www.ice.gov/news/library/factsheets/access.htm.

[31] *See generally* U.S. Immigration and Customs Enforcement, Fact Sheet: Criminal Alien Program, Nov. 19, 2008, *available at* http://www.ice.gov/news/library/factsheets/cap.htm (last updated Mar. 29, 2011); Andrea Guttin, Immigration Policy Center, *The Criminal Alien Program: Immigration Enforcement in Travis County, Texas*, Feb. 2010, at 4-6 (discussing development and implementation of CAP).

[32] The template for agreements which have traditionally been entered between ICE and state identification bureaus relating to implementation of the Secure Communities initiative can be viewed at http://www.ice.gov/doclib/foia/secure_communities/securecommunities moatemplate.pdf. Under the initiative, ICE has deployed biometric information-sharing capability to a growing number of jurisdictions. As of August 2, 2011, this capability has been activated in 1,508 jurisdictions in 44 states and territories, and ICE expects such capability to be available nationwide in 2013. U.S. Immigration and Customs Enforcement, Secure Communities: Activated Jurisdictions, *available at* http://www.ice.gov/doclib/secure-communities/pdf/sc-activated.pdf (last viewed on Aug. 2, 2011).

[33] Indeed, legal authority supporting the establishment of CAP and Secure Communities does not derive from INA §287(g), but instead from a number of other provisions. *See, e.g.,* INA §236, 8 U.S.C. §1226 (authorizing the establishment and implementation of a system by which federal immigration authorities may identify aliens convicted of aggravated felonies who are in state or local custody); INA §238, 8 U.S.C. §1228 (requiring the provision of expedited removal proceedings of certain criminal aliens at federal, state, and local correctional facilities); INA §287(d), 8 U.S.C. §1357(d) (authorizing federal immigration authorities, when informed by state or local law enforcement that an alien is within their custody on account of a controlled substance violation, to place a detainer on the alien authorizing his detention until federal authorities may assume custody); Consolidated Appropriations Act, 2008, P.L. 110-161, Div. E, U.S. Immigration and Customs Enforcement, Salaries and Expenses, 121 Stat. 2051 (Dec. 26, 2007) (providing appropriations to DHS to improve methods to identify criminal aliens for removal, and requiring DHS to submit to Congress "a strategy for [ICE] to identify every criminal alien, at the prison, jail, or correctional institution in which they are held … [and thereafter] make every reasonable effort to remove, upon their release from custody, all criminal aliens judged deportable").

[34] Although INA §103(a)(10) refers to the Attorney General, the authority described in the provision now appears to be exercised by the Secretary of Homeland Security, as a result of the transfer of immigration enforcement functions to DHS. *See supra* text accompanying footnote 17.

[35] 8 U.S.C. §1103(a)(10).

[36] Codified at 28 C.F.R. §65.84. *See also* Powers of the Attorney General to Authorize State or Local Law Enforcement Officers to Exercise Federal Immigration Enforcement Authority During a Mass Influx of Aliens, 67 Fed. Reg. 48354 (Jul. 24, 2002).

[37] Abbreviation or Waiver of Training for State or Local Law Enforcement Officers Authorized to Enforce Immigration Law During a Mass Influx of Aliens, 68 Fed. Reg. 8820-22 (Feb. 26, 2003) (codified at 28 C.F.R. §65.84(a)(4)).

[38] *See* Immigration and Naturalization Service, Press Release, *INS and Florida Sign Historic Agreement on Response to a Mass Migration*, Oct. 19, 1998.

[39] 8 U.S.C. §1252c.

[40] 142 CONG. REC. 4619 (Rep. Doolittle offering amend. no. 7 to H.R. 2703).

[41] United States v. Arizona, 641 F.3d 339, 364-64 (9th Cir. 2011).

[42] United States v. Vasquez-Alvarez, 176 F. 3d 1294, 1299-1300 (10th Cir. 1999) (holding that AEDPA §439 was not "intended to displace preexisting state or local authority to arrest individuals violating federal immigration laws").

[43] 8 U.S.C. §1324.

[44] 8 U.S.C. §1324(c) (emphasis added).

[45] 98 CONG. REC. 810 (1952) (emphasis added).

[46] CONF. REP. NO. 1505, 82 Cong., 2d Sess. (1952). Representative Walter offered the amendment to strike the words "of the United States." He stated that the purpose of the amendment was "to make it possible for any law enforcement officer to make an arrest." 98 CONG. REC. 1414-15 (1952).

[47] *See, e.g.*, Gonzales v. City of Peoria, 722 F.2d 468, 474-75 (9th Cir. 1983) (examining legislative history of INA and concluding that state and local law enforcement were not intended to be precluded from enforcing the INA's criminal provisions).

[48] In *Terry v. Ohio*, 392 U.S. 1 (1968), the Supreme Court held that law enforcement may briefly stop and investigate an individual when there is "reasonable suspicion" that the person is involved in criminal activity, without infringing upon the person's right under the Fourth Amendment to be free from unreasonable searches and seizures. Questioning a suspect regarding his identity may be a part of many *Terry* stops. *See, e.g.*, Hiibel v. Sixth Judicial District Court of Nevada, Humboldt County, 542 U.S. 177, 186 (2004) ("Obtaining a suspect's name in the course of a *Terry* stop serves important government interests."); Hayes v. Florida, 470 U.S. 811, 816 (1985) ("[I]f there are articulable facts supporting a reasonable suspicion that a person has committed a criminal offense, that person may be stopped in order to identify him, question him briefly, or to detain him briefly while attempting to obtain additional information."). Additionally, the Fourth Amendment is not implicated in consensual encounters with and questioning by law enforcement. Florida v. Bostick, 501 U.S. 429, 434 (1991) ("Since *Terry*, we have held repeatedly that mere police questioning does not constitute a seizure."). In *INS v. Delgado*, for example, the Supreme Court held that questioning by federal immigration authorities regarding the immigration status of employees during a worksite inspection did not constitute a "seizure" under the Fourth Amendment because, in view of the surrounding circumstances, "most workers could have had no reasonable fear that they would be seized upon leaving." 466 U.S. 210, 219 (1984). In consensual encounters, "even when officers have no basis for suspecting a particular individual, they may generally ask questions of that individual; ask to examine the individual's identification; and request consent to search his or her luggage." *Bostick*, 501 U.S. at 434.

[49] Nonetheless, there may be circumstances where inquiries by state or local police into the immigration status of an individual may raise preemption issues, even in cases where the person has been stopped and detained on nonimmigration related grounds and the questioning does not result in the person's extended detention. *See* United States v. Arizona, 703 F.Supp. 2d 980 (D. Ariz. 2010) (preliminarily enjoining state measure requiring state and local police to verify the immigration status of persons stopped for a state or local offense who are reasonably suspected of being unlawfully present, on the grounds that the measure was likely preempted by federal immigration law, in part because the "mandatory"

nature of the state requirement would unduly burden those federal agencies responsible for responding to immigration status verification requests coming from the state).

[50] For example, in *Muehler v. Mena*, the Supreme Court held that local police officers' questioning of the defendant about her immigration status while they searched the premises of a house she occupied for dangerous weapons did not violate the Fourth Amendment, because it did not prolong her detention. 544 U.S. 93, 101 (2005). *See also* Illinois v. Cabelles, 543 U.S. 405, 407 (2005) ("A seizure that is justified solely by [an] interest ... can become unlawful if it is prolonged beyond the time reasonably required to complete that mission."); Estrada v. Rhode Island, 594 F.3d 56, 64 (1st Cir. 2010) (applying *Muehler* in case where police officer inquired into the immigration status of passengers of stopped vehicle).

[51] In addition to the cases discussed in this section, a few other federal appellate courts have considered cases where state or local law enforcement have investigated or arrested persons for suspected violations of federal immigration law. However, these cases generally have not contained clear pronouncements regarding the ability of state or local police to enforce the civil provisions of federal immigration law. *See, e.g., Estrada*, 594 F.3d at 64-65 (state police officer who stopped a van for traffic violations and subsequently inquired into passengers' immigration status and thereafter transferred them to federal immigration authorities was entitled to qualified immunity in case brought by passengers which claimed he had violated their constitutional and statutory rights; court noted that the officer contended he had probable cause to believe petitioners had committed "immigration violations," and cited to provisions in INA carrying criminal penalties); United States v. Laville, 480 F.3d 187 (3rd Cir. 2007) (finding that state police officer's warrantless arrest of alien was supported by probable cause that he had committed the criminal offense of unlawfully entering the United States); United States v. Rodriguez-Arreola, 270 F.3d 611 (8th Cir. 2001) (reversing lower court's finding that a state trooper, after stopping the vehicle which defendant occupied for speeding, violated the defendant's Fourth Amendment rights by questioning him and the driver of the vehicle about the defendant's immigration status). In *Lynch v. Cannatella*, a three-judge panel of the U.S. Court of Appeals for the Fifth Circuit considered civil claims brought by several foreign stowaways who alleged mistreatment by local police when they were apprehended and detained, pending transfer to federal authorities, after having attempted to enter the United States unlawfully. 810 F.2d 1363 (5th Cir. 1987). In dismissing plaintiffs' claim that they were detained in a manner that was contrary to federal law, the court found that although the process used by local authorities was not expressly authorized by federal statute, it was also not prohibited by it. It further stated that no federal statute "precludes other federal, state, or local law enforcement agencies from taking other action to enforce this nation's immigration laws." *Id.* at 1371. Given the context in which this statement was made, it is unclear whether the court intended to convey a broad recognition of the ability of state and local police to enforce the criminal and civil provisions of federal immigration law, or whether the court was only referring to the ability of state, local, and federal law enforcement to arrest persons attempting to enter the United States unlawfully.

[52] *See, e.g.,* Buquer v. City of Indianapolis, 2011 U.S. Dist. LEXIS 68326, 1:11-cv-708 (S.D. Ind. Jun. 24, 2011) (granting preliminary injunction to prevent enforcement of Indiana law authorizing state and local law enforcement to arrest aliens for non-criminal immigration violations); Ga. Latino Alliance for Human Rights v. Deal, 2011 U.S. Dist. LEXIS 69600, 1:11-CV-1804 (N.D. Ga. Jun. 27, 2011) (granting preliminary injunction to prevent implementation of aspects of Georgia law targeting unlawfully present aliens).

[53] Arizona v. United States, petition for cert., filed Aug. 10, 2011.

[54] 722 F.2d 468, 474 (9th Cir. 1983). *Gonzales* was subsequently overruled by *Hodgers-Durgin v. de la Vina*, 199 F.3d 1037 (9th Cir. 1999), on grounds unrelated to issues discussed in this report.

[55] United States v. Arizona, 641 F.3d 339 (9th Cir. 2011) [hereinafter "*Arizona II*"].

[56] 8 U.S.C. §1325. The plaintiffs alleged that the city police engaged in the practice of stopping and arresting persons of Mexican descent without reasonable suspicion or probable cause and based only on their race. Furthermore, they alleged that those persons stopped under this policy were required to provide identification indicative of legal presence in the United States, and that anyone without acceptable identification was detained at the jail for release to immigration authorities.

[57] *Gonzales*, 722 F.2d at 474.

[58] *Id.* at 475 (*quoting De Canas v. Bica*, 424 U.S. 351, 356 (1976)).

[59] *Id.*

[60] *Id.*

[61] *Id.* at 474-75.

[62] The text of S.B. 1070, as amended by H.B. 2162, can be viewed at http://www. azleg. Gov /alispdfs/council/SB1070-HB2162.PDF. For further discussion, see CRS Report R41221, *State Efforts to Deter Unauthorized Aliens: Legal Analysis of Arizona's S.B. 1070*, by Kate M. Manuel, Michael John Garcia, and Larry M. Eig.

[63] United States v. Arizona, 703 F. Supp. 2d 980 (D. Ariz., 2010) [hereinafter "*Arizona I*"].

[64] *Arizona II*, 641 F.3d at 348-349.

[65] *Id.* at 348. The majority was concerned that reading INA §287(g)(10) without reference to subsections (g)(1)-(9) would "nullify" these provisions. Specifically, the majority pointed to use of the word "removal" in subsection (g)(10)(B) as indicating that "cooperation" is generally limited to assistance under a 287(g) agreement because states and localities cannot remove aliens, only the federal government can. *Id.* at 349-350. Apparently taking the view that the federal government must authorize state and local enforcement of federal immigration law, the majority found that INA §287(g)(10) does not "operate as a broad alternative grant of authority" for state and local officers to enforce federal law absent a 287(g) agreement, or permit them to "adopt laws dictating how and when state and local officers *must* communicate with the Attorney General regarding the immigration status of an individual." *Id.* at 349-350. The majority did not address the argument that states and localities have inherent authority to enforce federal immigration law in its discussion of Section 2(B), although it did in its discussion of Section 6.

[66] *Id.* at 352, 354. The district court had similarly expressed concern that Section 2(B) could potentially interfere with the federal government's responsibility "to maintain international relationships, for the protection of American citizens abroad as well as to ensure uniform national foreign policy." *Arizona* I, 703 F. Supp. 2d at 997 (citing *Hines*, 312 U.S. at 62-63, and also quoting Zadvaydas v. Davis, 533 U.S. 678, 700 (2001) ("We recognize ... the Nation's need to 'speak with one voice' in immigration matters.")). In addition to joining the majority opinion, Judge John T. Noonan wrote a separate concurrence to emphasize his view that provisions of S.B. 1070 were inconsistent with federal foreign policy. He further characterized the regulation of immigration as a subset of foreign policy, and argued that the "foreign policy of the United States preempts the field entered by Arizona." *Arizona II*, 641 F.3d at 368 (Noonan, J., concurring).

[67] *See Arizona II*, 641 F.3d at 384-87 (Bea, J., dissenting) (citing and discussing, *inter alia*, United States v. Di Re, 332 U.S. 581 (1948) (involving arrest by state officers of person for

knowingly possessing counterfeit gasoline ration coupons, in violation of federal law); Muehler v. Mena, 544 U.S. 93 (2005) (holding that that local police officers' questioning of an individual regarding her immigration status while they searched the premises of a house she occupied for dangerous weapons did not violate the Fourth Amendment)).

[68] *See Arizona II*, 641 F.3d at 387-91 (Bea, J., dissenting).

[69] *Id.* at 382 (Bea, J., dissenting).

[70] *Id.* at 349-50 (noting that state and local authorities can communicate immigration status information obtained or needed in the performance of "regular state duties," so long as these duties do not entail the systematic enforcement of federal immigration law absent a 287(g) agreement).

[71] United States v. Arizona, Plaintiff's Motion for a Preliminary Injunction and Memorandum of Law in Support Thereof, at 25 (D. Ariz. filed Jul. 6, 2010) [hereinafter "Arizona PI Motion"] available at http://www.justice.gov/usao/az/press_releases/ 2010/Arizona%20PI%20Brief%20(2).pdf. ("Before passage of S.B. 1070, Arizona police had the same discretion to decide whether to verify immigration status during the course of a lawful stop as any other state or federal law enforcement officer.").

[72] 520 F.3d 569 (6th Cir. 2008).

[73] *Id.* at 574.

[74] Prior to searching the defendant's vehicle, the stopping officer contacted federal authorities to determine whether the defendant was legally in the country, and learned that there was no record of the defendant. The majority noted that this lack of information was significant, because it indicated that the defendant was not present in the country after previously having been deported, which is a criminal offense. *See* INA §276, 8 U.S.C. §1326. The majority opinion found the lack of a deportation record to be "significant because illegal reentry after deportation is the only immigration violation that [the local officer] had the authority to enforce." *Urrieta*, 520 F.3d at 571-72.

[75] Further, the court also recognized that a person's false or evasive statements regarding immigration status do not provide law enforcement with reasonable suspicion to believe that the alien is engaged in unrelated criminal activity which could justify his continued detention. The court reasoned that: Although false or evasive statements to a law enforcement officer might indicate criminal activity, *see* United States v. $67,220.00 in U.S. Currency, 957 F.2d 280, 286 (6th Cir.1992), the fact is that very few undocumented immigrants are likely to admit to law enforcement that they are in the country illegally. The government's reasoning that dishonesty about one's immigration status suggests drug running, therefore, opens the door to allowing millions of undocumented immigrants to be detained for further questioning on that basis. To hold that one's illegal presence in this county is a sign of anything more than an immigration violation stretches the Fourth Amendment much too far. *Id.* at 579.

[76] *Id.* at 574-75.

[77] Although one judge of the panel dissented from the court's ruling, believing that the officer had reasonable suspicion to detain the defendant following the issuance of a traffic citation in order to investigate possible criminal activity, he agreed with the majority that the officer "had no authority to arrest [the defendant and his passenger] for an immigration violation because neither of them [had committed the criminal offense of having] reentered the country illegally." *Id.* at 580 (McKeague, J., dissenting).

[78] 728 F.2d 1298 (10th Cir. 1984).

[79] *Id.* at 1301 n.3.

[80] *Id.* at 1301.

[81] 176 F.3d 1294 (10th Cir. 1999).

[82] *Id.* at 1296.

[83] *Id.* at 1295.

[84] *See supra* at "Authorization to Arrest and Detain Previously Removed Criminal Aliens."

[85] *Vasquez-Alvarez*, 176 F.3d at 1296-97 (citing *Salinas-Calderon*, 728 F.2d at 1301-02 & n.3).

[86] *Id.* at 1296-97.

[87] *Id.* at 1295.

[88] *Id.*

[89] 264 F.3d 1188 (10th Cir. 2001).

[90] *Id.* at 1190.

[91] *Id.* at 1193-94. The court, nonetheless, cited Utah's peace officer statute (UTAH CODE ANN. §77-7-2), which empowers Utah state troopers to make warrantless arrests for "any public offense." The court also found the defendant's acknowledgment in *Vasquez-Alvarez* that the relevant state law specifically authorized local law enforcement officials to make arrests for violations of federal law unnecessary to that decision. *Id.* at 1194 n.7.

[92] *Id.* at 1193-94. The circuit court also approvingly cited to a few non-immigration-related decisions in other circuits which recognized state and local law enforcement's general authority to make arrests for federal offenses, presuming that the exercise of such authority is not barred under state law. *Id.* (citing *United States v. Janik*, 723 F.2d 537, 548 (7th Cir. 1983) and *United States v. Bowdach*, 561 F.2d 1160, 1167 (5th Cir. 1977)).

[93] *Santana-Garcia*, 264 F.3d at 1194 n.8 (*citing* UTAH CODE ANN. §77-7-2).

[94] The Tenth Circuit reaffirmed its prior recognition of the inherent authority of state and local police to enforce federal immigration law in an unpublished 2002 opinion, without appearing to distinguish between criminal and civil offenses. United States v. Favela-Favela. 41 Fed. App'x. 185 (10th Cir. 2002) (upholding alien smuggling conviction of person stopped by local law enforcement for a traffic violation and thereafter questioned regarding the immigration status of his passengers). As with prior cases, however, the case involved a stop made pursuant to an investigation of an offense under state law (a traffic violation), rather than being solely premised on an investigation into the immigration status of the occupants of the stopped vehicle. Moreover, the defendant's extended detention occurred during an investigation of illegal activity carrying criminal penalties under federal immigration law (unlawfully transporting unauthorized aliens).

[95] Interpreter Releases, vol. 55, Aug. 9, 1978, at 306 (quoting DOJ press release).

[96] *Id.*

[97] Interpreter Releases, vol. 60, Mar. 4, 1983, at 172-73 (quoting guidelines approved by the Attorney General on Feb. 10, 1983).

[98] Dep't of Justice, Office of Legal Counsel, *Handling of INS Warrants of Deportation in Relation to NCIC Wanted Person File*, at 4, 5, & n.11 (April 11, 1989).

[99] Dep't of Justice, Office of Legal Counsel, *Assistance by State and Local Police in Apprehending Illegal Aliens*, 1996 OLC LEXIS 76, at *2-*3 (Feb. 5, 1996) [hereinafter "1996 OLC Opinion"].

[100] *Id.* at *8 (citing, *inter alia*, *Ker v. California*, 374 U.S. 23 (1963); *Florida Avocado Growers, Inc. v. Paul*, 373 U.S. 132 (1963)). The opinion also discussed a number of legal authorities that recognized that state and local police were not preempted from enforcing the criminal provisions of federal immigration law. 1996 OLC Opinion, *supra* footnote 99, at *8-*13 (discussing, *inter alia*, *Gonzales v. City of Peoria*, 722 F.2d 468, 474 (9th Cir. 1983); *People v. Barajas*, 81 Cal. App. 3d 999 (1978) (state appellate court decision recognizing

ability of state police to arrest persons who commit criminal offenses under the INA relating to unlawful entry and reentry)).

[101] 1996 OLC Opinion, *supra* footnote 99, at *9.

[102] *Id.* at *16.

[103] *Id.* at *14 (quoting *Gonzales*, 772 F.2d at 476). The OLC Opinion also noted a California case which recognized that "[t]he civil provisions of the INA constitute a pervasive regulatory scheme such as to grant exclusive federal jurisdiction over immigration, thereby preempting state enforcement."). 1996 OLC Opinion, *supra* footnote 99, at *14 (quoting *Gates v. Superior Court*, 193 Cal. App. 3d 205, 213 (1987)).

[104] Dep't of Justice, Office of Legal Counsel, *Non-preemption of the Authority of State and Local Law Enforcement Officials to Arrest Aliens for Immigration Violations*, at 8 (Apr. 3, 2002) [hereinafter "2002 OLC Opinion"]. Initially, the DOJ did not make the 2002 OLC Opinion publicly available. Several immigration and public interest groups sought disclosure under the Freedom of Information Act. *See* Nat'l Council of La Raza v. Dep't of Justice, 411 F.3d 350 (2d Cir. 2005). As a result of this litigation, the DOJ was required to release a redacted version of the opinion, which can be viewed at http://www.aclu.org/FilesPDFs/ACF27DA.pdf or http://www.fairus.org/site/DocServer/ OLC_Opinion_2002.pdf?docID=1041.

[105] 2002 OLC Opinion, *supra* footnote 104, at 8.

[106] *Id.*

[107] *Id.* at 13.

[108] *Id.* at 7.

[109] *Id.* (italics in original).

[110] *Id.*

[111] *See* American Civil Liberties Union, *Re: 2002 OLC Opinion on State and Local Immigration Enforcement*, Mar. 6, 2009, *available at* http://www.aclu.org/files/assets/olc-exp-ag-4.pdf.

[112] *Id.* at 3.

[113] 2002 OLC Opinion, *supra* footnote 104, at 7-8.

[114] Tenaska Washington Partners, L.P. v. United States, 34 Fed. Cl. 434, 439 (Fed. Cl. 1995) ("Memoranda issued by the OLC ... are binding on the Department of Justice and other Executive Branch agencies and represent the official position of those arms of government.").

[115] Christensen v. Harris County, 529 U.S. 576, 587 (2000). *See also* Committee on Judiciary, U.S. House of Representatives v. Miers, 558 F.Supp.2d 53, 104 (D.D.C. 2008) (OLC opinions are entitled by the courts "to only as much weight as the force of their reasoning will support"); *Tenaska,* 34 Fed. Cl. at 440 ("[T]he fact that the Department of Justice asserts a legal theory does not bind the court to accept the reasoning as legally correct.").

[116] The text of the challenged Arizona statute, as amended, can be viewed at http://www.azleg.gov/alispdfs/council/SB1070-HB2162.PDF, and the text of the Alabama statute is available at http://alisondb.legislature.state.al.us/acas/searchablein struments /2011rs/bills/hb56.htm. For discussion and analysis of the Arizona statute, see CRS Report R41221, *State Efforts to Deter Unauthorized Aliens: Legal Analysis of Arizona's S.B. 1070*, by Kate M. Manuel, Michael John Garcia, and Larry M. Eig.

[117] Arizona PI Motion, *supra* footnote 71, at 33.

[118] Arizona PI Motion, *supra* footnote 71, at 25-34; United States v. Alabama, Plaintiff's Motion For Preliminary Injunction, No. 11-J-2746-S, at 58-65 (S.D. Ala., filed Aug. 1, 2011) [hereinafter "Alabama PI Motion"], available at http://www.justice.gov/opa/documents/motion-preliminary-injunction.pdf.

[119] Alabama PI Motion, *supra* footnote 118, at 54.
[120] *See* Arizona PI Motion, *supra* footnote 71, at 25.
[121] Alabama PI Motion, *supra* footnote 118, at 54 n.4 (italics in original).
[122] *Id.*
[123] *Arizona II*, 641 F.3d at 365 n. 24.

In: Illegal Aliens
Editor: K. Downs and D. Rasmussen
ISBN: 978-1-61942-631-3
© 2012 Nova Science Publishers, Inc.

Chapter 2

STATE AND LOCAL RESTRICTIONS ON EMPLOYING UNAUTHORIZED ALIENS*

Kate M. Manuel

SUMMARY

In May 2011, the Supreme Court ruled in Chamber of Commerce of the United States of America v. Whiting that federal immigration law did not preempt an Arizona statute that authorized or required the suspension or termination of the licenses of businesses that knowingly or intentionally hire unauthorized aliens, and also required that employers within Arizona use the federal government's E-Verify database to check employees' work authorization.

The doctrine of preemption derives from the Supremacy Clause of the U.S. Constitution, which establishes that federal law, treaties, and the Constitution itself are "the supreme Law of the Land." Thus, one essential aspect of the federal structure of government is that states can be precluded from taking actions that are otherwise within their authority if federal law is thereby thwarted. An act of Congress may preempt state or local action in a given area in any one of three ways: (1) the statute expressly states preemptive intent (express preemption); (2) a court concludes that Congress intended to occupy the regulatory field, thereby implicitly precluding state or local action in that area (field preemption);

---

* This is an edited, reformatted and augmented version of a Congressional Research Service publication, CRS Report for Congress R41991, from www.crs.gov, dated September 9, 2011.

or (3) state or local action directly conflicts with or otherwise frustrates the purpose of the federal scheme (conflict preemption).

When it was enacted in 1952, the Immigration and Nationality Act (INA) did not regulate the employment of unauthorized aliens, and several states subsequently enacted measures prohibiting the employment of individuals who were not lawful residents of the United States. In a 1976 decision declining to find one such measure preempted, the Supreme Court recognized that it was "within the mainstream of [a state's] police power" to restrict the employment of aliens within their jurisdiction whose presence in the United States was not authorized by the federal government. However, in 1986, Congress enacted the Immigration Reform and Control Act (IRCA), which amended the INA to sanction employers of unauthorized aliens and expressly preempt states and localities from sanctioning employers other than through "licensing and similar laws." Then, in 1996, Congress enacted the Illegal Immigration Reform and Immigrant Responsibility Act (IIRIRA), which authorized the creation of a pilot program for verifying work authorization that ultimately developed into the program known as E-Verify. Under federal law, use of E-Verify by private entities is generally voluntary, and the Secretary of Homeland Security may not require persons or entities not specified in IIRIRA to participate.

Prior to the Supreme Court's decision in Whiting, the federal courts of appeals had disagreed as to whether IRCA and IIRIRA preempted state and local measures like the Arizona statute. Some courts found that state licensing measures were within IRCA's "savings clause" even when the state independently determined whether an employer employed unauthorized aliens, and that IIRIRA did not prohibit states from requiring use of E-Verify. Others found that such measures were preempted because the licensing provisions disrupted the balance struck by Congress between deterring illegal immigration, minimizing burdens on employers, and preventing discrimination, and Congress did not want use of E-Verify to be mandatory.

In reaching its decision, the majority in Whiting relied primarily upon the "plain meaning" of IRCA and IIRIRA, while two dissents relied more heavily upon the legislative history and overall purpose of IRCA, in particular. The majority's decision apparently opens the door to additional state and local restrictions upon employing unauthorized aliens. However, it is unclear how closely such measures must parallel federal law to avoid being found to be preempted because they conflict with federal law, or how courts may apply the Whiting decision when reviewing other state and local immigration measures, such as those restricting access to housing or benefits.

INTRODUCTION

This report discusses state and local restrictions upon employing unauthorized aliens in light of the May 26, 2011, decision by the Supreme Court in *Chamber of Commerce of the United States of America v. Whiting.*[1] The Court's decision in *Whiting* arose from a facial challenge to the Legal Arizona Workers Act (LAWA), a predecessor of S.B. 1070,[2] which authorized or required the suspension or termination of the licenses of businesses that knowingly or intentionally hire unauthorized aliens, as well as required that employers in Arizona use the federal government's E-Verify database to check employees' work authorization.[3] Business, labor, and civil rights organizations had asserted that LAWA's licensing provisions were expressly and impliedly preempted by federal law and that its E-Verify provision was impliedly preempted.[4]

The doctrine of preemption derives from the Supremacy Clause of the Constitution, which establishes that federal law, treaties, and the Constitution itself are "the supreme Law of the Land."[5] Thus, one essential aspect of the federal structure of government is that states can be precluded from taking actions that are otherwise within their authority if federal law is thereby thwarted. An act of Congress may preempt state or local action in a given area in any one of three ways: (1) the statute expressly states preemptive intent (express preemption); (2) a court concludes that Congress intended to occupy the regulatory field, thereby implicitly precluding state or local action in that area (field preemption);[6] or (3) state or local action directly conflicts with or otherwise frustrates the purpose of the federal scheme (conflict preemption).[7]

In finding that LAWA was not preempted by federal immigration law, a majority of the Court apparently opens the door to additional state and local restrictions upon employing unauthorized aliens.[8] However, it is unclear how closely such measures must parallel federal law to avoid being found to be preempted because they conflict with federal law, or how courts may apply the *Whiting* decision when reviewing other state and local immigration measures, such as those restricting access to housing or benefits.[9]

This report does not address state and local authority to enforce federal immigration law, or state and local measures designed to deter unauthorized aliens from entering into or settling within a jurisdiction by restricting their ability to obtain housing or state or local benefits. The report also does not address potential due process or other issues that could be raised by state and local measures restricting the employment of unauthorized aliens.[10]

BACKGROUND

The Immigration and Nationality Act (INA) of 1952 established a "comprehensive federal statutory scheme for regulation of immigration and naturalization" and set "the terms and conditions of admission to the country and the subsequent treatment of aliens lawfully in the country."[11] However, the INA did not originally regulate employment of unauthorized aliens.[12] A number states subsequently enacted measures prohibiting the employment of individuals who were not lawful residents of the United States.[13] The constitutionality of one such measure—a California law providing that "[n]o employer shall knowingly employ an alien who is not entitled to lawful residence in the United States if such employment would have an adverse effect on lawful resident workers"—was at issue in the Supreme Court's 1976 decision in *De Canas v. Bica*.[14] There, in declining to hold that the California statute was preempted by federal immigration law,[15] the Court noted that

> Power to regulate immigration is unquestionably exclusively a federal power. But the Court has never held that every state enactment which in any way deals with aliens is a regulation of immigration and thus per se pre-empted by this constitutional power, whether latent or exercised.[16]

Further, the Court characterized prohibiting the employment of persons not entitled to work in the United States as "within the mainstream of [the State's] police power," and observed that the federal government had "at best" expressed a "peripheral concern" with the employment of unlawfully present aliens.[17]

Federal regulation of the employment of unauthorized aliens expanded significantly in 1986, when the Immigration Reform and Control Act (IRCA) was enacted.[18] IRCA amended the INA to make it unlawful for a person or other entity to hire, or to recruit or refer for a fee for employment in the United States, an alien, knowing that the alien is unauthorized.[19] IRCA also required employees to attest their eligibility to work and present specified identification documents, which employers are to examine and attest that they appear to be genuine.[20] The employer and employee attestations are accomplished through "I-9 forms," which are key to the verification process under IRCA. Employers who attempt to comply in good faith with these requirements are generally deemed to have complied notwithstanding technical or procedural failures to comply.[21]

Employers who violate IRCA's prohibitions on the unlawful employment of aliens may be subject to civil and/or criminal penalties under federal law.[22] However, IRCA provides that, "[t]he provisions of this section preempt any State or local law imposing civil or criminal sanctions (*other than through licensing and similar laws*) upon those who employ, or recruit or refer for a fee for employment, unauthorized aliens."[23] The language within the parentheses is commonly referred to as the "savings clause" because it potentially saves state and local "licensing and similar laws" from preemption. However, even when a state and local measure is not expressly preempted, as is the case here, the possibility of implied preemption remains.[24]

Ten years later, Congress expanded upon IRCA's employment verification regime when it enacted the Illegal Immigration Reform and Immigrant Responsibility Act (IIRIRA).[25] IIRIRA directed the Attorney General (later the Secretary of Homeland Security) to conduct three pilot programs for electronic employment eligibility confirmation, one of which, the Basic Pilot Program, ultimately developed into the E-Verify program.[26] IIRIRA also provided that participation by private parties in the pilot programs is generally voluntary,[27] and the Secretary of Homeland Security "may not require any person or other entity to participate."[28] However, as an incentive for participation, IIRIRA provides that entities which opt to participate and obtain confirmation of the identify and employment eligibility of employees establish a rebuttable presumption that they have not violated IRCA.[29]

Despite the enactment of IRCA and IIRIRA, concerns about the employment of unauthorized aliens persisted, particularly in states and localities that are significantly affected by unauthorized immigration.[30] Beginning in 2006, several of these states and localities enacted or considered measures that would deter unauthorized aliens from entering or settling in their jurisdiction by restricting access to work, housing, and benefits.[31] Those measures seeking to limit unauthorized aliens' ability to obtain work typically sanctioned employers of unauthorized aliens and/or required employers to use E-Verify to verify employees' work authorization.

As discussed below, the federal courts of appeals reached differing conclusions as to whether these measures were preempted by federal immigration law before the Supreme Court issued its decision in *Whiting*. Some courts found that state licensing measures were within IRCA's "savings clause" even when the state independently determined whether an employer employed unauthorized aliens, and that IIRIRA did not prohibit a state from requiring use of E-Verify. Others found that such measures were preempted because the licensing provisions disrupted the balance struck by Congress between deterring illegal immigration, minimizing burdens on employers, and preventing discrimination against those perceived as "foreign," and Congress did not want use of E-Verify to be mandatory. The Supreme Court granted certiorari in *Whiting*, in part, because of these differences among the courts of appeals.[32]

PRE-WHITING JURISPRUDENCE

Prior to the Supreme Court's decision in *Whiting*, some reviewing federal and state courts found that state and local measures suspending or revoking the licenses of businesses found to have employed unauthorized aliens and/or requiring employers within the jurisdiction to use E-Verify were not preempted by federal immigration law.[33] For example, in *Chicanos por la Causa v. Napolitano*, the U.S. Court of Appeals for the Ninth Circuit unanimously rejected the plaintiffs' argument that the Legal Arizona Workers Act was expressly preempted because it provided for the suspension and termination of licenses of employers whom state officers determined had hired unauthorized aliens.[34] The plaintiffs had asserted both that LAWA's savings clause "encompass[es] only licenses to engage in specific professions, such as medicine or law,"[35] and that Congress intended to permit revocation of the licenses of only those entities whom the federal government had determined violated IRCA.[36] However, in an opinion that gave rise to the Supreme Court's decision in *Whiting*, the Ninth Circuit rejected these arguments based on the "plain" or dictionary meaning of "license," as well as the legislative history of IRCA.[37] The Ninth Circuit also declined to find that LAWA's licensing provisions were impliedly preempted because of a "speculative, hypothetical possibility" of conflict in the practical operation of state and federal laws.[38] The Ninth Circuit similarly found that LAWA's E-Verify requirements are not impliedly preempted by IIRIRA since Congress's making E-Verify voluntary at the federal level "did not in and of itself" indicate that Congress intended to prohibit states from requiring participation.[39] A majority of the U.S. Court of Appeals for the Tenth Circuit also concluded that the E-Verify requirement of the Oklahoma Taxpayer and Citizen Protection Act of 2007 was not impliedly preempted in its decision in *Chamber of Commerce of the United States of America v. Edmondson*.[40]

Other courts reached contrary conclusions, finding that state and local licensing measures and/or E-Verify requirements are preempted by federal immigration law. In particular, in *Lozano v. City of Hazleton*, the U.S. Court of

Appeals for the Third Circuit unanimously found that a city ordinance with licensing provisions and an E-Verify requirement like those in LAWA was impliedly preempted. Although it reversed the district court's finding that the ordinance's licensing provisions were expressly preempted because they constituted "sanctions" under IRCA,[41] the Third Circuit nonetheless found that the provisions impermissibly conflicted with IRCA because they disrupted the balance that Congress had crafted between the "competing policy objectives of effectively deterring employment of unauthorized aliens, minimizing the resulting burden on employers, and protecting unauthorized aliens and citizens perceived as 'foreign' from discrimination."[42] According to the Third Circuit, the ordinance "substantially undermine[d]" this balance by prioritizing deterring the employment of unauthorized aliens over Congress's other objectives.[43] The Third Circuit further found that the ordinance "contravene[d] congressional objectives by requiring the use of E-Verify when Congress had declined to do so."[44] In so doing, the Third Circuit noted that other courts, including the Ninth Circuit, had found otherwise, but suggested that these decisions "fail[ed] to afford proper weight to the purposes underlying Congress's decision to retain E-Verify as a voluntary program."[45]

SUPREME COURT'S DECISION IN WHITING

In *Whiting*, the Supreme Court upheld LAWA's licensing provisions and E-Verify requirements in a 5-3 decision authored by Chief Justice Roberts. Justice Thomas concurred in the outcome and in those parts of the opinion which found that the statute's licensing provisions are not expressly preempted given the plain meaning of the relevant passages of IRCA and LAWA,[46] and that the statute's E-Verify requirement is not impliedly preempted because it does not conflict with federal law.[47] Three Justices dissented in two separate opinions which would have found LAWA's licensing provisions expressly preempted and its E-Verify requirements impliedly preempted. Justice Kagan recused herself.[48]

The Controlling Opinion

The controlling opinion, written by Chief Justice Roberts, focused first upon the "plain wording" of IRCA's savings clause and the Arizona statute, noting that federal law saves from express preemption "licensing and similar laws" and that the Arizona law, "on its face, purports to impose sanctions through licensing laws."[49] The petitioners had argued that LAWA does not constitute a licensing law under IRCA because LAWA defines "license" broadly, to include "any agency permit, certificate, approval, registration, charter or similar form of authorization," and governs only the suspension or termination of licenses, not their issuance.[50] However, the Court rejected both arguments. It found that LAWA was a licensing law, in part, because LAWA's definition of "license" largely "parroted" the definition of "license" given in the Administrative Procedure Act (APA).[51] The Court also found that laws which do not purport to govern the issuance of licenses constitute "licensing laws" under IRCA because a contrary construction would "run[] contrary to the definition [of license] that Congress itself has codified" in the APA, and "is also contrary to common sense."[52] Further, the Court suggested that even if LAWA were not a "licensing law" for purposes of IRCA, IRCA's savings clause also encompasses "similar laws."[53] While the petitioners had also asserted that the legislative history of IRCA supported a narrow interpretation of the savings clause, the Court found these arguments unpersuasive given that

> no such limit is remotely discernible in the statutory text. Absent any textual basis, we are not inclined to limit so markedly the otherwise broad phrasing of the savings clause. ... Congress's authoritative statement is the statutory text, not the legislative history.[54]

The controlling opinion also found that LAWA's licensing provisions are not impliedly preempted by IRCA.[55] In so finding, the Court noted that IRCA "specifically preserved authority for states" to impose sanctions through licensing and similar laws upon persons who employ unauthorized aliens.[56] According to the Court, because Congress specifically preserved this authority, "it stands to reason" that Congress did not intend that the federal system would be exclusive and necessarily conflict with any state system.[57] The Court further noted that Arizona's system, in particular, did not conflict with federal law, but rather "closely tracks IRCA's provisions in all material respects," adopting IRCA's definition of "unauthorized alien" and prohibiting state investigators from independently determining aliens' work authorization.[58] The Court also cited 8 U.S.C. §1373(c), which requires federal officials to respond to state and local inquiries regarding persons' immigration status, as evidence that Congress did not intend for the federal system to be exclusive.[59] In addition, the Court rejected petitioners' argument that LAWA upsets the balance that Congress sought to strike when enacting IRCA.[60] It did so, in part, because "[r]egulating instate businesses through licensing laws has never been ... an area of dominant federal concern," and LAWA does not "directly interefere[] with the operation of [any federal] program."[61] It also rejected petitioners' assertion that LAWA's penalties for licensing violations, which the petitioners and Justice Breyer characterized as a "business death penalty," are such significant sanctions that they disrupt the balance struck by Congress.[62] Instead, the Court viewed these sanctions as "typical attributes of a licensing regime," and noted that IRCA sought to balance state and federal interests, not just deterring unauthorized immigration, minimizing burdens on employers, and preventing discrimination against those perceived as "foreign."[63] According to the Court, in enacting IRCA,

> The principle that Congress adopted was not that the Federal Government can impose large sanctions, and the States only small ones. ... [I]n preserving to the States the authority to impose sanctions through licensing laws, Congress did not intend to preserve only those state laws that would have no effect.[64]

The Court further found that LAWA's E-Verify requirements were not impliedly preempted by federal law. The petitioners had asserted that these requirements conflicted with federal law because mandatory use of E-Verify impedes Congress's purpose in establishing a reliable and non-burdensome system of work authorization.[65] However, the Court found that Arizona's requiring the use of E-Verify does not conflict with federal law because the text of IIRIRA only prohibits the Secretary of Homeland Security from requiring the use of E-Verify, not anyone else.[66] The Court also emphasized that LAWA's E-Verify requirement is "entirely consistent" with federal law given that the consequences of using E-Verify were the same under federal and state law (i.e., the person was not entitled to a presumption that they had not violated IRCA). [67] The Court further found that "the Federal Government has consistently expanded and encouraged the use of E-Verify."[68] In addition, the Court noted that even the federal government disagreed with the petitioners' assertion that the E-Verify system would be overwhelmed—and Congress's purposes defeated—if other jurisdictions also required use of E-Verify.[69]

Dissenting Opinions

Three justices dissented in two separate opinions. Justice Breyer, in an opinion which Justice Ginsburg joined, rejected with the majority's characterization of LAWA as a "licensing law" falling within IRCA's savings clause.[70] According to this dissent, LAWA should be found to be expressly preempted because the legislative history of IRCA,[71] coupled with the balance that IRCA established between deterring unauthorized immigration, minimizing burdens on employers, and preventing discrimination against those perceived as "foreign,"[72] demonstrate that Congress intended to exempt from preemption only a narrow class of state laws, such as those governing the licensing of agricultural labor contractors.[73] Justice Breyer specifically objected to the majority's resort to the plain meaning of "license" in determining Congress's intent, asserting that the "statutory context" of the phrase, not its dictionary meaning, should be used to ascertain its meaning.[74] He also criticized the majority opinion on the grounds that the opinion would create obstacles to the accomplishment and execution of the full purposes and objectives of Congress by "permit[ing] States to turn virtually every permission-related state law into an employment-related 'licensing' law."[75] The dissent similarly would have found LAWA's E-Verify requirements preempted because, "[b]y making mandatory that which federal law seeks to make voluntary, the state provision stands as a significant 'obstacle to the accomplishment and execution of the full purposes and objectives of Congress.'"[76] In particular, Justice Breyer suggested that the majority was mistaken in inferring permission for states to make the program mandatory from language in IIRIRA prohibiting the Secretary of Homeland Security from requiring the use of E-Verify.[77]

Justice Sotomayor would also have found LAWA's licensing provisions expressly preempted. However, unlike Justice Breyer, she would have done so on the grounds that IRCA expressly preempts laws that permit states and localities to determine whether an employer has violated IRCA.[78] Her dissent reached this conclusion primarily because the legislative history of IRCA evidenced Congress's desire to replace the pre-IRCA "patchwork" of state laws prohibiting the employment of unauthorized aliens with a "uniformly" enforced federal law.[79] Accordingly, the dissent would find that states and localities are preempted from independently adjudicating whether an employer has employed an unauthorized alien.[80] In support of this conclusion, the dissent also noted the limitations on use of I-9 forms under federal law,[81] as well as the fact that federal law provides no mechanism for states to access information regarding aliens' work authorization.[82] The dissent similarly would have found LAWA's E-Verify requirement impliedly preempted because it is "in contravention of the significant policy objectives motivating Congress' decision to make participation in the E-Verify program voluntary."[83] While noting that the fact that state law makes mandatory something Congress made voluntary does not, *per se*, result in preemption, Justice Sotomayor emphasized that LAWA differs from other state laws in that it directly regulates the relationship between the federal government and private parties by requiring private employers to use the federal E-Verify database.[84] The dissent also noted the U.S. government's "uniquely federal interest" in managing the use of the E-Verify database, and that Congress's decision not to create a mandatory program was based, in part, on the costs of such a program.[85]

IMPLICATIONS

The Supreme Court's decision in *Whiting* apparently opens the door to the enactment of additional state and local measures restricting the employment of unauthorized aliens.[86] However, it remains to be seen what state and local measures—beyond those exactly paralleling LAWA— are permissible under *Whiting*. The controlling opinion in *Whiting* repeatedly emphasized how closely LAWA "tracks IRCA's provisions in all material respects,"[87] and reviewing courts could potentially still find that state and local measures that "track" IRCA less closely are preempted.[88] Also, the *Whiting* decision does not directly address the permissibility of state and local measures directly targeting unauthorized workers, as opposed to their employers. Such measures have been viewed by reviewing courts as preempted because they "conflict[] with ... Congress' IRCA intent."[89] IRCA itself imposes no penalties upon unauthorized workers who seek or obtain work, but its silence here, coupled with the sanctions it imposes on those who hire unauthorized workers, have been seen by some courts as "justif[ying] a preemptive inference that Congress intended to prohibit states from criminalizing work."[90] The U.S. Court of Appeals for the Ninth Circuit recently reached this conclusion in upholding a district court's decision to preliminarily enjoin those sections of S.B. 1070 that make it an Arizona crime for an unlawfully present alien to apply for or solicit work in the state, or work as an employee or an independent contractor in the state.[91] However, the State of Arizona has appealed this decision to the

Supreme Court,[92] and a challenge to a similar provision in an Alabama law is currently pending before a federal district court.[93]

It also remains to be seen whether and how other courts might apply the *Whiting* decision and, particularly, heed the controlling opinion's skepticism about the role that congressional balancing of competing interests plays in determining whether state or local measures addressing unauthorized alien employment are preempted. For example, in its challenge to Alabama's "omnibus" immigration bill, which authorizes state and local police to participate in immigration enforcement activities, sanctions certain conduct which may facilitate the presence of unlawfully present aliens, and denies unlawfully present aliens access to certain government services, the Department of Justice repeatedly claimed that the bill disrupts the balance established by Congress and, thus, is preempted.[94]

There have been calls for Congress to preempt state and local E-Verify requirements, in particular, because of the burdens that complying with various state and local requirements would impose on employers.[95] Legislation (H.R. 2164) has been introduced in the House that would do this.[96] Legislation has also been introduced that would expressly preempt state and local measures that prohibit employers from verifying new hires or current employees through E-Verify (S. 1196),[97] as well as amend the employer sanctions provisions of the INA to establish that neither they nor any other federal law preempt state or local measures imposing civil or criminal sanctions upon those who employ unauthorized aliens (H.R. 2670). Along with the Supreme Court's decision in *Whiting*, the enactment of such legislation could also potentially shape the extent and nature of state and local restrictions on employing unauthorized aliens.

End Notes

[1] 131 S. Ct. 1968, __ U.S. __ (2011).

[2] S.B. 1070 is a more comprehensive Arizona law on unauthorized aliens. The Ninth Circuit recently upheld a district court decision enjoining implementation of those provisions of S.B. 1070 requiring state and local law enforcement officials to facilitate the detection of unauthorized aliens in their daily enforcement activities, among other things. For more on S.B. 1070, see generally CRS Report R41221, *State Efforts to Deter Unauthorized Aliens: Legal Analysis of Arizona's S.B. 1070*, by Kate M. Manuel, Michael John Garcia, and Larry M. Eig.

[3] *See* ARIZ. REV. STAT. ANN. §§23-211 to 23-214. To prevail on a facial challenge, the challenger must establish that "no set of circumstances exists under which the Act would be valid." United States v. Salerno, 481 U.S. 739 (1987). The U.S. Court of Appeals for the

Ninth Circuit recently suggested, in a case challenging another Arizona statute targeting unauthorized immigrants, that "there can be no constitutional application of a statute that, on its face, conflicts with Congressional intent and therefore is preempted by the Supremacy Clause." United States v. Arizona, 641 F.3d 339, 345-46 (9th Cir. 2011). The Ninth Circuit's application of *Salerno* here is one thing Arizona has challenged in its petition to the Supreme Court for certiorari. *See* Arizona v. United States, Petition for a Writ of Certiorari (S. Ct. filed Aug. 10, 2011), at 16, 30 (copy on file with the author). The U.S. Court of Appeals for the Third Circuit had previously raised questions about the applicability of *Salerno* to a facial challenge to a Hazleton, Pennsylvania, ordinance sanctioning those who employ or rent housing to unauthorized aliens. *See* Lozano v. City of Hazleton, 620 F.3d 170, 203 n.25 (3d Cir. 2010), *aff'g, in part*, 496 F. Supp. 2d 477 (M.D. Pa. 2007).

[4] *See, e.g.*, Chamber of Commerce v. Whiting, No. 09-115, Brief for the Petitioners (S. Ct. filed Sept. 1, 2010), at 20, 37, 47, *available at* http://www.americanbar.org/content/dam/aba/publishing/preview/publiced_preview_briefs_pdfs_09_10_09_115_Petitioner.authcheckdam.pdf.

[5] U.S. Const. art. VI, cl. 2.

[6] Congressional intent to "occupy the field" to the exclusion of state law can be inferred when "[1] the pervasiveness of the federal regulation precludes supplementation by the States, [2] where the federal interest in the field is sufficiently dominant, or [3] where the object sought to be obtained by the federal law and the character of obligations imposed by it ... reveal the same purpose." Schneidewind v. ANR Pipeline Co., 485 U.S. 293, 300 (1988) (internal quotations omitted).

[7] *See, e.g.*, Crosby v. Nat'l Foreign Trade Council, 530 U.S. 363, 373 (2000); English v. Gen. Elec. Co., 496 U.S. 72, 78-79 (1990); Silkwood v. Kerr-McGee Corp., 464 U.S. 238, 248-49 (1984); Pac. Gas & Elec. Co. v. State Energy Res. Conservation & Dev. Comm'n, 461 U.S. 190, 203-04 (1983). The delineation between these categories, particularly between field and conflict preemption, is not rigid. *See English*, 462 U.S. at 79 n.5 ("By referring to these three categories, we should not be taken to mean that they are rigidly distinct. Indeed, field pre-emption may be understood as a species of conflict pre-emption: A state law that falls within a pre-empted field conflicts with Congress' intent (either express or plainly implied) to exclude state regulation."); *Crosby*, 530 U.S. at 373 n.6.

[8] *See, e.g.*, *Uptick in State Immigration Laws May Force Congress to Act, Speakers Say*, 5 WORKPLACE IMMIGR. REP. 381 (July 25, 2011).

[9] As discussed below, the majority in *Whiting* focused primarily upon questions of statutory interpretation pertaining to state restrictions upon employing unauthorized aliens and seemed skeptical of arguments that state enactments in this area disrupted the balance established by Congress between deterring unauthorized immigration, protecting employers from burdensome requirements, and preventing discrimination.

[10] All persons within the United States, including unauthorized aliens, are protected by the Fourteenth Amendment, which provides that no state may "deprive any person of life, liberty, or property, without due process of law." *See, e.g.*, Zadvydas v. Davis, 533 U.S. 678, 693 (2001); Board of Regents v. Roth, 408 U.S. 564, 572 (1972) (recognizing liberty interests in the right to contract and engage in the "common occupations of life"); Bell v. Burson, 402 U.S. 535, 539 (1971) (recognizing property interests in the revocation of a business license). The types of procedures necessary to ensure due process can vary depending upon the circumstances and interests involved. *See* Mathews v. Eldridge, 424 U.S. 319, 335 (1976) (holding that "[i]dentification of the specific dictates of due process"

requires consideration of (1) the private interests that would be affected by the action; (2) the risk of erroneous deprivation of such interests, and the probable value of alternative procedural safeguards; and (3) the government's interests, including the burdens that would be entailed by alternate procedures). However, states and localities must generally provide, at a minimum, notice of the proposed deprivation and a hearing before an impartial tribunal. State and local restrictions upon the hiring or employment of unauthorized aliens have been challenged on the grounds that they deprive employers and/or employees of due process. *See, e.g.*, Chicanos Por La Causa, Inc. v. Napolitano, 558 F.3d 856, 867-69 (9th Cir. 2009), *aff'g* Ariz. Contractors Ass'n v. Candelaria, 534 F. Supp. 2d 1036 (D. Ariz. 2008); Gray v. City of Valley Park, No. 4:07CB00881 ERW, 2008 U.S. Dist. LEXIS 7238, at *84-*97 (E.D. Mo. Jan. 31, 2008); *Lozano*, 496 F. Supp. 2d at 533-37. Such challenges have generally not succeeded, but could become more prevalent now that certain preemption-based challenges appear to be foreclosed by the Supreme Court's decision in *Whiting*.

[11] De Canas v. Bica, 424 U.S. 351, 353, 359 (1976).

[12] When it was enacted, the INA did contain a provision establishing that "employment (including the usual and normal practices incident to employment) shall not be deemed to constitute harboring." *See* 8 U.S.C. §1324 note.

[13] *See* Brief for the Petitioners, *supra* note 4, at 25 (noting that approximately 12 states had such laws at the time IRCA was enacted).

[14] *De Canas*, 424 U.S. at 352 n.1.

[15] *Id.* at 365 (remanding the case for California courts to construe the California statute and determine whether it conflicts with federal law). The California Court of Appeals, in a decision which the California Supreme Court declined to review, had found that the statute was preempted because Congress intended to occupy the field. *See* 115 Cal. Rptr. 444, 446 (1974). Arguments expressly based on field preemption have not figured prominently in the litigation over state and local measures targeting the employment of unauthorized aliens since *De Canas*. However, the line between field and conflict preemption "is not rigid," and those challenging LAWA argued, among other things, that Congress intended the federal system to be exclusive, and any state system necessarily conflicts with federal law. *See* Brief for the Petitioners, *supra* note 4, at 39 ("There is no room in this scheme [IRCA] for alternative investigatory and adjudicatory systems.").

[16] *De Canas*, 424 U.S. at 354, 356 (internal citations omitted).

[17] *Id.* at 356, 360.

[18] P.L. 99-603, 100 Stat. 3359 (Nov. 6, 1986) (codified, as amended, at 8 U.S.C. §§1324a-1324b). *Cf.* Hoffman Plastic Compounds v. NLRB, 535 U.S. 137, 147 (2002) (noting that IRCA created a "comprehensive scheme prohibiting the employment of illegal aliens in the United States" and "forcefully made combating the employment of illegal aliens central to the policy of immigration law").

[19] 8 U.S.C. §1324a(a)(1)(A). IRCA also defined an "unauthorized alien" as one who is not admitted for permanent residence, or not authorized to be employed by IRCA or the Secretary of Homeland Security. 8 U.S.C. §1324a(h)(3).

[20] 8 U.S.C. §1324a(b)(1)(A).

[21] 8 U.S.C. §1324a(b)(6)(A). There are exceptions for those who do not correct failures to comply after notice, or have engaged or are engaging in a pattern or practice of violations. 8 U.S.C. §1324a(b)(6)(B)-(C).

[22] 8 U.S.C. §1324a(e)-(f). For a discussion of current penalties, see CRS Report R40002, *Immigration-Related Worksite Enforcement: Performance Measures*, by Andorra Bruno.

[23] 8 U.S.C. §1324a(h)(2) (emphasis added).

[24] *See, e.g.*, Geier v. Am. Honda Motor Co., 529 U.S. 861, 869-70 (2000) (construing the language of the savings clause in question to find that "[n]othing in [its language] suggests an intent to save state-tort actions that conflict with federal law").

[25] P.L. 104-208, div. C., title IV, subtitle A, §§401-405, 110 Stat. 3009-655 to 3009-666 (Sept. 30, 1996) (codified in various sections of Titles 8 and 18 of the United States Code).

[26] *Id.* at §401, 110 Stat. 3009-655 to 3009-656. Originally, the three pilot programs established by IIRIRA were to last for a four year period. *Id.* However, the Basic Pilot Program, in particular, was subsequently extended. *See, e.g.*, Consolidated Security, Disaster Assistance & Continuing Appropriations Act, 2009, P.L. 119-329, §143, 122 Stat. 3574, 3580 (Sept. 30, 2008); Basic Pilot Program Extension and Expansion Act of 2003, P.L. 108-156, 117 Stat. 1944 (Dec. 3, 2003); Basic Pilot Program Extension Act of 2001, P.L. 107-128, 115 Stat. 2407 (Jan. 16, 2002). For more on E-Verify, see generally CRS Report R40446, *Electronic Employment Eligibility Verification*, by Andorra Bruno.

[27] Use of E-Verify is required for federal government entities and federal contractors, and private entities that unlawfully employ unauthorized aliens may be required to use it. *See* Chamber of Commerce of the United States of America v. Napolitano, 648 F. Supp. 2d 726 (S.D. Md. 2009) (upholding Executive Order 13465 and its implementing regulations, which generally require federal contractors to use E-Verify to check the work authorization of employees performing federal contracts). In rejecting arguments that the executive order and regulations violated IIRIRA because they "required" contractors to use E-Verify, the court noted that the "decision to be a government contractor is voluntary and ... no one has a right to be a government contractor." *Id.* at 733. The court also found that IIRIRA only prohibits the Secretary of Homeland Security from requiring use of E-Verify, not the President. *Id.* at 734. In his dissenting opinion in *Whiting*, Justice Breyer similarly emphasized that contractors "voluntarily" enter a "special relation with the Government" in explaining why the majority was mistaken in implying permission for states to require use of E-Verify from the language in IIRIRA prohibiting the Secretary of Homeland Security from requiring the use of E-Verify. *Whiting*, 131 S. Ct. at 1997.

[28] P.L. 104-208, div. C., title IV, subtitle A, §402(a), 110 Stat. 3009-656.

[29] *Id.*, at §402(b), 110 Stat. 3009-656 to 3009-657.

[30] For example, Arizona notes that it is the "gateway for nearly half of the nation's illegal border crossings" in its petition to the Supreme Court for certiorari in the S.B. 1070 litigation. *See* Petition for a Writ of Certiorari, *supra* note 3, at 2.

[31] *See* S. Karthick Ramakrishnan and Tom (Tak) Wong, University of California – Riverside Campus, "Immigration Policies Go Local: The Varying Responses of Local Governments to Undocumented Immigration," Nov. 9, 2007, *available at* http://www.law.berkeley.edu/files/RamakrishnanWongpaperfinal(1).pdf (finding that less than 1% of all municipalities had enacted measures addressing unlawfully present aliens). *See also* National Conference of State Legislatures, "State Laws Related to Immigration and Immigrants," http://www.ncsl.org/default.aspx?tabid=19897 (surveying state measures enacted or proposed between 2009 and the present).

[32] *See* 130 S. Ct. 3498 (2010).

[33] Other state and local measures targeting employers of unauthorized aliens have been found to be expressly preempted by IRCA. *See* Chamber of Commerce of the United States of America v. Edmondson, 594 F.3d 742 (10th Cir. 2010), *aff'g, in part*, Chamber of Commerce v. Henry, No. CIV-08-109-C, 2008 U.S. Dist. LEXIS 44168 (W.D. Okla. June 4, 2008) (finding that IRCA expressly preempted provisions of a state statute that would have (1) made it a "discriminatory practice" for an employer to terminate an authorized

worker while retaining an employee that is known, or reasonably should have been known, to be unauthorized, and (2) required contractors to verify the work eligibility of their independent contractors or withhold certain taxes from them). The court found the latter requirement preempted, in part, because it disrupted the balance that Congress had constructed in excluding independent contractors from verification obligations. 594 F.3d at 767, 769. Concerns about the effects of state and local legislation upon the balance struck by Congress also formed the basis for the decision by the U.S. Court of Appeals for the Third Circuit in *Lozano v. City of Hazleton*, discussed below. However, as is also discussed below, the controlling opinion in *Whiting* seemed skeptical of arguments that state enactments targeting employers of unauthorized aliens disrupt the balance established by Congress between deterring unauthorized immigration, protecting employers from burdensome requirements, and preventing discrimination.

[34] 558 F.3d at 864-66.

[35] *Id.* at 865. It should be noted that LAWA expressly excludes professional licenses from its definition of "license." ARIZ. REV. STAT. §23-211(9)(c)(ii).

[36] *Id.*

[37] *Id.* (quoting BLACK'S LAW DICTIONARY 940 (8th ed. 2004) and H.R. REP. NO. 99-682(i), at 58, *as reprinted in* 1986 U.S.C.C.A.N. 5649, 5662). In particular, the district and appellate courts noted that the language from the House Report which the plaintiffs relied upon as evidence that Congress did not intend to preempt state or local "processes" concerning the suspension, revocation, or refusal to issue a license to anyone "found to have violated the sanctions provisions of this legislation" was "contradicted" by a later statement that Congress did not intend to preempt licensing or "fitness to do business" laws. Under the plaintiffs' proposed reading, only those whom the federal government found to have violated IRCA could be sanctioned (pursuant to state or local "processes") because Congress provided that only those "found to have violated the sanctions provisions *of this legislation*" could be sanctioned, and federal officials adjudicate violations under IRCA. *But see Gray*, 2008 U.S. Dist. LEXIS 7238, at *36 ("There is no requirement in the statute that a finding be made by the federal government that a person has employed, recruited, or referred for a fee for employment, unauthorized aliens, only that those individuals are subject to penalty.").

[38] 558 F.3d at 866. The Ninth Circuit did, however, acknowledge the possibility of as-applied challenges in the future. *Id.* at 861. *See also* Transcript of Oral Argument, at 41-42, *Chamber of Commerce v. Whiting*, 131 S. Ct. 1968 (copy on file with author) (counsel for Arizona noting the possibility of as-applied challenges). As of April 2010, there had been few legal actions brought under LAWA. *See, e.g.*, Nicole Santa Cruz, *Arizona Has Rarely Invoked Its Last Tough Immigration Law*, LOS ANGELES TIMES, Apr. 19, 2010, *available at* http://articles.latimes.com/2010/apr/19/nation/lana-employer-sanctions19-2010apr19 (reporting that 12 of the state's 15 counties had not taken legal action against any business for failure to comply with LAWA, although Maricopa County reported that complaints had been brought against three businesses).

[39] 558 F.3d at 866-67. The court further noted that Congress had "plainly envisioned and endorsed" increased usage of E-Verify, and that LAWA is consistent with and furthers Congress' purpose here. *Id.* at 866.

[40] *Edmondson*, 594 F.3d at 768. The dissenting judge in *Edmonson*, as well as the district court, would have found the E-Verify requirement to be expressly preempted. The dissenting judge, in particular, emphasized that this requirement disputed the balance struck by Congress between the competing goals of deterring unauthorized immigration, minimizing

the burden on employers, and preventing discrimination against those perceived as "foreign." *See id.* at 768.

[41] 620 F.3d at 208-10 (relying on MERRIAM-WEBSTER'S DICTIONARY and BLACK'S LAW DICTIONARY to establish the plain meaning of "license"). The Third Circuit also reversed the district's court's finding that a presumption against preemption should be applied when reviewing the ordinance. *See id.* 206-07 (presumption against preemption applies when legislation involves areas within states' historic police powers, even if Congress subsequently legislates in these areas). While the Ninth Circuit similarly concluded that a presumption against preemption should be applied when reviewing LAWA, the Tenth Circuit reached a contrary conclusion. *Compare Chicanos Por La Causa*, 558 F.3d at 865 *with Edmonson*, 594 F.3d at 768 n.2. In *Whiting*, the Supreme Court did not address whether a presumption against preemption is to be accorded to state and local measures regulating the employment of unauthorized aliens.

[42] 620 F.3d at 210.

[43] *Id.* at 211. In reaching this conclusion, the court noted that the ordinance increased the burden on employers by creating a "separate and independent adjudicative system;" provided "substantially fewer" procedural protections than IRCA; and would subject employers to a "patchwork" of state and local laws. *Id.* at 212-17. The court also noted that the ordinance failed to balance its sanctions with anti-discrimination provisions, but instead "impos[ed] additional sanctions on employers who hire unauthorized aliens, while not penalizing those who discriminate." *Id.* at 217-19. IRCA specifically prohibits discrimination by employers on the basis of nationality or citizenship, and its fines for violations of this prohibition correspond to those for knowingly employing an unauthorized alien. *See* 8 U.S.C. §1324b.

[44] 620 F.3d at 214.

[45] *Id.* at 216. Hazleton appealed the Third Circuit's decision to the Supreme Court, which remanded the case for reconsideration in light of its decision in *Whiting*. *See* 180 L. Ed. 2d 243.

[46] 131 S. Ct. at 1977-81.

[47] *Id.* at 1985-86. Justice Thomas did not join in those sections of the controlling opinion which found that LAWA's licensing provisions are not impliedly preempted because they do not conflict with federal law or impermissibly upset the balance among competing objectives that Congress sought to strike when enacting IRCA. *See id.* at 1981-84. Although Justice Thomas did not state his reasons for not joining these portions of the *Whiting* opinion, in prior preemption cases he has expressed skepticism regarding the Court's reliance on the implied preemption doctrine and indicated an unwillingness to join portions of any opinion which expressly or implicitly endorses its usage. *See Wyeth v. Levine,* 555 U.S. 555, __, 129 S. Ct. 1187, 1205 (2009) (Thomas, J., concurring) (agreeing with Court's judgment that federal law did not preempt state law claim relating to drug company's labeling of product, but stating that he could not "join the majority's implicit endorsement of far-reaching implied pre-emption doctrines").

[48] *Id.* at 1972.

[49] *Id.* at 1977.

[50] *Id.* at 1978-79 (quoting ARIZ. REV. STAT. ANN. §23-212(A) & (F) and §23-212.01(A) & (F)).

[51] *Id.* at 1978. The APA's definition of "license" includes "the whole or a part of an agency permit, certificate, approval, registration, charter, membership, statutory exemption or other form of permission." 5 U.S.C. §551(8).

[52] 131 S. Ct. at 1978 (quoting 5 U.S.C. §551(9), which defines "licensing" as encompassing any "agency process respecting the grant, renewal, denial, revocation, suspension, annulment, withdrawal, limitation, amendment, modification, or conditioning of a license").

[53] *Id.* at 1978 ("[E]ven if a law regulating articles of incorporation, partnership certificates, and the like is not itself a 'licensing law,' it is at the very least 'similar' to a licensing law, and therefore comfortably within the savings clause.").

[54] *Id.* at 1980. In particular, the Court noted that the House Report, which the petitioners said evidenced Congress's intent to permit *only* state and local licensing measures targeting farm labor contractors whom the federal government determined had violated IRCA, had previously been dismissed by the Court as "'a rather slender reed' from 'one House of a politically divided Congress.'" *Id.* (quoting *Hoffman*, 535 U.S. at 149-50).

[55] *Id.* at 1981-85. Justice Thomas concurred in the result, but not in the Chief Justice's opinion here. *See supra* note 47 and accompanying text.

[56] *Id.* at 1981.

[57] *Id.*

[58] *Id.*

[59] *Id.* at 1982. *See also* 8 U.S.C. §1373(c) ("The Immigration and Naturalization Service shall respond to an inquiry by a Federal, State, or local government agency, seeking to verify or ascertain the citizenship or immigration status of any individual within the jurisdiction of the agency for any purpose authorized by law, by providing the requested verification or status information.").

[60] 131 S. Ct. at 1982.

[61] *Id.* at 1983. According to the controlling opinion, these factors differentiated the instant case from the precedents that the petitioners cited.

[62] *Id.* at 1983-84.

[63] *Id.*

[64] *Id.* at 1984-95.

[65] Brief for the Petitioners, *supra* note 4, at 47-51.

[66] 131 S. Ct. at 1985.

[67] *Id.* at 1985-86.

[68] *Id.* at 1986.

[69] *Id. See also* Chamber of Commerce v. Whiting, Brief for the United States as Amicus Curiae Supporting Petitioners, No. 09-115 (S. Ct. filed Sept. 2010), at 34, *available at* http://www.americanbar.org/content/dam/aba/publishing/preview/publiced_preview_briefs_pdfs_09_10_09_115_PetitionerAmCuUSA.authcheckdam.pdf ("[T]he E-Verify system can accommodate the increased use that the Arizona statute and existing similar laws would create.").

[70] 131 S. Ct. at 1987 ("[The] statute strays beyond the bounds of the federal licensing exception, for it defines 'license' to include articles of incorporation and partnership certificates, indeed *virtually every* state-law authorization for *any* firm, corporation, or partnership to do business in the State.").

[71] *Id.* at 1994.

[72] *Id.* at 1989-90.

[73] *Id.* at 1992 ("The federal licensing exception cannot apply to a state statute that, like Arizona's statute, seeks to bring virtually all articles of incorporation and partnership within its scope. I would find the scope of the exception to federal pre-emption to be far more limited. Context, purpose, and history make clear that the 'licensing and similar laws' at issue involve *employment-related* licensing systems.").

[74] *Id.* at 1988.

[75] *Id.* at 1993 (noting that, under the majority's approach, a "state need only call the permission a 'license' and revoke the license should its holder hire an unauthorized alien. If what was not previously an employment-related licensing law can become one simply by using it as a sanction for hiring unauthorized aliens or simply by state definition, indeed, if the State can call a corporate charter an employment-related licensing law, then why not an auto licensing law (amended to revoke the driver's licenses of those who hire unauthorized aliens)? Why not a dog licensing law?"). In particular, the dissent noted a South Carolina law imputing licenses to all employers within the state that are conditioned on not hiring unauthorized aliens, and suggested that the exception would "swallow" the rule under the majority approach. *Id.* (citing S.C. CODE ANN. §41-8-20 (Supp. 2010) ("All private employers in South Carolina ... shall be imputed a South Carolina employment licenses, which permits a private employer to employ a person in this State").

[76] *Id.* at 1995.

[77] *Id.* at 1997. In particular, Justice Breyer emphasized that the requirements of Executive Order 13465 are different from those in LAWA because federal contractors "enter voluntarily into a special relation with the Government." *Id. See supra* note 27.

[78] *Id.* at 1998.

[79] *Id.* at 1999-2000 (quoting P.L. 99-603, §115, 100 Stat. 3384 ("It is the sense of the Congress that ... the immigration laws of the United States should be enforced vigorously and uniformly."). Justice Sotomayor emphasized that the majority's approach would "subject[] employers to a patchwork of enforcement schemes similar to the one that Congress sought to displace when it enacted IRCA." *Id.* at 2001-02.

[80] *Id.* at 2000-01. *See also id.* at 2003 ("I can discern no reason why Congress would have intended for state courts inexperienced in immigration matters to adjudicate, in the context of licensing sanctions, the very same question that IRCA commits to federal officers, [administrative law judges], and the courts of appeals.").

[81] *Id.* at 2001 (discussing 8 U.S.C. §1324a(b)(5), which provides that neither I-9 forms nor the information contained in or appended to them may be used "for purposes other than for enforcement of this chapter and sections 1001, 1028, 1546, and 1621 of title 18" of the United States Code).

[82] *Id.* In further support of this conclusion, the dissent contrasted IRCA's provisions regarding the employment of unauthorized aliens with those regarding aliens' eligibility for Medicaid and food stamps, noting that while IRCA created a mechanism whereby states and localities could verify the latter, it did not create a similar mechanism whereby they could verify the former. Also, like Justice Breyer, Justice Sotomayor noted that 8 U.S.C. §1373(c) does not require federal officials to provide states and localities with information on aliens' work authorization status.

[83] *Id.* at 1998.

[84] *Id.* at 2005-06.

[85] *Id.* at 2006. The dissent further noted that the executive branch's view that it is now capable of handling the demands of increased usage of E-Verify is immaterial because only Congress's intent at the time it enacted IRCA is relevant. *Id.* at 2006-07.

[86] The petitioners in *Whiting* cited over a dozen such measures in their September 1, 2010, brief to the Supreme Court. Brief for the Petitioners, *supra* note 4, at 14 (citing Arizona, Colorado, Georgia, Louisiana, Mississippi, Missouri, Oklahoma, South Carolina, Tennessee, Virginia, and West Virginia statutes, as well as ordinances of Albertville, Alabama; Apple Valley, California; Hazleton, Pennsylvania; and Mission Viejo,

California). However, this number has increased since then, with lawmakers in 14 states and Puerto Rico reportedly enacting 23 employment-related immigration bills in the first half of 2011. *See In First Half of 2011 States Enacted 23 Immigration-Related Immigration Measures*, 5 WORKPLACE IMMIGR. REP. 381 (July 25, 2011). Another five states reportedly enacted six omnibus bills with employment provisions. Many of these measures would require the use of E-Verify by at least some employers within the state. However, at least one state has tried to preclude use of E-Verify. *See* 820 ILL. COMP. STAT. ANN. 55/12 (2007) (prohibiting employers, with certain exceptions, from using E-Verify "until the Social Security Administration (SSA) and Department of Homeland Security (DHS) databases are able to make a determination on 99% of the tentative non-confirmation notices issued to employers within 3 days, unless otherwise required by federal law"). This law was found to be preempted. United States v. Illinois, No. 07-3261, 2009 U.S. Dist. LEXIS 19533 (C.D. Ill. Mar. 12, 2009).

[87] S. Ct. at 1981 (noting that LAWA adopted IRCA's definition of "unauthorized alien" and prohibited state investigators from independently determining aliens' work authorization). Had LAWA authorized state officials to independently determine aliens' work authorization, it could potentially have been struck down as an impermissible regulation of immigration under *De Canas*. *See* 424 U.S. at 355 (characterizing a regulation of immigration as "essentially a determination of who should or should not be admitted into the country, and the conditions under which a legal entrant may remain"). *See, e.g.*, League of United Latin Am. Citizens v. Wilson, 908 F. Supp. 755, 770 (C.D. Cal. 1995) (finding that California's Proposition 187, which would have required state personnel to verify the immigration status of persons with whom they came into contact, was preempted, in part, because it "created an entirely *independent* set of criteria by which to classify individuals based on immigration status"); Villas at Parkside Partners v. City of Farmers Branch, 577 F. Supp. 2d 858, 869-70 (N.D. Tex. 2008) (finding that an ordinance that relied upon classifications used by the U.S. Department of Housing and Urban Development in determining eligibility for housing subsidies to determine who could rent private housing constituted an impermissible regulation of immigration because it did not rely on the INA's classification of aliens' status).

[88] *See supra* note 33 (discussing those provisions of the Oklahoma Taxpayer and Citizen Protection Act of 2007 that were found to be preempted because they conflict with federal immigration law).

[89] *Arizona*, 641 F.3d at 358.

[90] *Id.* at 359.

[91] *Id. See also* S.B. 1070, §5, as amended by H.B. 2162, *available at* http://www.azleg.gov/alispdfs/council/SB1070-HB2162.PDF.

[92] Petition for a Writ of Certiorari, *supra* note 3.

[93] *See* Complaint, United States v. Alabama, No. 2:11-cv-02746-IPJ, at 27-28 (N.D. Ala. filed Aug. 1, 2011).

[94] *Id.* at 4 ("By emphasizing one goal—maximum enforcement—H.R. 556 ignores the many other objectives that Congress has established for the federal immigration system. This failure to abide by the set of interests animating federal immigration law provides sufficient reason that H.B. 56 is preempted."); Plaintiff's Motion for Preliminary Injunction, United States v. Alabama, No. 11-J-2746-S, at 7 (N.D. Ala. filed on Aug. 1, 2011) (noting that "federal immigration laws do not focus on one singular interest, but instead seek to further multiple and sometimes competing objectives").

[95] *See, e.g.*, Uptick in State Immigration Laws, *supra* note 8.

[96] H.R. 2164 would expressly preempt state and local E-Verify measures, along with other measures "relat[ing] to the hiring, continued employment, or status verification for employment eligibility purposes, of unauthorized aliens." However, it would allow states and localities to revoke the business or other licenses of employers who fail to electronically verify the employment eligibility of their workers.

[97] An Illinois statute that would have prohibited Illinois employers, with certain exceptions, from using E-Verify until certain conditions were met was found to be preempted by a federal district court in 2009. *See Illinois*, 2009 U.S. Dist. LEXIS 19533.

In: Illegal Aliens
Editor: K. Downs and D. Rasmussen
ISBN: 978-1-61942-631-3
© 2012 Nova Science Publishers, Inc.

Chapter 3

STATE AND LOCAL RESTRICTIONS ON EMPLOYING, RENTING PROPERTY TO, OR PROVIDING SERVICES FOR UNAUTHORIZED ALIENS: LEGAL ISSUES AND RECENT JUDICIAL DEVELOPMENTS*

Kate M. Manuel, Jody Feder, and Alison M. Smith

SUMMARY

An estimated 37 million foreign-born persons currently reside in the United States, almost a third of whom may be present without legal authorization. The reaction of state and local jurisdictions to unauthorized immigration has varied. In some cases, states and localities have adopted measures intended to deter unlawfully present aliens from arriving and settling within their jurisdictions, including by restricting such aliens' access to work, housing, and benefits. Typically, such measures have sought to (1) limit the hiring and employment of unauthorized aliens, including through the denial of permits to persons that employ unauthorized aliens and the regulation of day labor centers; (2) restrict the ability of unlawfully present aliens to rent or occupy dwellings within the

* This is an edited, reformatted and augmented version of a Congressional Research Service publication, CRS Report for Congress RL34345, from www.crs.gov, dated December 20, 2010.

state or locality; and/or (3) deny unlawfully present aliens access to state or local services or benefits.

State or local restrictions upon unlawfully present aliens' access to employment or housing and eligibility for public benefits have been challenged on various grounds, including on the grounds that they (1) are preempted by federal law, including the Immigration and Nationality Act (INA), and thus unenforceable by federal or state courts; (2) deprive persons of equal protection of the law in violation of the Fourteenth Amendment to the U.S. Constitution; (3) deprive persons of property or liberty interests without providing them due process in violation of the Fourteenth Amendment; and (4) run afoul of federal civil rights statutes, including the Fair Housing Act, Title VII of the Civil Rights Act, and 42 U.S.C. § 1981. The outcomes of such challenges have varied, depending upon the specific restrictions at issue and the jurisdiction of the courts reviewing the restrictions. However, based upon the cases decided to date, these challenges appear to be more significant with regard to state and local restrictions on employing or renting property to unlawfully present aliens than they are with regard to state and local restrictions on unlawfully present aliens' access to public services and benefits. This term, the Supreme Court is considering the case of Chamber of Commerce v. Whiting, which involves arguments as to whether federal law preempts a 2007 Arizona statute that requires employers to use the federal government's E-Verify system to determine the work eligibility of employees and suspends or revokes the business licenses of entities found to have hired unauthorized aliens.

This report discusses the constitutional issues raised by state and local laws intended to deter the presence of unauthorized aliens by limiting their access to housing, employment, and public benefits, as well as the implications that federal civil rights statutes might have for the implementation and enforcement of these laws. It also discusses recent federal court cases addressing the constitutionality of such measures. The report does not discuss recent state laws that seek to deter the presence of unauthorized aliens by requiring state law enforcement to enforce federal immigration law, or that criminalize conduct that may facilitate the presence of unauthorized aliens within the state.

INTRODUCTION

In recent years, some states and localities have considered, and in a few cases enacted, measures intended to deter the presence of aliens who entered and/or remain in the United States without legal authorization. Typically, these measures have sought to (1) limit the hiring and employment of unauthorized aliens, including through the denial of permits to persons that employ unauthorized aliens and the regulation of day labor centers; (2) restrict the ability of unlawfully present aliens to rent or occupy dwellings within a state or locality's jurisdiction; and/or (3) deny unlawfully present aliens access to state or local services or benefits. More recently, some states have arguably gone further by imposing criminal or civil penalties upon activities that may facilitate unauthorized immigration.[1]

Several such measures have been challenged in court, including on federal preemption and Fourteenth Amendment grounds. Legal challenges brought in federal court concerning restrictions on employment, in particular, have led to conflicting court rulings. In some cases, the relevant state or local measure has been upheld as constitutionally and legally valid.[2] In other cases, the measure has been struck down.[3] In still other instances, the parties have reached a settlement agreement that precludes enforcement of the contested law; the government has repealed the challenged provision; or the presiding court has enjoined the enforcement of the challenged provisions pending trial.[4]

These cases illustrate the difficulties that states and localities face in attempting to regulate the presence and rights of aliens within their jurisdictions in a manner consistent with federal law. Over time, the courts have narrowed the legal bases upon which states and localities may enact legislation affecting aliens. State and local authority to regulate aliens has also been limited, directly or impliedly, by the growing scope of federal immigration law. With the enactment of federal employer sanctions, welfare reform, and other recent immigration laws, Congress has left increasingly few opportunities for states and localities to legislate. Significantly, these laws have not only broadened the substantive regulation of aliens (e.g., employment eligibility), but also established discrete procedures for determining alien eligibility for employment and certain benefits. Perhaps ironically then, even as new state and local measures to deter illegal immigration are motivated in part by a perceived lack of federal enforcement of immigration law,[5] the degree to which states and localities may regulate immigration-related matters has arguably been curbed by the growing breadth of federal immigration law. Conflicting court rulings regarding the permissibility of state and local measures targeting unlawfully present aliens have further contributed to this legal ambiguity. In particular, the U.S. Courts of Appeals for the Third, Ninth, and Tenth Circuits have reached differing conclusions as to whether federal law preempts state or local measures that would require employers within their jurisdiction to use E-Verify, the online federal employment eligibility verification system, to check the work authorization of employees.[6] This term, the Supreme Court is considering the case of *Chamber of Commerce v. Whiting*, which involves arguments as to whether federal law preempts an Arizona statute that requires employers to use the federal government's E-Verify system to determine the work eligibility of employees and suspends or revokes the business licenses of entities found to have hired unauthorized aliens.[7]

FACTUAL BACKGROUND

An estimated 37 million foreign-born persons currently reside in the United States, almost a third of whom may be present without authorization.[8] Over the past two decades, the number of aliens who unlawfully reside in the United States has grown significantly, from an estimated 3.2 million in 1986 to a high of more than 11 million in 2008.[9] While this number dropped to 10.8 million in 2009 and the level of unauthorized migration into the United States has declined in recent years,[10] some states and localities, concerned about the perceived negative effects of illegal immigration, have enacted measures intended to deter the presence of unauthorized aliens within their jurisdiction.

Since early 2006, some states and localities have considered legislation that would (1) limit the hiring and employment of unauthorized aliens, including through the denial of permits to persons that employ unauthorized aliens and the regulation of day labor centers; (2) restrict the ability of unlawfully present aliens to rent or occupy dwellings within a state or locality's jurisdiction; and/or (3) deny unlawfully present aliens access to state or local services or benefits. Although local measures to restrict unlawfully present aliens' access to employment or housing have received considerable attention, relatively few of the measures reportedly introduced appear to have been enacted.[11] State action on these matters has arguably been more significant, with several states adopting measures that restrict employers from hiring or employing unauthorized aliens or aliens' eligibility for public benefits.[12] No state appears to have enacted legislation specifically barring unlawfully present aliens from renting private dwellings,[13] although such measures have been enacted by some localities.

Relevant Immigration-Related Legal Issues

State or local restrictions upon unlawfully present aliens' access to employment or housing and eligibility for public benefits have been challenged upon various grounds. Among other things, plaintiffs challenging such restrictions have alleged that they: (1) are preempted by federal immigration law and thus unenforceable by federal or state courts; (2) deprive persons of equal protection of the law in violation of the Fourteenth Amendment to the U.S. Constitution; and/or (3) deprive persons of property or liberty interests without providing them due process of law in violation of the Fourteenth Amendment.

The following sections describe the legal concepts of preemption, equal protection, and procedural due process in more detail, particularly as they may apply to state and local regulation of unlawfully present aliens within their jurisdiction.

Preemption

The doctrine of preemption derives from the Supremacy Clause of the Constitution, which establishes that federal law, treaties, and the Constitution itself are "the supreme Law of the Land."[14] Thus, one essential aspect of the federal structure of government is that states can be precluded from taking actions that are otherwise within their authority if federal law is thereby thwarted. "States cannot, inconsistently with the purpose of Congress, conflict or interfere with, curtail or complement, the federal law, or enforce additional or auxiliary regulations."[15] An act of Congress may preempt state or local action in a given area in any one of three ways: (1) the statute expressly states preemptive intent (express preemption); (2) a court concludes that Congress intended to occupy the regulatory field,[16] thereby implicitly precluding state or local action in that area (field preemption); or (3) state or local action directly conflicts with or otherwise frustrates the purpose of the federal scheme (conflict preemption).[17] The delineation between these categories, particularly between field and conflict preemption, is not rigid.[18]

The power to set rules for which aliens may enter and remain in the United States is undoubtedly federal, and the breadth and detail of regulation Congress has established in the Immigration and Nationality Act (INA) of 1952,[19] as amended, precludes substantive state regulation concerning which noncitizens may enter or remain. With the INA, Congress established a comprehensive framework to regulate the admission and removal of aliens, as well as the conditions of aliens' continued presence in the United States.[20] Later, Congress enacted the Immigration Reform and Control Act (IRCA) of 1986,[21] which amended the INA to establish a system to combat the employment of unauthorized aliens. The Supreme Court has characterized this system as "central to the policy of immigration law."[22] On the one hand, the INA sets forth various categories of legal aliens and grants certain rights to aliens falling within those categories. On the other hand, the INA establishes an enforcement regime to deter the unlawful presence of aliens, including through the use of employer sanctions, criminal and/or civil penalties, and deportation.

Nevertheless, the Supreme Court has never held that "every state enactment which in any way deals with aliens is a regulation of immigration and thus, *per se*, pre-empted by this constitutional power, whether latent or exercised."[23] In the 1976 case of *De Canas v. Bica*, the Court held that state regulation of matters within their jurisdiction that were only tangentially related to immigration would, "absent congressional action[,] ... not be an invalid state incursion on federal power."[24] The Court further indicated that field preemption claims against state action that did not conflict with federal law could only be justified when the "complete ouster of state power ... was the clear and manifest purpose of Congress."[25] Still, the *De Canas* Court recognized that, even in situations where federal immigration law "contemplates some room for state legislation," a state measure might nonetheless be unenforceable on conflict preemption grounds if it "stands as an obstacle to the accomplishment and execution of the full purposes and objectives of Congress in enacting the INA."[26]

Equal Protection

The Equal Protection Clause of the Fourteenth Amendment provides that no state shall "deny to any person within its jurisdiction the equal protection of the laws."[27] However, being entitled to "equal protection" does not mean that persons are entitled to "equal treatment,"[28] and not all classifications distinguishing between persons are invalid under the Equal Protection Clause. Generally, the standard of judicial review applied to state and local laws that treat different categories of persons differently—the "rational basis" test—is highly deferential to the government.[29] Under this test, persons challenging the constitutionality of a law must show that it is not rationally related to a legitimate government interest.[30] In contrast, if a distinction disadvantages a "suspect class" or relates to a "fundamental right," a reviewing court will apply "strict scrutiny." Under strict scrutiny, the state or locality must demonstrate that the distinction is justified by a compelling government interest.[31] Other tests falling between rational basis review and strict scrutiny have also been applied on occasion, depending upon the nature of the classifications involved.[32]

All persons in the United States are entitled to equal protection under the Fourteenth Amendment, and states are limited in the degree to which they may restrict persons' rights and privileges because they are unauthorized aliens.[33] In the 1982 case of *Plyler v. Doe*, the Supreme Court held that a Texas statute that would have prohibited students who were unauthorized aliens from receiving free public elementary and secondary education violated the Constitution.[34] The Court first determined that the Equal Protection Clause of the Fourteenth Amendment protects unlawfully present aliens.[35] Then, finding that unauthorized immigrants are not a "suspect class" and education is not a "fundamental right," but also sensitive to the hardship that could result to a discrete class of children who were not accountable for their being present in the United States without authorization, the Court evaluated the Texas statute under an "intermediate" standard of review, requiring that the statute further a "substantial state interest." Ultimately, it found that none of the interests alleged by the state as justifications for the statute—which included conserving the state's educational resources, preventing an influx of illegal immigrants, and maintaining high-quality public education—constituted such an interest.[36] As a result, the Court struck down the Texas statute.

Procedural due Process

The Fourteenth Amendment provides that no state may "deprive any person of life, liberty, or property, without due process of law."[37] The Supreme Court has long recognized that the Due Process Clause contained in the Fifth and Fourteenth Amendments[38] "applies to all 'persons' within the United States, including aliens, whether their presence here is lawful, unlawful, temporary, or permanent."[39]

Procedural due process operates to ensure that states and localities do not arbitrarily interfere with certain key interests (i.e., life, liberty, and property). However, procedural due process rules are not meant to protect persons from the deprivation of these interests, *per se*. Rather, they are intended to prevent the "*mistaken or unjustified* deprivation of life, liberty, or property" by ensuring that states and localities use fair and just procedures when taking away such interests.[40] The type of procedures necessary to satisfy due process can vary depending upon the circumstances and interests involved. In *Mathews v. Eldridge*, the Supreme Court announced the prevailing standard for assessing the requirements of due process, finding that:

> Identification of the specific dictates of due process generally requires consideration of three distinct factors: first, the private interest that will be affected by the official action; second, the risk of erroneous deprivation of such interest through the procedures used, and probable value, if any, of additional or substitute procedural safeguards; and finally, the Government's interest, including the function involved and the administrative and fiscal burdens that the additional or substitute procedural requirements would entail.[41]

Although the requirements of due process may vary depending on the particular context, states and localities must provide persons with the ability to contest the basis upon which they are to be deprived of a protected interest. This generally entails notice of the proposed deprivation and a hearing before an impartial tribunal.[42] Additional procedural protections, such as discovery of evidence or an opportunity to confront adverse witnesses, may also be required in certain circumstances to minimize the occurrence of unfair or mistaken deprivations of protected interests.[43]

The procedural protections of the Due Process Clause apply only to direct government action that deprives a person of a protected interest.[44] They "do[] not apply to the indirect adverse effects of governmental action."[45] While persons who are indirectly affected by government action may, in some cases, possess a legal cause of action against the government or another party, this cause of action generally would not be based upon a procedural due process claim.

Issues Raised by State or Local Restrictions on the Employment of Unauthorized Aliens

The ability of states and localities to restrict the hiring or employment of unauthorized aliens may depend upon the form that those restrictions take, although any such restrictions could potentially be subject to preemption and procedural due process challenges.[46]

Preemption

With IRCA, Congress amended the INA to establish a comprehensive federal scheme regulating the employment of unauthorized aliens. Section 274A of the INA generally prohibits the hiring, referring, recruiting for a fee, or continued employment of aliens who lack legal authorization to work in the United States. Violators may be subject to cease and desist orders, civil monetary penalties or, in the case of serial offenders, criminal fines and/or imprisonment for up to six months. Subsection (h)(2) of INA § 274A, in particular, expressly preempts

> ... any State or local law imposing civil or criminal sanctions (other than through licensing and similar laws) upon those who employ, or recruit or refer for a fee for employment, unauthorized aliens.[47]

This provision means that states and localities cannot constitutionally enact measures that would impose "civil or criminal sanctions"—other than through "licensing and similar laws"—upon employers of unauthorized aliens.

Neither "civil or criminal sanctions" nor "licensing and similar laws" is defined by IRCA. However, courts have found that state and local measures creating a private right of action against employers who discharge authorized workers while retaining unauthorized workers impose civil sanctions and are expressly preempted.[48] They have also found that "licensing and similar laws" include laws pertaining to the issuance of business licenses, not just those pertaining to the issuance of professional licenses.[49] Such laws have, thus, been found not to be expressly preempted, although they could potentially be impliedly preempted, as discussed below. The "inclusion of an express pre-emption clause does *not* bar the ordinary working of [implied] preemption principles,"[50] and measures that fall within the savings clause of an express preemption provision could still potentially be found unconstitutional either because Congress has evidenced an intent to occupy the field or because the state or local enactment conflicts with or otherwise frustrates the purpose of federal law. It is also possible that state and local measures could be found to be expressly preempted if they would sanction employers who purportedly employ unauthorized aliens, but have not been found by federal authorities to have violated the INA.[51] However, most courts to date appear to have addressed this as conflict preemption, rather than express preemption.[52]

In determining whether state and local measures targeting employers of unauthorized aliens through "licensing and similar laws" are constitutional, courts generally apply a presumption against preemption because the regulation of employment has traditionally been within states' police powers.[53] This presumption appears to apply even though federal regulation of the employment of unauthorized aliens expanded significantly with the enactment of IRCA. As the Third Circuit recently noted:

> We are aware, of course, that the landscape of federal immigration law has changed dramatically since the Court decided De Canas. In enacting IRCA, Congress clearly made the regulation of the employment of unauthorized aliens a central concern of federal immigration policy. However, while this sea change in the federal regulatory scheme is incredibly important for purposes of our substantive analysis, it does not negate the operation of the presumption against pre-emption. The applicability of the presumption turns on a state's historic police powers. By definition, that means that the presumption depends on the past balance of state and federal regulation, not the present.[54]

Notwithstanding this presumption, depending upon their terms and the jurisdiction of any reviewing courts, state or local measures could still potentially be found to be impliedly preempted. The "pervasiveness" of the INA's provisions regarding employment of unauthorized aliens could potentially lead a court to find that Congress has preempted the field. However, the exclusion of "licensing and similar laws" from the express preemption of INA § 274A(h)(2) could perhaps be said to indicate that Congress has not evidenced an intent to wholly occupy the regulatory field with respect to alien employment, and, thus far, few courts have found that state or local restrictions on the employment of unauthorized aliens are precluded on field preemption grounds.[55]

Conflict preemption, in contrast, has been the primary focus of parties' arguments and judicial analysis to date. State and local measures could potentially be found to be unconstitutional on conflict preemption grounds if their requirements can be characterized as inconsistent or incompatible with federal law. Preemption challenges might, thus, be raised against state or local measures that (1) establish standards independent from those contained in the INA for determining whether a person has employed an unauthorized alien, and impose sanctions upon persons who violate these standards;[56] (2) rely on state or local determinations that employers have violated the INA requirements concerning work eligibility, instead of relying upon federal determinations;[57] (3) establish state and local procedures for verification of employees' work eligibility that differ from federal procedures (e.g., giving employers less time to resolve the status of an employee whose eligibility has been questioned than is provided for in federal law);[58] (4) sanctioning persons for employing unauthorized aliens using a lower *scienter* (i.e., degree of awareness) threshold than provided for in federal law;[59] or (5) imposing verification requirements upon persons who would not qualify as "employers" under federal law.[60] However, it should be noted that not all differences between state and local measures and federal law would necessarily constitute grounds for finding conflict preemption,[61] and reviewing courts could potentially interpret the relevant provisions of federal law differently in determining whether state and local measures are preempted on conflict grounds.

Courts have, for example, reached differing conclusions as to the constitutionality of state and local measures requiring employers to use E-Verify, the online federal employment eligibility verification system, to check the work authorization of employees, because of their differing interpretations of federal law. The U.S. Court of Appeals for the Third Circuit has held that such measures are preempted on conflict grounds because, when Congress enacted the Illegal Immigration Reform and Immigrant Responsibility Act (IIRIRA) of 1996 and established the pilot program that developed into E-Verify, it expressly prohibited the Secretary of Homeland Security from "requir[ing] any person or other entity to participate" in the program.[62] Because of this prohibition, the Third Circuit found that state and local measures requiring the use of E-Verify conflict with federal law and frustrate congressional intent regarding the use of E-Verify.[63] In contrast, the U.S. Courts of Appeals for the Ninth and Tenth Circuits have found that state and local measures requiring use of E-Verify are not conflict preempted because Congress intended for E-Verify to be used widely and/or did not prohibit states and localities from requiring the use of E-Verify.[64] The Supreme Court heard oral arguments on this issue, as well as whether measures that would suspend or revoke the licenses of businesses that hire unauthorized aliens are preempted, this term.[65]

Additionally, even when state or local measures requiring employers to verify the work authorization of employees mirror the specific provisions of federal law, there is also the possibility that these measures could nonetheless be found to be preempted on conflict grounds if the broader policies they would promote are inconsistent with federal policies, or if the proliferation of similar local measures would have effects that are inconsistent with federal policies. The Third Circuit, in particular, recently found that the federal verification requirements established in IRCA reflect a deliberate balancing by Congress of policies relating to (1) deterring undocumented immigration (through the imposition of sanctions upon employers who hire unauthorized aliens); (2) minimizing the burdens imposed upon employers by the employment verification process; and (3) protecting aliens who are authorized to work and others who might be perceived as "foreign" from discrimination.[66] It thus found that a local verification requirement, which it viewed as imposing additional burdens upon employers and which failed to provide its own protections against discrimination, was conflict preempted because it promoted deterrence over minimizing the burdens on employers and preventing discrimination.[67] While the ordinance in question also diverged from federal law in its requirements, the Third Circuit's view that Congress intended all three policies to be promoted equally when it enacted IRCA could, if widely adopted, potentially lead courts to strike down state and local verification requirements that do not conflict with federal law in their provisions regarding deterrence, but that do not include protections against discrimination.[68] Similarly, state or local measures could also be found to be conflict preempted if a court determines that the enactment of similar measures by other jurisdictions would have effects that are inconsistent with federal policy.[69] It is also possible that a statute which is not unconstitutional on its face could be found to be unconstitutional as applied.[70]

Moreover, there is the possibility that, because of its terms, a state or local measure could be found to constitute a "regulation of immigration," rather than a regulation affecting aliens. In *De Canas*, the Supreme Court noted that while the latter may be permissible, the former is always preempted because the power to regulate immigration is exclusively federal.[71] Some plaintiffs and commentators have asserted that state and local licensing and/or verification requirements constitute impermissible regulations of immigration because they would deter the employment of aliens, and persons generally cannot enter or remain in the United States without the ability to earn a livelihood.[72] Courts have, thus far, declined to adopt this reasoning,[73] and may be unlikely to do so given the precedent of *De Canas*. The *De Canas* Court rejected arguments that a California statute restricting the employment of unlawfully present aliens was *per se* preempted as a regulation of immigration, and instead suggested that states and localities could have legitimate interests in restricting employment of unauthorized aliens within their jurisdiction.[74] However, the INA's regulation of the employment of aliens has expanded since *De Canas* was decided, and arguments that licensing and/or verification provisions constitute impermissible regulations of immigration could perhaps be made with more success in future litigation, especially in situations where the state or local measure is not narrowly tailored and/or based on legitimate purposes.

In contrast, state or local regulations prohibiting *or* establishing day labor centers would, on their face, appear to raise fewer preemption issues.[75] Nothing in federal law addresses day labor centers, much less expressly preempts state or local measures concerning them,[76] and both zoning and employment matters are within states' historical police powers.[77] Moreover, certain restrictions upon the operation of day labor centers, in particular, could plausibly be characterized as targeting "essentially local problems" and tailored to "combat effectively the perceived evils," as would appear to be permitted under *De Canas*.[78] Depending upon their implementation, however, particular state or local measures could potentially be subject to preemption challenges on an as-applied basis. Restrictions upon day labor centers or solicitations of or by day laborers could also raise other constitutional issues that are outside the scope of this report, such as infringement of the rights to freedom of speech and association provided for in the First Amendment.[79]

Procedural due Process

State and local restrictions on the hiring and employment of unauthorized aliens could also be challenged on procedural due process grounds, depending upon the form such restrictions take. If, for example, a state or locality revoked the business permit of an entity that employed or hired unauthorized aliens, the employer's interests under the Due Process Clause would be implicated. The granting of a business license can accord the licensee a property interest that may not be *revoked* unless certain procedural due process requirements are met,[80] although no such property interest exists which guarantees the *issuance* of a license.[81] Additionally, the liberty interest protected by the Due Process Clause extends to the "right of the individual to contract, to engage in any of the common occupations of life,"[82] and this interest would appear to be abridged by state and local measures penalizing employers on account of the employment contracts they enter.

State and local measures could be found unconstitutional if they fail to provide employers with the ability to contest the basis upon which they are to be deprived of protected property or liberty interests.[83] This would generally entail notice of the proposed deprivation and a hearing before an impartial tribunal, during which they could challenge state or local findings regarding their employment practices. Additional procedural protections could potentially also be required. However, based upon the case law to date, employers would not necessarily be found to have been denied procedural due process if the state or local measure does not (1) provide employers with guidance on how to determine employees' work eligibility; (2) give employers the opportunity to review the contents of any third-party complaints against them which trigger state or local investigations; or (3) afford the employer a chance to contest, before state or local officials, any federal determinations that an employee is not authorized to work.[84] State and local measures that provide employers with procedural protections similar to those accorded to businesses by the federal government under INA § 274A may be more likely to withstand a procedural due process challenge than those measures that do not.[85]

Issues Raised by State or Local Restrictions upon Tenancy or Dwelling

State and local measures barring unlawfully present aliens from renting or occupying private dwellings raise issues under both the preemption doctrine and the Fourteenth Amendment. These issues are, however, potentially more significant than those raised by state or local restrictions on employment because denial of housing can be seen as a regulation of immigration.[86]

Preemption

State or local measures barring unlawfully present aliens from renting or occupying private dwellings within the jurisdiction could be susceptible to preemption challenges. Some have argued that such measures constitute impermissible "regulation of immigration" and are thus, *per se*, preempted.[87] The *De Canas* Court described a "regulation of immigration" as one that attempts to determine "who should and should not be admitted into the country, and the conditions under which a legal entrant may remain,"[88] and at least one court has noted that it is "difficult to conceive of a more effective method of ensuring that persons do not enter or remain in a locality than by precluding their ability to live in it."[89] Some courts have found that state or local measures constitute impermissible regulations of immigration because they classify persons using their own categories, instead of those used in the INA, when determining which aliens may rent housing, and/or they rely upon state or local personnel to determine individuals' immigration status.[90] Other courts have found that such measures are impermissible regulations of immigration because denying persons an abode is tantamount to denying them permission to remain in the country.[91] This argument might have less force in situations where the state or local measure relies on federal classifications and authorities in determining eligibility. However, the potential effects of similar restrictions in other areas could raise additional concerns.[92]

Even if state or local measures barring unlawfully present aliens from renting or occupying private dwellings do not constitute regulations of immigration that are, *per se*, preempted, they could still be found to be unconstitutional because of field or conflict preemption. The INA, particularly its provisions regarding harboring, could potentially be seen as preempting the field.[93] Section 274 of the INA criminalizes various activities relating to the bringing in and harboring of aliens who are not authorized to enter or remain in the United States, as well as certain other activities related to the transportation of unlawfully present aliens or the encouragement or inducement of unlawfully present aliens to reside in the United States. Courts have generally interpreted this provision broadly, and it could be construed to cover renting property to an illegal alien or otherwise permitting him to dwell in a residence, at least when it is done in knowing or reckless disregard of the alien's illegal status.[94] There is also the possibility of conflict preemption because of the broad discretion that the federal government has regarding which aliens to remove and/or the burden that state or local verification requirements would place on the federal government.[95] Imposing burdens on aliens whose unauthorized presence the federal government has declined to sanction could be said to frustrate the federal scheme, as could "requiring" the federal government to devote resources to activities based upon state or local—as opposed to federal—priorities.[96]

Equal Protection

State or local measures could also potentially be challenged on the grounds that they deprive prospective tenants, in particular, of equal protection in violation of the Fourteenth Amendment, although the outcome of such challenges remains somewhat uncertain, at least where no U.S.- born children of unlawfully present aliens are involved. The degree to which states and localities may restrict persons' ability to obtain private housing on account of alienage remains unsettled. As early as 1886, the Supreme Court recognized that the Equal Protection Clause applied to state classifications based on alienage.[97] Nevertheless, during the early part of the twentieth century, the Supreme Court upheld a number of state laws denying rights and privileges to persons on account of their alienage (regardless of whether such aliens were lawfully present in the United States),[98] in part because states were able to demonstrate a "special public interest" that was advanced through such measures.[99]

However, these decisions came at an earlier period of Fourteenth Amendment jurisprudence, and over time "the [Supreme] Court's decisions gradually have restricted the activities from which States are free to exclude aliens."[100] Although none of the Court's earlier decisions has been expressly overruled, in at least some cases their precedential value has been questioned.[101] Nevertheless, it appears well established, even following the Court's decision in *Plyler*, that states may impose greater restrictions upon the rights of unauthorized aliens than may be imposed upon citizens or legal immigrants, at least where the direct subjects of regulation are not children.[102] At least one federal district court has found that an ordinance regulating the leasing of housing to unauthorized aliens did not violate the Equal Protection clause because it did not facially discriminate against a suspect class because of race, ethnicity, or national origin, and it was otherwise rationally related to a legitimate government interest in reducing crime by unauthorized immigrants and safeguarding community resources.[103] This decision was not appealed.

In contrast, alienage-based restrictions that directly or indirectly affect the legal rights of those children or spouses of unlawfully present aliens who lawfully reside in the United States might face more significant legal challenges. In the 1948 case of *Oyama v. California*,[104] the Supreme Court found that a California statute banning alien landholding impermissibly discriminated against the citizen child of an alien, because it required the child to prove that his alien parent did not purchase property in the child's name to circumvent alien ownership restrictions—a burden not imposed upon the children of U.S. citizens.[105] Depending on the manner and scope of a state or local housing restriction on unlawfully present aliens, the measure could trigger an *Oyama*-like challenge by a U.S. citizen directly or indirectly affected by the rule, such as a citizen child or spouse of an illegal immigrant whose property rights are impaired on account of family membership.

Procedural due Process

Additionally, state or local measures that would bar unlawfully present aliens from renting or occupying private dwellings could implicate property interests of landlords and/or tenants that are affected by the Due Process Clause.[106] The right to "maintain control over ... [one's] home, and to be free from governmental interference, is a private interest of historic and continuing importance."[107] A government measure requiring the termination of a lease between a property owner and lessee deprives one or both of the parties of several property-related interests, including "the right of sale, the right of occupancy, the right to unrestricted use and enjoyment, and the right to receive rents."[108] In addition, some measures barring persons from leasing real property to unlawfully present aliens are enforced through the imposition of monetary penalties upon offenders.[109] Those who are compelled to pay such fines are deprived of an additional property interest. Ordinances that subject violators to incarceration would also deprive offenders of a liberty interest.[110] State or local measures prohibiting the rental of housing to unlawfully present aliens therefore appear likely to deprive property owners and/or tenants of an interest protected by the Fourteenth Amendment's Due Process Clause.[111] Accordingly, states and localities enacting such measures must provide procedural protections to minimize the occurrence of unfair or mistaken deprivations of protected interests, such as providing landlords with notice and an opportunity for a hearing before suspending their licenses and providing tenants with the opportunity to challenge their designation as unlawfully present.[112]

Issues Raised by State or Local Restrictions on Public Benefits or Services

Some localities have attempted to deter the presence of illegal aliens within their borders via the denial of services and/or benefits.[113] Such denials may be less prone to legal challenges than measures pertaining to employment and housing, partly because such measures appear less likely to raise preemption and equal protection challenges and partly because federal law expressly requires or authorizes states and localities to deny certain benefits to unlawfully present aliens. The outcome of any such challenge thus seems likely to hinge upon the scope of the benefits being denied, as well as whether the state or local measure in question would involve state or local personnel making independent assessments of persons' immigration status when determining whether to deny benefits.[114]

The degree to which states and localities may deny services or benefits based on unlawful presence in the United States remains unclear. During the 1970s and early 1980s, the U.S. Supreme Court decided a series of cases on governmental authority to discriminate against aliens in providing government benefits. Collectively, these cases set forth the following basic constitutional principles: state governments generally cannot discriminate between aliens who are authorized to live here indefinitely and U.S. citizens when setting eligibility requirements for state benefits;[115] states have broader, but still limited, authority to discriminate against aliens who are here without authorization;[116] and the federal government, by contrast, has wide discretion to discriminate both between citizens and legal aliens, as well as between classes of legal aliens.[117]

After these cases were decided, Congress enacted the Personal Responsibility and Work Opportunity Reconciliation Act of 1996 (PRWORA), which both established a general rule as to which benefits *must be denied* to aliens unlawfully residing in the United States and delineated which local public benefits *must be provided* regardless of immigration status. PRWORA prohibits many classes of noncitizens, legal and illegal alike, from receiving assistance. Generally, unlawfully present aliens are denied federal benefits and may qualify for state benefits only under laws passed by the states after the PRWORA's enactment.[118] The class of benefits denied is broad and includes: (1) grants, contracts, loans, and licenses, and (2) retirement, welfare, health, disability, housing, food, unemployment, postsecondary education,[119] and similar benefits. There are, however, exceptions to the aforementioned bars, including exceptions for:

- treatment under Medicaid for emergency medical conditions (other than those related to an organ transplant);
- short-term, in-kind, emergency disaster relief;

- immunizations against immunizable diseases and testing for and treatment of symptoms of communicable diseases; and
- services or assistance (such as soup kitchens, crisis counseling and intervention, and short-term shelters) designated by the Attorney General as: (i) delivering in-kind services at the community level, (ii) providing assistance without individual determinations of each recipient's needs, and (iii) being necessary for the protection of life and safety.[120]

The PRWORA also expressly bars unlawfully present aliens from most state and locally funded benefits. The restrictions on these benefits parallel the restrictions on federal benefits.[121] As such, unauthorized aliens are generally barred from state and local government contracts, licenses, grants, loans, and assistance.[122] However, states and localities are prohibited from denying benefits and/or services for emergency medical care, disaster relief, and immunizations.

Although federal law has established a general framework as to what services may or may not be denied to unlawfully present aliens, courts have generally yet to weigh in on the issue of when localities may make lawful presence a requirement for services to be made available.[123] Some of the services states and localities may attempt to deny to unlawfully present aliens could include bus tours for senior citizens, leadership training programs for adults, rental and mortgage assistance, drug treatment, health care for the uninsured, access to libraries and parks, and use of day labor centers. Courts will have to interpret how broadly the term "local public benefit" should be interpreted and whether denial of particular benefits is consistent with congressional purpose. This interpretation may depend on which services can be construed as encouraging illegal immigration. While services such as health care for the uninsured or rental assistance arguably fall within the purview of "local public benefit," others such as access to parks or libraries are less clear cut. Implementation of the denial of services to unlawfully present aliens could also raise issues, particularly if state or local personnel would determine alien eligibility for benefits by means other than that provided for in federal law.[124]

POTENTIAL LIMITATIONS IMPOSED BY FEDERAL CIVIL RIGHTS STATUTES

Some state and local measures restricting the hiring or housing of unauthorized aliens could also potentially conflict with existing federal anti-discrimination laws. Under Title VII of the Civil Rights Act,[125] employers are prohibited from discriminating on the basis of race, color, religion, sex, or national origin.[126] The Supreme Court has ruled that, with respect to Title VII, "the term 'national origin' does not embrace a requirement of United States citizenship."[127] In reaching this result, the Court reasoned that national origin refers to the country in which someone is born or from which his or her ancestors came. Because individuals who share the same national origin do not necessarily share the same citizenship status, the Court determined that Title VII's prohibition on national origin discrimination does not necessarily make it illegal for employers to discriminate on the basis of citizenship status or alienage. Any state or local measure restricting the hiring or employment of unauthorized aliens must comply with Title VII requirements.[128] Thus, for example, a local ordinance that authorized the enforcement of an employment complaint that alleged violations solely on the basis of an employee's race or national origin would not be legally enforceable.

However, it is possible that an ordinance restricting the employment of unauthorized aliens could, when implemented, encourage violations of Title VII in situations where discrimination on the basis of citizenship would have the purpose or effect of discriminating on the basis of national origin. For example, employers who are concerned about inadvertently hiring unlawful workers may become reluctant to hire individuals from certain ethnic backgrounds, and such reluctance could have the unlawful effect of discriminating on the basis of national origin. In other cases, an employer might use a citizenship test as a pretext to disguise what is in fact national origin discrimination. As the Court has noted, "Title VII prohibits discrimination on the basis of citizenship whenever it has the purpose or effect of discriminating on the basis of national origin."[129] In an effort to comply with such ordinances, therefore, some employers may engage in practices that could give rise to legal challenges under Title VII.[130]

Like Title VII, the Fair Housing Act (FHA) prohibits discrimination in the sale or rental of housing on a number of grounds, including national origin.[131] In the housing context, as in the employment context, courts have found that citizenship discrimination does not automatically constitute national origin discrimination under the FHA, although they have held that the FHA would prohibit citizenship discrimination if such discrimination had the purpose or effect of discriminating on the basis of national origin.[132] As a result, any state or local measure that authorizes the enforcement of housing complaints based solely on the national origin of a dwelling's inhabitants would be impermissible.[133] Further, if landlords who are attempting to comply with an ordinance barring the tenancy of unlawfully present aliens engage in national origin discrimination, then such actions may give rise to legal challenges under the FHA.

Thus far, only one federal court appears to have directly addressed whether a local ordinance intended to deter the housing of unlawfully present aliens constitutes a violation of the FHA. In *Lozano v. City of Hazleton*,[134] the district court dismissed the plaintiffs' facial challenge, concluding that the plaintiffs had failed to show that there was no set of circumstances under which the ordinance would be valid. The court did, however, leave the door open to a possible "as applied" challenge to the local ordinances in question, noting, "Because the statutes have not yet gone into effect, we cannot know whether they would have the discriminatory effect that plaintiffs claim."[135] The plaintiffs did not appeal.

It is also possible that an employment or housing ordinance aimed at unauthorized aliens could give rise to violations of 42 U.S.C. § 1981. This provision, which was originally enacted as part of the Civil Rights Act of 1870, states that:

> All persons within the jurisdiction of the United States shall have the same right in every State and Territory to make and enforce contracts, to sue, be parties, give evidence, and to the full and equal benefit of all laws and proceedings for the security of persons and property as is enjoyed by white citizens, and shall be subject to like punishment, pains, penalties, taxes, licenses, and exactions of every kind, and to no other.

Although the Supreme Court has held that an alien is a "person" for purposes of § 1981,[136] the Court has not addressed whether *unauthorized* aliens are encompassed within the statute's definition of "person." The Court, however, has held that unauthorized aliens are "persons" in the context of the Fourteenth Amendment,[137] and, therefore, might be inclined to make a similar finding with respect to the definition of "person" under § 1981. If unauthorized aliens are protected from discrimination by governmental actors under the statute, then states or localities that pass employment or housing ordinances aimed at unauthorized aliens may be liable for violations of § 1981. Indeed, a federal district court held in the *Lozano* case that a local ordinance intended to deter the employment and housing of unauthorized aliens was a violation of § 1981.[138] The Third Circuit did not address this issue on appeal.

In addition, although the Supreme Court has held that § 1981 prohibits alienage discrimination by governmental actors,[139] the Court has never addressed the question of whether § 1981 bars alienage discrimination by private actors. Until 1991, when Congress amended § 1981, the federal courts of appeals that had considered the issue were split with regard to this question. Since the amendments to § 1981, some courts have confirmed that the statute applies to private discrimination against aliens.[140] As a result, it is possible, but not certain, that a court might find that an employer or landlord who, in complying with a state or local measure, refused to employ or rent to an unauthorized alien was in violation of § 1981.

RECENT DEVELOPMENTS IN ARIZONA

The State of Arizona has enacted several measures that place it in the vanguard of recent attempts to test the legal limits of state and local measures intended to deter unauthorized immigration. The Legal Arizona Workers Act of 2007 would, among other things, require employers to use E-Verify to check the work authorization of employees and suspend or revoke the licenses of employers found to have hired unauthorized aliens.[141] It has been challenged by several parties on various grounds, including that it is preempted by federal law and deprives employers of due process. Its E-Verify and licensing provisions, in particular, have been upheld by the district court and the U.S. Court of Appeals for the Ninth Circuit.[142] The plaintiffs appealed to the Supreme Court, which granted certiorari. Oral arguments in the case were heard on December 8, 2010, on the issue of whether these provisions are expressly or impliedly preempted.[143]

More recently, Arizona has arguably gone further in seeking to deter the presence of unauthorized aliens by enacting a measure in April 2010 that is commonly referred to as S.B. 1070. In addition to requiring state and local police to facilitate the detection of unauthorized aliens in their daily enforcement activities, S.B. 1070 would also criminalize certain conduct that may help bring about the presence of unlawfully present aliens within the state, including: willful failure to complete or carry an alien registration document; certain activities relating to the transport or harboring of unlawfully present aliens; and the application for, solicitation of, or performance of work within the state by unauthorized aliens.[144] A federal district court has enjoined enforcement of many provisions of S.B. 1070—including those requiring state and local law enforcement to attempt to ascertain the immigration status of certain persons within their custody reasonably suspected to be unlawfully present—in response to the federal government's suit alleging that these provisions are preempted.[145] A decision on the merits in this suit is still pending, as is the State of Arizona's appeal to the Ninth Circuit of the district court's grant of a preliminary injunction barring enforcement of many provisions of S.B. 1070. Private parties have also filed suit challenging S.B. 1070, including on the grounds that it would "cause widespread racial profiling."[146]

End Notes

[1] See generally CRS Report R41221, State Efforts to Deter Unauthorized Aliens: Legal Analysis of Arizona's S.B. 1070, by Kate M. Manuel, Michael John Garcia, and Larry M. Eig (discussing Arizona statute criminalizing conduct that may facilitate unauthorized immigration, including alien smuggling and the hiring of persons picked up along busy roadways).

[2] See, e.g., Chicanos Por La Causa, Inc. v. Napolitano, 558 F.3d 856 (9th Cir. 2009) (Arizona statute that would require use of E-Verify, as well as suspend or revoke the licenses of businesses that hire unauthorized aliens), cert. granted, Chamber of Commerce of U.S. v. Candelaria, 130 S. Ct. 3498 (2010); Gray v. City of Valley Park, No. 4:07CB00881 ERW, 2008 U.S. Dist. LEXIS 7238 (E.D. Mo., Jan. 31, 2008) (municipal ordinance providing for the suspension or revocation of the licenses of businesses that hire unauthorized aliens).

[3] See, e.g., Lozano v. City of Hazleton, 620 F.3d 170 (3d Cir. 2010) [hereinafter "Lozano II"] (municipal ordinance that would require use of E-Verify, suspend or revoke the licenses of businesses that hire unauthorized aliens, and prohibit rental of private housing to unlawfully present aliens); Chamber of Commerce of the United States of Am. v. Edmondson, 594 F.3d 742 (10th Cir. 2010) (upholding the district court's determination that a measure allowing employees to sue for reinstatement, back pay and attorneys' fees was expressly preempted).

[4] See, e.g., Gray, 2008 U.S. Dist. LEXIS 7238, at *15 (noting that Valley Park had repealed an ordinance prohibiting the rental of private dwellings to unlawfully present aliens); Garrett v. City of Escondido, 465 F. Supp. 2d 1043 (S.D. Cal. 2006) (granting a temporary restraining order against enforcement of the ordinance, which prohibited the rental of housing to unlawfully present aliens).

[5] See, e.g., Mark B. Evans, Text of Gov. Brewer's Speech After Signing SB 1070, TUCSON CITIZEN, Apr. 23, 2010, available at http://tucsoncitizen.com/mark-evans/archives/236 ("The bill I'm about to sign into law – Senate Bill 1070 – represents another tool for our state to use as we work to solve a crisis we did not create and the federal government has refused to fix.").

[6] Chicanos Por La Causa, 558 F.3d at 867; Lozano II, 620 F.3d at 214; Edmondson, 594 F.3d at 768-69. There is also an apparent circuit split as to whether measures providing for the suspension or revocation of the business licenses of employers who hire or employ unauthorized aliens are preempted. However, there are substantive differences between the specific state or local measures underlying the courts' decisions that could, in part, account for differences in outcomes.

[7] Chamber of Commerce of the United States of Am. v. Whiting, No. 09-115. Oral arguments in this case were held on December 8, 2010.

[8] The other two-thirds of foreign-born U.S. residents are legal permanent residents (i.e., "legal immigrants") or naturalized citizens. See CRS Report RL33874, Unauthorized Aliens Residing in the United States: Estimates Since 1986, by Ruth Ellen Wasem.

[9] See CRS Report RL33874, Unauthorized Aliens Residing in the United States: Estimates Since 1986, by Ruth Ellen Wasem, supra note 8. See also Jeffrey S. Passel, Pew Hispanic Center, Trends in Unauthorized Immigration: Undocumented Inflow Now Trails Legal Inflow, Oct. 2, 2008, available at http://pewhispanic.org/files/reports/94.pdf.

[10] See, e.g., Jeffrey S. Passel and D'Vera Cohn, Pew Hispanic Center, U.S. Unauthorized Immigration Flows Are Down Sharply Since Mid-Decade, Sept. 1, 2010, available at http://pewhispanic.org/reports/report.php?ReportID=126. The increase in the number of unlawfully present aliens was particularly marked in the period between 2000 and 2005, when an estimated 850,000 people entered the United States each year without authorization. However, it subsequently dropped to 550,000 persons annually in 2005-2007 and 300,000 persons annually in 2007-2009. Id.

[11] See S. Karthick Ramakrishnan and Tom (Tak) Wong, University of California – Riverside Campus, "Immigration Policies Go Local: The Varying Responses of Local Governments to Undocumented Immigration," Nov. 9, 2007, available at http://www.law.berkeley.edu/files/RamakrishnanWongpaperfinal(1).pdf (finding that less than 1% of all municipalities have enacted measures addressing unlawfully present aliens); Emily Gunn, et al., "Assessment of Local Ordinances to Reduce Illegal Immigration," Texas A & M University, George Bush School of Government and Public Service (2008) (on file with author) (finding 21 localities that had passed legislation between 2006 and early 2008 restricting unlawfully present aliens' access to employment or housing).

[12] See, e.g., National Conference of State Legislatures, Immigration Enactments Database, available at http://www.ncsl.org/default.aspx?TabId=19209.

[13] Some states have, however, enacted statutes that would prohibit "harboring" unlawfully present aliens. See, e.g., 21 OKLA. ST. § 446 (B) (2010) ("It shall be unlawful for any person to conceal, harbor, or shelter from detection any alien in any place within the State of Oklahoma, including any building or means of transportation, knowing or in reckless disregard of the fact that the alien has come to, entered, or remained in the United States in violation of law.").

[14] U.S. CONST. art. VI, cl. 2.

[15] Hines v. Davidowitz, 312 U.S. 52, 66-67 (1941) (internal citations omitted).

[16] Congressional intent to "occupy the field" to the exclusion of state law can be inferred when "[1] the pervasiveness of the federal regulation precludes supplementation by the States, [2] where the federal interest in the field is sufficiently dominant, or [3] where the object sought to be obtained by the federal law and the character of obligations imposed by it ... reveal the same purpose." Schneidewind v. ANR Pipeline Co., 485 U.S. 293, 300 (1988) (internal quotations omitted).

[17] See, e.g., Crosby v. Nat'l Foreign Trade Council, 530 U.S. 363, 373 (2000); English v. Gen. Elec. Co., 496 U.S. 72, 78-79 (1990); Silkwood v. Kerr-McGee Corp., 464 U.S. 238, 248-49 (1984); Pac. Gas & Elec. Co. v. State Energy Res. Conservation & Dev. Comm'n, 461 U.S. 190, 203-04 (1983).

[18] See English, 462 U.S. at 79 n.5 ("By referring to these three categories, we should not be taken to mean that they are rigidly distinct. Indeed, field pre-emption may be understood as a species of conflict pre-emption: A state law that falls within a pre-empted field conflicts with Congress' intent (either express or plainly implied) to exclude state regulation."); Crosby, 530 U.S. at 373 n.6.

[19] 8 U.S.C. § 1101 et seq.

[20] See, e.g., Hoffman Plastic Compounds, Inc. v. Nat'l Labor Relations Board, 535 U.S. 137, 147 (2002).

[21] P.L. 99-603 (1986).

[22] Hoffman Plastic Compounds, 535 U.S. at 147 (internal quotations omitted).

[23] De Canas v. Bica, 424 U.S. 351, 355 (1976). Indeed, during the nineteenth century, when federal regulation of immigration was far more limited in scope, state legislation limiting the rights and privileges of certain categories of aliens was common. See Gerald L. Neuman, The Lost Century of American Immigration Law (1776-1875), 93 COLUM. L. REV. 1833 (1993). Many of these restrictions would now be preempted by federal immigration law.

[24] De Canas, 424 U.S. at 356.

[25] Id. at 357.

[26] Id. at 363 (internal quotations omitted). See also Crosby, 530 U.S. at 373 (2000) (quoting Hines, 312 U.S. at 67). De Canas concerned a California statute that imposed sanctions on employers who hired unlawful aliens if that employment adversely affected lawful workers. When Congress added federal employer sanctions to the INA in 1986, it expressly preempted state or local laws that sanctioned employers (other than through licensing or similar laws) for hiring unauthorized workers. See INA § 274a(h)(2), 8 U.S.C. § 1324a(h)(2).

[27] U.S. CONST., amend. XIV, § 1.

[28] See, e.g., Tigner v. Texas, 310 U.S. 141, 147 (1940) (noting that the Constitution does not require things which are "different in fact or opinion to be treated in law as though they were the same").

[29] See, e.g., Abdulah v. Comm'n of Insurance, 907 F. Supp. 13 (D. Mass. 1995) (quoting New Orleans v. Dukes, 427 U.S. 297, 303-04 (1976).

[30] See, e.g., Lehnhausen v. Lake Shore Auto Parts Co., 410 U.S. 356, 364 (1973).

[31] See, e.g., Loving v. Virginia, 388 U.S. 1, 11 (1967) (racial classifications must be shown to be necessary to some "legitimate overriding purpose"); McLaughlin v. Florida, 379 U.S. 184, 192, 194 (1964) (racial classifications "bear a far heavier burden of justification" than other classifications and are invalid absent an "overriding statutory purpose").

[32] See, e.g., United States v. Virginia, 518 U.S. 515 (1996) (requiring the state to provide an "exceedingly persuasive justification" for its policy of maintaining an all-male military academy).

[33] Because of its broad plenary power over immigration and naturalization, the federal government has significantly greater leeway than states in the measures that it may take with respect to aliens. See Mathews v. Diaz, 426 U.S. 67, 84-87 (1976). "The equal protection analysis also involves significantly different considerations because it concerns the relationship between aliens and the States rather than between aliens and the Federal

Government." Id. at 84-85. However, the Supreme Court has suggested that "undocumented status, coupled with some articulable federal policy, might enhance state authority with respect to the treatment of undocumented aliens." Plyler v. Doe, 457 U.S. 202, 226 (1982).

[34] 457 U.S. at 231.

[35] Id. at 210.

[36] Id. at 230.

[37] U.S. CONST., amend. XIV, § 1.

[38] Both the Fifth and Fourteenth Amendments protect persons from government action depriving them of life, liberty, or property. However, the Fifth Amendment concerns obligations owed by the federal government, whereas the Fourteenth Amendment covers those owed by state and local governments.

[39] Zadvydas v. Davis, 533 U.S. 678, 693 (2001). See also, e.g., Plyler, 457 U.S. at 210 ("Aliens, even aliens whose presence in this country is unlawful, have long been recognized as 'persons' guaranteed due process of law by the Fifth and Fourteenth Amendments.").

[40] Carey v. Piphus, 435 U.S. 247, 259 (1978).

[41] 424 U.S. 319, 335 (1976) (emphasis added).

[42] See, e.g., Mullane v. Central Hanover Trust Co., 339 U.S. 306, 314 (1950) (describing notice of a proposed deprivation of a protected interest as "[a]n elementary and fundamental requirement of due process"); Mathews, 424 U.S. at 333 ("[S]ome form of hearing is required before an individual is finally deprived of a ... [protected] interest."); In re Murchison, 349 U.S. 133, 135 (1955) ("A fair trial in a fair tribunal is a basic requirement of due process.").

[43] See CONGRESSIONAL RESEARCH SERVICE, CONSTITUTION OF THE UNITED STATES: ANALYSIS AND INTERPRETATION, Fourteenth Amendment: Rights Guaranteed: The Requirements of Due Process, available at http://www.crs.gov/conan/default.aspx?doc=Amendment14.xml&mode=topic&s=1&t=5|1|3.

[44] See, e.g., O'Bannon v. Town Court Nursing Center, 447 U.S. 773 (1980) (finding that nursing home residents had no constitutional right to a hearing before a state or federal agency revoked the home's authority to provide them with nursing care at government expense); Legal Tender Cases, 79 U.S. 457, 551 (1870) ("[The Due Process Clause] has always been understood as referring only to a direct appropriation, and not to consequential injuries resulting from the exercise of lawful power. It has never been supposed to have any bearing upon, or to inhibit laws that indirectly work harm and loss to individuals.").

[45] O'Bannon, 447 U.S. at 789.

[46] State and local measures could also potentially be challenged on the grounds that they deprive employees who are racial or ethnic minorities of equal protection in violation of the Fourteenth Amendment. However, to date, there does not appear to have been a successful challenge on these grounds. See, e.g., Gray, 2008 U.S. Dist. LEXIS 7238, at *69-*70 (finding that employers lacked standing to assert an equal protection claim on behalf of their employees); Lozano v. City of Hazleton, 496 F. Supp. 2d 477, 540-42 [hereinafter "Lozano I"] (finding that the "ordinances do not implicate a fundamental right or use a suspect classification" and that plaintiffs failed to demonstrate discriminatory intent in enacting the ordinance). The Third Circuit did not address this issue on appeal.

[47] INA § 274A(h)(2); 8 U.S.C. § 1324a.

[48] Edmondson, 594 F.3d at 765 (upholding the district court's determination that a measure allowing employees to sue for reinstatement, back pay and attorneys' fees was expressly preempted). The district court also found that taxing employers who hired unauthorized aliens at the maximum rate and revoking any government contracts they held were

expressly preempted. See Chamber of Commerce of the United States of Am. v. Henry, No. CIV-08-109-C, 2008 U.S. Dist. LEXIS 44168, at *20 (W.D. Okla., June 4, 2008). However, these findings were reversed on appeal. Edmondson, 594 F.3d at 765-66.

[49] Some plaintiffs and commentators have argued that measures allowing for the revocation of business licenses should be excluded from the scope of "licensing and similar laws" and, therefore, subject to express preemption. For example, on appeal, the plaintiffs in Lozano argued that "IRCA's express pre-emption provision would be toothless if a state or municipality could effectively circumvent the general prohibition on imposing sanctions by imposing sanctions of this severity … [T]he loss of a business license is the 'death penalty' for a business, and the express pre-emption clause would be swallowed by its exception if a law regulating business licenses is held to be a licensing law." 620 F.3d at 208. See also Mark S. Grube, Preemption of Local Regulations Beyond Lozano v. City of Hazleton: Reconciling Local Enforcement with Federal Immigration Policy, 95 CORNELL L. REV. 391, 413 (2010) (noting the apparent incongruity between prohibiting a $250 fine and allowing a business to be shut down). The district court in Lozano found for the plaintiffs on this argument. Lozano I, 496 F. Supp. 2d at 519. However, this holding was reversed on appeal, and no other court appears to have found for plaintiffs on similar arguments. See, e.g., Chicanos Por La Causa, 558 F.3d at 865; Gray, 2008 U.S. Dist. LEXIS 7238, at *31.

[50] Sprietsma v. Mercury Marine, a Division of Brunswick Corporation, 537 U.S. 51, 65 (2002) (internal quotations omitted). See also Geier v. Am. Honda Motor Co., 529 U.S. 861 (2000) (recognizing that a state law that falls within an express preemption savings clause is still subject to the ordinary workings of implied preemption principles).

[51] See, e.g., Lozano II, 496 F. Supp. 2d at 519 (finding that an ordinance providing for the suspension or revocation of the business licenses of employers who hire unauthorized aliens was expressly preempted because it would have relied upon its own requirements, not those of INA § 274A, in determining which employers had hired unauthorized aliens), rev'd, 620 F.3d at 210-11.

[52] Lozano II, 620 F.3d at 210-14 (finding that an ordinance providing for the suspension or revocation of the business licenses of employers who hire unauthorized aliens was preempted on conflict grounds because it would have relied upon its own requirements, not those of INA § 274A, in determining which employers had hired unauthorized aliens). See also Ariz. Contractors Ass'n v. Candelaria, 534 F. Supp. 2d 1036, 1045-48 (D. Ariz. 2008) (relying on the plain meaning of INA § 274A(h)(2) and its legislative history to reject plaintiffs' argument that state or local measures are expressly preempted unless they would impose licensing sanctions only upon employers who have already been found liable in completed federal proceedings under IRCA), affirmed by Chicanos Por La Causa, 558 F.3d at 866 (finding that, for purposes of determining whether the statute in question is expressly preempted, "plaintiffs' reading of the second sentence, as permitting enforcement only of state licensing regulations conditioned on federally adjudicated violations, is contradicted by the third sentence, which recognizes states can condition an employer's 'fitness to do business' on hiring documented workers"); Gray, 2008 U.S. Dist. LEXIS 7238, at *36 ("There is no requirement in the statute that a finding be made by the federal government that a person has employed, recruited, or referred for a fee for employment, unauthorized aliens, only that those are the individuals who are subject to penalty.").

[53] See, e.g., Meditronic, Inc. v. Lohr, 518 U.S. 470 (1996) (discussing the presumption against preemption); Gray, 2008 U.S. Dist. LEXIS 7238, at *25 (characterizing the regulation of business as being within states' historic police powers).

[54] Lozano II, 620 F.3d at 206-07 (finding that the district court erred in failing to accord this presumption against preemption when reviewing the Hazleton ordinance).

[55] But see Lozano I, 496 F. Supp. 2d at 521-25 (finding that the ordinance in question was field preempted). The Third Circuit did not adopt this analysis on appeal, but instead focused on conflict preemption. See Lozano II, 620 F.3d at 213 n.34 (noting the possibility of field preemption, but focusing on conflict preemption).

[56] See, e.g., Lozano II, 620 F.3d at 209-10 (focusing on conflict preemption when striking down a local measure that would sanction employers for violating local law regarding the employment of unauthorized aliens, not federal law).

[57] Courts taking the view that such measures are preempted have generally based their findings on the grounds that employment authorization depends upon immigration status, which can only be determined by the federal government because of the government's broad discretion in determining which unauthorized aliens to take action against and/or the difficulties inherent in determining whether particular aliens are unlawfully present. See e.g., Lozano II, 620 F.3d at 210-19. In fact, the Third Circuit has even gone so far as to suggest that the federal courts have the final say in determining whether an alien is unlawfully present in the United States. Lozano II, 620 F.3d at 197-98 ("[W]hile any alien who is in the United States unlawfully faces the prospect of removal proceedings being initiated against her/him, whether s/he will actually be ordered removed is never a certainty until all legal proceedings have been concluded."). It should also be noted that state or local measures that call for state or local personnel to determine the immigration status of individual aliens have traditionally been viewed as regulations of immigration that are per se preempted. See, e.g., League of United Latin Am. Citizens v. Wilson, 908 F. Supp. 755, 769-71 (C.D. Cal. 1995) (finding that California's Proposition 187, which would have required state personnel to verify the immigration status of persons with whom they came into contact, was preempted, in part, because it required the state to make an independent determination as to whether a person was in violation of federal immigration law); Villas at Parkside Partners v. The City of Farmers Branch, 577 F. Supp. 2d 858, 869-70 (N.D. Tex. 2008) (finding that an ordinance that relied upon classifications used by the U.S. Department of Housing and Urban Development in determining eligibility for housing subsidies to determine who could rent private housing constituted an impermissible regulation of immigration because it did not rely on the INA's classification of aliens' status). However, the situation could potentially be viewed differently if state or local personnel relied on federal determinations of immigration status, such as those provided pursuant to 8 U.S.C. § 1373(c). This statutory provision requires that "[t]he Immigration and Naturalization Service ... respond to an inquiry by a Federal, State, or local government agency, seeking to verify or ascertain the citizenship or immigration status of any individual within the jurisdiction of the agency for any purpose authorized by law, by providing the requested verification or status information." 8 U.S.C. § 1373(c).

[58] See, e.g., Lozano II, 620 F.3d at 214-15 ("[T]he [ordinance in question] contravenes congressional objectives by altering the verification scheme created by IRCA, and supplemented by IIRIRA and subsequent legislation."). But see Gray, 2008 U.S. Dist. LEXIS 7238, at *50 (finding that a municipal ordinance was not conflict preempted because it gave employers three days to respond to allegations that they had hired unauthorized workers, while federal law provides an 18-day period after receipt of a "tentative nonconfirmation" of an employee's eligibility).

[59] For example, a state or locality would likely be preempted from penalizing a business solely because it has hired an unauthorized alien, given that federal law only penalizes employers

who knowingly hire such persons (except in cases where the employer fails to comply with the prescribed employment verification requirements). See INA § 274A(a)(1); 8 U.S.C. 1324a(a)(1).

[60] See, e.g., Edmondson, 594 F.3d 769-70 (striking down an Oklahoma statute that would have required verification by persons who employ independent contractors or domestic help because such persons are not defined as "employers" and, thus, are not subject to verification requirements under federal law); Lozano II, 620 F.3d at 216 (same). But see Gray, 2008 U.S. Dist. LEXIS 7238, at *45 (upholding a local ordinance imposing verification requirements upon persons who employ independent contractors after finding that the federal regulations excluding persons who hire independent contractors from the definition of "employer" do not constitute a reasonable interpretation of the governing statute and are, thus, unenforceable). IRCA does not itself define "employer," although regulations promulgated under its authority provide such a definition. See 8 C.F.R. § 274a.1(f)-(h) (defining "employee," "employer," and "employment").

[61] See Lozano II, 620 F.3d at 210 ("We … have concerns about the district court's approach, … because it did at times equate difference with conflict."). See also Gray, 2008 U.S. Dist. LEXIS 7238 at *53 (suggesting that discrepancies in time frames between state or local measures and federal ones do not necessarily mean that state or local measures are preempted, so long as state or local procedures are "tolled" while federal procedures play out).

[62] P.L. 104-208, div. C, tit. IV, subtit. A, § 402(a) (1996) (codified, as amended, at 8 U.S.C. § 1324a note). But see Chamber of Commerce of the United States of Am. v. Napolitano, 648 F. Supp. 2d 726 (Md. 2009) (upholding the legality of Executive Order 13465 and the Federal Acquisition Regulation, which require government contractors to use E-Verify). Key to the court's reasoning in Chamber of Commerce was that (1) the President, not the Secretary of Homeland Security, imposed the "requirement" to use E-Verify on federal contractors and (2) no one is "required" to use E-Verify because "the decision to be a government contractor is voluntary." Id. at 733. It should be noted that IIRIRA also states that "any person or other entity that conducts any hiring (or recruitment or referral) in a State in which a pilot program is operating may elect to participate in that pilot program," and this language has been found to preempt states and localities from prohibiting employers within their jurisdiction from participating in E-Verify. See United States v. Illinois, No. 07-3261, 2009 U.S. Dist. LEXIS 19533 (C.D. Ill., Mar. 12, 2009).

[63] Lozano II, 620 F.3d at 214.

[64] Chicanos Por La Causa, 558 F.3d at 867 ("Though Congress did not mandate E-Verify, Congress plainly envisioned and endorsed an increase in its usage."); Edmondson, 594 F.3d at 767-69. The Ninth Circuit, in particular, has emphasized the significance of Congress's failure to prohibit use of E-Verify: "Congress could have, but did not, expressly forbid state laws from requiring E-Verify participation. It certainly knew how to do so because, at the same time, it did expressly forbid 'any State or local law imposing civil or criminal sanctions (other than through licensing and similar laws) upon those who employ, or recruit or refer for a fee for employment, unauthorized aliens.'" Chicanos Por La Causa, 558 F.3d at 867. See also Gray, 2008 U.S. Dist. LEXIS 7238, at *58 ("The court does not see Congress's decision not to make the program mandatory as restricting a state or local government's authority under the police powers."). Although the Eighth Circuit issued a decision in Gray, its decision did not reach the merits of this argument. See Gray v. City of Valley Park, 567 F.3d 976 (8th Cir. 2009).

[65] See supra note 7.

[66] Lozano II, 620 F.3d at 211 (noting that undermining the balance of policy interests struck by federal law constitutes a "significant conflict"); Edmondson, 595 F.3d at 768-69. See also Bonito Boats, Inc. v. Thunder Craft Boats, Inc., 489 U.S. 141 (1989) (Florida law preempted because it struck a balance between the encouragement of invention and free competition in patented ideas different from that struck by federal patent law); Rogers v. Larson, 563 F.2d 617, 626 (3d Cir. 1977) (Virgin Islands law preempted because it struck a balance between ensuring an adequate labor force and protecting citizens' jobs different from that struck in federal immigration law). See also 132 Cong. Rec. H10583-01 (daily ed., Oct. 15, 1986) ("[We should] put the burden of enforcing the law on the Government, where it belongs, not on private employers."); H.R. Rep. No. 99-682 (II), at 4 ("[I]f there is to be sanctions enforcement and liability, there must be an equally strong and readily available remedy if resulting employment discrimination occurs.").

[67] Lozano II, 620 F.3d at 219 ("Simply put, Hazleton has enacted a single regulatory scheme that is designed to further the single objective of federal law that it deems important—ensuring unauthorized aliens do not work in the United States. It has chosen to disregard Congress's other objectives. ... Regulatory 'cherry picking' is not concurrent enforcement and it is not constitutionally permitted."). See also Immigrants Rights, Inc. v. INS, 913 F.2d 1350, 1366 (9th Cir. 1990), (characterizing IRCA as "a carefully crafted political compromise which at every level balances specifically chosen measures discouraging illegal employment with measures to protect those who might be adversely affected"), rev'd on other grounds, 502 U.S. 183 (1991).

[68] Lozano II, 620 F.3d at 218 ("To be consistent with federal law, states and localities that use regulatory enactments to sanction employers who have been found guilty of employing unauthorized aliens under IRCA must impose sanctions of equal severity on employers found guilty of discriminating."). From this decision, it would appear that a state or local measure could not rely on the protections against discrimination provided for in federal law, but instead must include its own protections. But see Gray, 2008 U.S. Dist. LEXIS 7238, at *49-*50 (ordinance need not prohibit discrimination in the same way that IRCA does). Some plaintiffs have also suggested that "harsh" employer sanctions encourage discrimination and, therefore, disrupt the balance between deterring illegal immigration, minimizing employers' burdens, and preventing discrimination established by federal law. However, the Ninth Circuit has rejected this claim as "essentially speculative," at least when made in a facial challenge. Chicanos Por La Causa, 558 F.3d at 867.

[69] See, e.g., Lozano II, 620 F.3d at 213. See also Rowe v. N.H. Motor Transp. Ass'n, 552 U.S. 364 (2008) (reasoning that allowing one state to implement its own monitoring stem "would allow other States to do the same ... easily lead[ing] to a patchwork of state ... laws, rules, and regulations").

[70] United States v. Salerno, 481 U.S. 739, 745 (1987) ("A facial challenge to a legislative Act is, of course, the most difficult challenge to mount successfully, since the challenger must establish that no set of circumstances exists under which the Act would be valid."); Chicanos Por La Causa, 558 F.3d at 861 ("If and when the statute is enforced, and the factual background is developed, other challenges to the Act as applied in any particular instance or manner will not be controlled by our decision.").

[71] 424 U.S. at 355. See also Henderson v. Mayor of City of New York, 92 U.S. 259, 274 (1875) (holding that states are not permitted to restrict immigration because it "has been confided to Congress by the Constitution"). The Court in De Canas characterized a "regulation of immigration" as one that attempts to determine "who should and should not be admitted

into the country, and the conditions under which a legal entrant may remain." 424 U.S. at 355.

[72] See, e.g., Lozano I, 496 F. Supp. 2d at 518; Karla Mari McKanders, Welcome to Hazleton! "Illegal" Immigrants Beware: Local Immigration Ordinances and What the Federal Government Must Do About It, 39 LOY. U. CH. L.J. 1, 32 (2007).

[73] See, e.g., Lozano I, 496 F. Supp. 2d at 524 n.45; Gray, 2008 U.S. Dist. LEXIS 7238, *25.

[74] De Canas, 424 U.S. at 356-57 ("Employment of illegal aliens in times of high unemployment deprives citizens and legally admitted aliens of jobs; acceptance by illegal aliens of jobs on substandard terms as to wages and working conditions can seriously depress wage scales and working conditions of citizens and legally admitted aliens; and employment of illegal aliens under such conditions can diminish the effectiveness of labor unions.").

[75] To date, most legal challenges to day labor centers appear to allege that their establishment and/or operation violates federal laws regarding the employment of unauthorized aliens, the harboring of unlawfully present persons, and/or aiding and abetting violations of the INA. See, e.g., Karunakarum v. Town of Herndon, 70 Va. Cir. 208 (2006) (finding that the plaintiffs had standing to challenge a day labor center on these grounds).

[76] However, had it been enacted, the Border Protection, Antiterrorism, and Illegal Immigration Control Act of 2005 would have amended the INA to require that day labor centers verify the immigration status of all clients, as well as expanded the INA's provisions regarding smuggling, transporting, and harboring undocumented aliens so as to reach certain types of conduct by day labor centers. H.R. 4437, 109th Cong.

[77] Village of Euclid v. Ambler Realty Co., 272 U.S. 365 (1926) (zoning); Gray, 2008 U.S. Dist. LEXIS 7238, at *25 (regulation of employment).

[78] See 424 U.S. at 356-57.

[79] Compare Xiloj-Itzep v. City of Agoura Hills, 29 Cal. Rptr. 2d 879 (Cal. App. 1994) (upholding a municipal ordinance prohibiting occupants of vehicles from soliciting work from any person within the public right-of-way because it constituted a valid non-content based restriction on speech) and Coalition for Humane Immigrant Rights of Los Angeles v. Burke, No. CV 98-4863-GHK 2000, 2000 U.S. Dist. LEXIS 16520 (C.D. Cal. Sept. 12, 2000) (striking down a similar provision as a content-based restriction of speech because it was too broad geographically and left no alternatives for solicitation).

[80] Bell v. Burson, 402 U.S. 535, 539 (1971). In addition, "[t]he assets of a business (including its good will) unquestionably are property, and any state taking of those assets is unquestionably a 'deprivation' under the Fourteenth Amendment ... [, although] business in the sense of the activity of doing business, or the activity of making a profit is not property in the ordinary sense. " College Sav. Bank v. Florida Prepaid Postsecondary Educ. Expense Bd., 527 U.S. 666, 675 (1999) (emphasis in original). See also Duplex Printing Press Co. v. Deering, 254 U.S. 443, 465 (1921) ("[C]omplainant's business ... is a property right, entitled to protection against unlawful injury or interference.").

[81] Bell, 402 U.S. at 539.

[82] Board of Regents v. Roth, 408 U.S. 564, 572 (1972).

[83] It is less clear that employees would be denied due process by state or local measures. As a general rule, the procedural requirements of the Due Process Clause are triggered by a direct deprivation of a protected interest by the government. See supra notes 45-46 and accompanying text. Persons who are indirectly affected by the government's deprivation of a third party's protected interest(s) "have no constitutional right to interject themselves into the dispute." O'Bannon, 447 U.S. at 788. However, one district court has found that a local measure providing for the suspension or revocation of the business license of employers

who hire or employ unauthorized aliens deprives employees of due process. Lozano I, 496 F. Supp. 2d at 533-37. This question was not addressed in the Third Circuit's opinion in Lozano, and no other court appears to have reached this conclusion.

[84] See, e.g., Chicanos Por La Causa, 558 F.3d at 867-69; Gray, 2008 U.S. Dist. LEXIS 7238, at *84-*97.

[85] Before the federal government may sanction a business for unlawful employment practices relating to unauthorized aliens, the business must be provided with notice of the proposed action and a hearing before an administrative law judge in which the basis for the proposed order may be challenged. The administrative judge's decision is subject to administrative appellate and judicial review within specified time periods. INA § 274A(e); 8 U.S.C. § 1324a(e).

[86] Villas at Parkside Partners v. The City of Farmers Branch, 701 F. Supp. 2d 835, 855 (N.D. Tex. 2010) ("Local regulation that conditions the ability to enter private contract for shelter on federal immigration status is of a fundamentally different nature than the sorts of restrictions on employment or public benefits that have been found not to be preempted regulations of immigration [in certain cases].").

[87] See, e.g., Villas at Parkside Partners, 577 F. Supp. 2d at 869. But see Garrett v. City of Escondido, 465 F. Supp. 2d 1043, 1055 (S.D. Cal. 2006) (rejecting plaintiffs' claim that restrictions on ability to rent property were tantamount to regulation of immigration). Where regulation of immigration is involved, there is no possibility of concurrent enforcement even if the state or local measure "mirrors" the federal one. See, e.g., Lozano II, 620 F.3d at 222. The court in Lozano further suggested that the local measure in question could not mirror the federal harboring provisions, discussed below, because these provisions have not been construed to reach the landlord/tenant relationship. Id. at 222-24.

[88] 424 U.S. at 355-56.

[89] Lozano II, 620 F.3d at 220-21.

[90] In one early case, a federal district court struck down California's Proposition 187, which would have relied on state screening to prevent unlawfully present aliens from receiving certain public benefits, because it classified individuals differently than the federal government did, and it relied upon state agents' determinations of immigration status. League of United Latin Am. Citizens, 908 F. Supp. at 770-72. More recently, a district court in Texas found that an ordinance that would have relied on classifications used by the U.S. Department of Housing and Urban Development (HUD) in determining eligibility for housing subsidies to determine who could rent private housing was preempted because it did not rely on the INA's classification of aliens' status. Villas at Parkside Partners, 577 F. Supp. 2d at 870 ("The court determines that the city's reliance on the HUD regulations and documents demonstrates that the city is doing more than adopting federal immigration requirements; the city adopts federal regulations regarding housing benefits to noncitizens and uses those regulations to define which noncitizens may rent an apartment in Farmers Branch."). The court was particularly concerned that there are certain persons who are lawfully in the country, but who are not entitled to federal housing assistance (e.g., alien visitors, tourists, diplomats, and students temporarily in the United States). Id.

[91] See Villas at Parkside Partners, 577 F. Supp. 2d at 868 (quoting Truax v. Raich, 239 U.S. 33, 42 (1915) ("The assertion of an authority to deny aliens the opportunity of earning a livelihood when lawfully admitted to the state would be tantamount to the assertion of the right to deny them entrance and abode.")); Lozano II, 620 F.3d at 220. The fact that people could potentially reside within the jurisdiction by purchasing homes or staying with friends

would not necessarily save a challenged measure from being found to be preempted. See, e.g., Lozano II, 620 F.3d at 221.

[92] See, e.g., Lozano II, 620 F.3d at 221.

[93] Garrett, 465 F. Supp. 2d at 1056.

[94] E.g., United States v. Aguilar, 883 F.2d 662 (9th Cir. 1989) (finding that a church official violated the harboring provision when he invited an illegal alien to stay in an apartment behind his church, and interpreting harboring statuteas not requiring an intent to avoid detection); United States v. Rubio-Gonzalez, 674 F.2d 1067 (5th Cir. 1982) (suggesting that "harboring" an alien is a broader concept than other smuggling provisions relating to the concealment of an alien or the shielding of an alien from detection); United States v. Acosta De Evans, 531 F.2d 428 (9th Cir. 1976) (upholding harboring conviction of defendant who provided illegal aliens with an apartment, and concluding that harboring provision was not limited to clandestine sheltering only). See also Cristina Rodriguez, et al., Migration Policy Institute, National Center on Immigrant Integration Policy, Testing the Limit: A Framework for Assessing the Legality of State and Local Immigration Measures, at 24-27 (discussing merits and weaknesses of argument that federal alien smuggling statute preempts local restrictions on renting to unauthorized aliens). A reviewing court might consider arguments that state or local measures barring persons from renting property to unauthorized aliens, or otherwise prohibiting such persons from occupying a dwelling unit, constitute "additional or auxiliary regulation[s]" to a federal scheme. This argument is probably strongest in cases where criminal penalties are imposed upon persons who violate a non-federal dwelling restriction, but it may also be applicable in cases where non-criminal penalties are imposed. Compare We Are America/Somos America, Coalition of Arizona v. Maricopa County Bd. of Sup'rs, 594 F. Supp. 2d 1104, 1114 (D. Ariz. 2009) (finding that Arizona's human smuggling statute was not preempted by federal law) and State v. Barragan-Sierra, 196 P.3d 879, 890-91 (Ariz. Ct. App. 2008) (same) with Garrett v. City of Escondido, 465 F. Supp. 2d 1043 (S.D. Cal. 2006) (granting temporary restraining order against local ordinance imposing civil and criminal penalties upon persons renting property to unauthorized aliens, in part because serious field preemption concerns were raised due to the existence of the federal alien smuggling statute) and State of New Hampshire v. Barros-Batistele, Case No. 05-CR-1474, 1475 (N.H. Dist. Ct., Aug. 12, 2005) (same).

[95] Garrett, 465 F. Supp. 2d at 1057.

[96] See, e.g., United States v. Arizona, 703 F. Supp. 2d at 995-96 (finding that the provision of Arizona's S.B. 1070 requiring state and local officials to verify the immigration status of all stopped persons who are suspected of being unlawfully present aliens was preempted, in part, because of the burden it imposed on the federal government).

[97] See Yick Wo v. Hopkins, 118 U.S. 356, 369 (1886).

[98] E.g., Heim v. McCall, 239 U.S. 175 (1915) (upholding state law barring noncitizens from being employed on public works projects); Patsone v. Pennsylvania, 232 U.S. 138 (1914) (upholding conviction of person under state law prohibiting an alien from owning a rifle or shotgun); Clarke v. Deckebach, 274 U.S. 392 (1927) (upholding local ordinance barring an alien from being licensed to operate a pool hall); Frick v. Webb, 263 U.S. 326 (1923); Porterfield v. Webb, 263 U.S. 225 (1923) (upholding states' ability to deny aliens the right to own or lease agricultural lands); Terrace v. Thompson, 263 U.S. 197, 220 (1923) (same); Webb v. O'Brien, 263 U.S. 313 (1923) (same).

[99] See Takahashi v. Fish & Game Comm'n, 334 U.S. 410, 420-21 (1948); see also Peter J. Spiro, The States and Immigration in an Era of Demi-Sovereignties, 35 VA. J. INT'L L. 121, 149-51 (1994).

[100] Ambach v. Norwick, 441 U.S. 68, 72-73 (1979).

[101] See Takahashi, 334 U.S. at 410 (1948) (finding that a California statute barring issuance of fishing licenses to lawfully present aliens who were ineligible for citizenship denied such aliens equal protection, and could not be justified as protecting a special interest of the state in conserving public fishing); Sei Fujii v. State 242 P.2d 617 (Cal. 1952) (finding a California law restricting land ownership by aliens violated the Fourteenth Amendment, and also concluding that earlier Supreme Court decisions upholding alien land laws were not in accord with subsequent Court jurisprudence).

[102] Compare Graham v. Richardson 403 U.S. 365, 372 (1971) (finding state classifications based on alienage, as such, to be "inherently suspect and subject to close judicial scrutiny") with Plyler, 457 U.S. at 219 n.19 (finding that the unauthorized presence of illegal aliens is not a "constitutional irrelevancy," and such aliens do not constitute a "suspect class").

[103] Lozano I, 496 F. Supp. 2d at 542.

[104] 332 U.S. 633 (1948).

[105] It should be noted that the Court only ruled that the California alien land law unconstitutional as applied in the case before it. It did not reach the question of whether states could constitutionally bar aliens from owning real property, nor expressly overrule earlier Court decisions upholding alien land laws. In separate concurrences, Justice Black (joined by Justice Douglas) and Justice Murphy (joined by Justice Rutledge) argued that the California statute unconstitutionally abridged the property rights of aliens. Id. at 647 (Black, J., concurring); id. at 650 (Murphy, J., concurring).

[106] Depending upon their terms, such measures could also be challenged as depriving landlords and/or tenants of due process on other grounds, most notably on the grounds that they are "void for vagueness." The void-for-vagueness doctrine requires that a "penal statute define the criminal offense with sufficient definiteness that ordinary people can understand what conduct is prohibited and in a manner that does not encourage arbitrary and discriminatory enforcement." Kolender v. Lawson, 461 U.S. 352, 357 (1983). At least one court has found that a local restriction on renting to unlawfully present aliens was void for vagueness because it did not define "eligible immigration status" and was not specific about its document requirements. Villas at Parkside Partners, 577 F. Supp. 2d at 876-77.

[107] United States v. James Daniel Good Real Property, 510 U.S. 43, 53-54 (1993) (holding that the Due Process Clause compels the government to give notice and a meaningful opportunity to be heard before seizing real property subject to civil forfeiture).

[108] Id.; Greene v. Lindsey, 456 U.S. 444, 450-51 (1982) (recognizing that tenants have a significant property interest in "the right to continued residence in their homes"); Garrett, 465 F. Supp. 2d at 1057-59 (noting that landlords could potentially lose rent and have to undertake eviction proceedings because of the ordinance in question).

[109] See, e.g., Garrett, 465 F. Supp. 2d at 1048 (subjecting repeat offenders to a monetary penalty of up to $1,000 per day per violation and/or a jail term of six months).

[110] See, e.g., id.

[111] Although some state or local housing restrictions may directly affect the property interests of both tenants and lessors, others may not. For example, a state or locality may choose to impose civil penalties upon persons who lease real property to unauthorized aliens, while imposing no direct penalty upon an alien who leases or occupies such property. An unauthorized alien might not be able to challenge such a measure on procedural due process grounds, as the government action only affects the alien's property interests indirectly (e.g., if a property owner breaks a lease with an unauthorized alien tenant to avoid incurring a civil fine). While the alien may have a cause of action against the government or, more

directly, the lessor (e.g., for breach of the lease agreement), he or she may not be able to raise a procedural due process claim against the government. See supra notes 45-46 and accompanying text.

[112] See, e.g., Garrett, 465 F. Supp. 2d at 1057-59 (noting serious due process concerns regarding an ordinance that failed to provide such protections).

[113] See e.g., Ariz. Stat. § 15-232 (restricting adult education services to U.S. citizens, legal residents or persons otherwise lawfully present in the United States); Ariz. Stat. §§ 15-1803 and 15-1825 (restricting in-state tuition and state financial aid for state university and community colleges to the same); Ariz. Stat. Rev. § 46-803 (denying child care assistance to unlawfully present aliens); Colo. Rev. Stat. § 24-76.5-103 (requiring agencies and state political subdivisions to verify the lawful presence in the United States of any applicant for state or local benefits excluding services needed for emergency medical conditions); Nick Miroff, Pr. William Passes Resolution Targeting Illegal Immigration, WASH. POST, July 11, 2007, available at http://www.washingtonpost.com/wp-dyn/content/article/2007/07/10/AR2007071002093.html (describing a resolution passed by the Board of Supervisors of Prince William County, Virginia, which, among other things, required the County Executive to provide the Board with a plan outlining which benefits the county has the discretion to deny to those who are illegally present). Services recommended for restriction included: adult services to allow elderly and disabled individuals to remain in their homes; in-home services; rental and mortgage assistance; substance abuse program; and elderly/disabled tax relief programs.

[114] See, e.g., Wilson, 908 F. Supp. 755, 769-71 (finding that a California measure constituted a regulation of immigration, in part, because it relied upon determinations about aliens' immigration status made by state and local personnel).

[115] See Graham v. Richardson, 403 U.S. 365 (1971) (declaring state-imposed welfare restrictions on legal immigrants unconstitutional, both because the state statutes violated the Fourteenth Amendment's equal protection clause and because they encroached upon the exclusive federal power to regulate immigration).

[116] See Plyler, 457 U.S. 202 (recognizing that unlawfully present aliens are due lesser constitutional protection than legal aliens are). For discussion of the Plyer decision, see CRS Report 97-542, The Right of Undocumented Alien Children to Basic Education: An Overview of Plyler v. Doe, by Larry M. Eig. 117 See Mathews v. Diaz, 426 U.S. 67, 84 (1976) (declaring that the federal government's broad plenary power over immigration and naturalization provides the government with leeway to draw distinctions among aliens in providing benefits, so long as the distinctions are not "wholly irrational").

[118] See 8 U.S.C. § 1621(d) (defining the term "federal public benefit").

[119] As discussed previously, the U.S. Supreme Court has held that the children of unlawfully present aliens cannot be denied equal access to public elementary and secondary schools. See supra notes 34 to 36 and accompanying text.

[120] In 2001, the Attorney General promulgated regulations under the authority of PRWORA that specified the types of community programs, services, and assistance for which all aliens are eligible under these provisions of PRWORA. See U.S. Dep't of Justice, Final Specification of Community Programs Necessary for Protection of Life or Safety Under Welfare Reform Legislation, 66 Fed. Reg. 3613 (Jan. 16, 2001). These include programs involving activities intended to protect life and safety generally, which some commentators have suggested include day labor centers. See Margaret Hobbins, The Day Laborer Debate: Small Town, U.S.A. Takes on Federal Immigration Law Regarding Undocumented Workers, 6 CONN. PUB. INT. L.J. 111, 136-37 (2006).

[121] 8 U.S.C. § 1621.

[122] 8 U.S.C. § 1621(c) (defining "state or local public benefit").

[123] See, e.g., Roe 1 v. Prince William County, 525 F. Supp. 2d 799 (E.D. Va. 2007) (finding that the possibility of future harms with respect to denial of services was too speculative to confer standing upon plaintiffs). In some cases, state or local actions have been challenged on the grounds that they provide public benefits to unlawfully present aliens in violation of PRWORA. See, e.g., Day v. Bond, 500 F.3d 1127 (10th Cir. 2007) (finding that plaintiffs lacked standing to challenge a Kansas statute allowing certain unlawfully present aliens to receive in-state tuition at public institutions of higher education); Martinez v. Regents of the University of California, 50 Cal. 4th 1277 (2010) (finding that a California statute allowing certain unlawfully present aliens to receive in-state tuition at public institutions of higher education was not preempted); Karunakarum, 70 Va. Cir. 208 (plaintiffs alleged that operation of a day labor center constituted provision of public benefits to unlawfully present aliens in violation of federal law).

[124] The Systematic Alien Verification for Entitlements (SAVE) system is intended to provide federal, state, and local government agencies with information on immigration status that is necessary to determine noncitizen eligibility for public benefits. Issues could arise if a state or local measure attempted to rely on some means other than SAVE to determine immigration status and/or eligibility.

[125] 42 U.S.C. §§ 2000e et seq.

[126] Id. at §2000e-2. INA § 274B contains a similar prohibition with respect to employment-based discrimination on the basis of national origin or citizenship. 8 U.S.C. § 1324b.

[127] Espinoza v. Farah Mfg. Co., 414 U.S. 86, 88 (1973).

[128] Title VII contains a preemption provision that states, "Nothing in this title shall be deemed to exempt or relieve any person from any liability, duty, penalty, or punishment provided by any present or future law of any State or political subdivision of a State, other than any such law which purports to require or permit the doing of any act which would be an unlawful employment practice under this title." 42 U.S.C. § 2000e-7. In other words, state laws that conflict with Title VII are preempted.

[129] Farah, 414 U.S. at 92.

[130] The possibility of this occurring may, however, be minimized by the fact that IRCA's penalties for discrimination on the basis of citizenship status and national origin are the same as its penalties for knowingly hiring an unauthorized alien. Compare 8 U.S.C. § 1324a(e)(4)(A)(i)-(iii) with 8 U.S.C. § 1324b(g)(2)(B)(iv)(I)-(III).

[131] 42 U.S.C. § 3604(a).

[132] See, e.g., Espinoza v. Hillwood Square Mut. Asso., 522 F. Supp. 559 (D. Va. 1981).

[133] Like Title VII, the FHA contains a preemption provision that states, "Nothing in this title shall be construed to invalidate or limit any law of a State or political subdivision of a State, or of any other jurisdiction in which this title shall be effective, that grants, guarantees, or protects the same rights as are granted by this title; but any law of a State, a political subdivision, or other such jurisdiction that purports to require or permit any action that would be a discriminatory housing practice under this title shall to that extent be invalid." 42 U.S.C. § 3615.

[134] Lozano I, 496 F. Supp. 2d 477.

[135] Id. at 546.

[136] Takahashi, 334 U.S. at 419.

[137] Plyler, 457 U.S. at 210.

[138] Lozano I, 496 F. Supp. 2d. at 547-48.

[139] Takahashi, 334 U.S. at 419.

[140] See, e.g., Anderson v. Conboy, 156 F.3d 167, 169 (2nd Cir. 1998).

[141] Relatedly, in 2004, Arizona voters enacted Proposition 200, which (1) required individuals to produce proof of citizenship before registering to vote or applying for public benefits; (2) made it a misdemeanor for public officials to fail to report persons who apply for benefits who are unable to produce documentation of citizenship; and (3) created a private right of action for Arizona citizens who believe public officials have given benefits to undocumented persons. The Ninth Circuit recently affirmed a lower court's holding that Proposition 200's provisions regarding voter identification are unconstitutional under the Elections Clause of the U.S. Constitution. See Gonzalez v. Arizona, No. 08-17094, No. 08-17115, 2010 U.S. App. LEXIS 22071 (9th Cir. 2010). The benefits provisions had been separately challenged. See Friendly House v. Napolitano, 419 F.3d 930 (9th Cir. 2007) (finding that plaintiffs lacked standing).

[142] Chicanos Por La Causa, 558 F.3d 856, aff'g Ariz. Contractors Assn., 534 F. Supp. 2d 1036.

[143] See supra note 7.

[144] The text of S.B. 1070, as amended by H.B. 2162, can be viewed at http://www.azleg.gov/alispdfs/council/SB1070-HB2162.PDF.

[145] United States v. Arizona, 703 F. Supp. 2d 980 (D. Ariz. 2010).

[146] See, e.g., Friendly House v. Whiting, No. CV 10-1061, Complaint (D. Ariz., filed May 17, 2010), at 6, available at http://www.aclu.org/files/assets/az_sb1070_complaint_ 20100517.pdf.

In: Illegal Aliens
Editor: K. Downs and D. Rasmussen
ISBN: 978-1-61942-631-3
© 2012 Nova Science Publishers, Inc.

Chapter 4

STATE EFFORTS TO DETER UNAUTHORIZED ALIENS: LEGAL ANALYSIS OF ARIZONA'S S.B. 1070*

Kate M. Manuel, Michael John Garcia, and Larry M. Eig

SUMMARY

On April 23, 2010, Arizona enacted S.B. 1070, which is designed to discourage and deter the entry or presence of aliens who lack lawful status under federal immigration law. Potentially sweeping in effect, the measure requires state and local law enforcement officials to facilitate the detection of unauthorized aliens in their daily enforcement activities. The measure also establishes criminal penalties under state law, in addition to those already imposed under federal law, for alien smuggling offenses and failure to carry or complete alien registration documents. Further, it makes it a crime under Arizona law for an unauthorized alien to apply for or perform work in the state, either as an employee or an independent contractor.

The enactment of S.B. 1070 has sparked significant legal and policy debate. Supporters argue that federal enforcement of immigration law has not adequately deterred the migration of unauthorized aliens into Arizona, and that state action is both necessary and appropriate to combat the

---

* This is an edited, reformatted and augmented version of a Congressional Research Service publication, CRS Report for Congress R41221, from www.crs.gov, dated June 7, 2011.

negative effects of unauthorized immigration. Opponents argue, among other things, that S.B. 1070 will be expensive and disruptive, will be susceptible to uneven application, and can undermine community policing by discouraging cooperation with state and local law enforcement. In part to respond to these concerns, the Arizona State Legislature modified S.B. 1070 on April 30, 2010, through the approval of H.B. 2162.

Whenever states enact laws or adopt policies to affect the entry or stay of noncitizens, including aliens present in the United States without legal authorization, questions can arise whether Congress has preempted their implementation. For instance, Congress may pass a law to preempt state law expressly. Further, especially in areas of strong federal interest, as evidenced by broad congressional regulation and direct federal enforcement, state law may be found to be preempted implicitly. Analyzing implicit preemption issues can often be difficult in the abstract. Prior to actual implementation, it might be hard to assess whether state law impermissibly frustrates federal regulation. Nevertheless, authority under S.B. 1070, as originally adopted, for law enforcement personnel to investigate the immigration status of any individual with whom they have "lawful contact," upon reasonable suspicion of unlawful presence, could plausibly have been interpreted to call for an unprecedented level of state immigration enforcement as part of routine policing. H.B. 2162, however, has limited this investigative authority.

Provisions in S.B. 1070 criminalizing certain immigration-related conduct also may be subject to preemption challenges. The legal vulnerability of these provisions may depend on their relationship to traditional state police powers and potential frustration of uniform national immigration policies, among other factors. In addition to preemption issues, S.B. 1070 arguably might raise other constitutional considerations, including issues associated with racial profiling. Assessing these potential legal issues may be difficult before there is evidence of how S.B. 1070, as modified, is implemented and applied in practice.

S.B. 1070, as amended, was scheduled to go into effect on July 29, 2010. However, the U.S. Department of Justice filed suit seeking to preliminarily enjoin the enforcement of certain sections of S.B. 1070 on the grounds that they are preempted. On July 28, 2010, a federal district court enjoined Arizona from enforcing those provisions of S.B. 1070 pertaining to immigration status verifications, among other things. Arizona appealed this decision, and on April 11, 2011, the U.S. Court of Appeals for the Ninth Circuit issued an opinion affirming the district court's decision. Arizona's governor has reportedly expressed a desire to appeal this decision, and the district court has yet to issue a final ruling as to the merits of the government's challenge.

On April 23, 2010, Arizona enacted legislation (commonly referred to as S.B. 1070) intended

> to make attrition through enforcement the public policy of all state and local government agencies in Arizona. The provisions of this act are intended to work together to discourage and deter the unlawful entry and presence of aliens and economic activity by persons unlawfully present in the United States.[1]

By so doing, Arizona arguably placed itself in the vanguard of recent attempts to test the legal limits of greater state involvement in immigration enforcement, and prompted significant debate regarding the desirability and effectiveness of S.B. 1070 and similar state or local measures. Supporters of S.B. 1070 argue that federal enforcement of immigration law has not adequately deterred the migration of unauthorized aliens into Arizona, and that state action is both necessary and appropriate to combat the negative effects of unauthorized immigration. Opponents argue, among other things, that S.B. 1070 will be expensive and disruptive, will be susceptible to uneven application, and can undermine community policing by discouraging cooperation with state and local law enforcement. In part to respond to some of these concerns, the Arizona State Legislature modified S.B. 1070 on April 30, 2010, through the approval of H.B. 2162 (unless otherwise specified, references to S.B. 1070 in this report refer to the version amended by H.B. 2162).

Following the enactment of S.B. 1070 but prior to its scheduled date to go into effect (July 29, 2010),[2] the U.S. Department of Justice (DOJ) and a number of private entities filed separate lawsuits challenging the legislation. The central argument made by the petitioners was that aspects of S.B. 1070, both separately and in conjunction, are preempted by federal law and are therefore unenforceable.[3]

On July 28, 2010, Judge Susan Bolton of the U.S. District Court for the District of Arizona granted DOJ's motion to preliminarily enjoin, pending a final ruling on the case, those provisions of S.B. 1070 pertaining to (1) immigration status determinations during stops, detentions, or arrests by state law enforcement; (2) the imposition of state criminal penalties for certain violations of federal alien registration requirements; (3) the criminalization of the solicitation or performance of work by unlawfully present aliens; and (4) the authorization of state law enforcement to make warrantless arrests for public offenses which constitute grounds for deportation under federal immigration law.[4] However, the district court did not enjoin other provisions of S.B. 1070 from taking effect, including provisions allowing legal residents of Arizona to bring suit to challenge state or local policies that restrict enforcement of federal immigration laws and provisions criminalizing activities related to the transportation or harboring of unlawfully present aliens.[5]

Arizona appealed the district court's decision,[6] and on April 11, 2011, a three-judge panel of the U.S. Court of Appeals for the Ninth Circuit issued a decision affirming the district court's decision to preliminarily enjoin enforcement of those provisions of S.B. 1070 pertaining to immigration status determinations during stops, detentions, and arrests; failure to apply for or carry alien registration papers; the solicitation or performance of work by unauthorized aliens; and warrantless arrests for certain public offenses.[7] The panel unanimously affirmed the district court's injunction order with respect to those provisions of S.B. 1070 relating to alien registration and the performance of work by unauthorized aliens, and split 2-1 in affirmation of those portions of the order relating to status determinations and warrantless arrests. Arizona Governor Jan Brewer announced on May 9, 2011, that Arizona would petition the Supreme Court to hear an appeal of the panel's decision, rather than seeking *en banc* review by the Ninth Circuit.[8] The district court has yet to issue a final ruling as to the merits of the federal government's challenge, but its preliminary injunction remains in effect.[9]

This report discusses S.B. 1070 and notable preemption issues raised by some of its provisions. It examines rulings made by the reviewing district and appellate court concerning the federal government's legal challenge. It also discusses other preemption issues potentially raised by S.B. 1070 or similar legislation, including some issues that have yet to be addressed by the reviewing courts. It should be noted that the upholding of the district court's preliminary injunction by the Ninth Circuit panel is not the final word as to the constitutionality of S.B. 1070 or similar measures which may be contemplated in other states. It is possible that the district court could analyze the preemption issues raised by S.B. 1070 differently when it issues its final ruling as to the merits of the government's challenge. Further, it remains to be seen whether the Ninth Circuit might potentially reconsider the issue *en banc.*[10] Moreover, if legislation similar to S.B. 1070 is enacted in another jurisdiction and subsequently faces legal challenge, it is possible that a reviewing court would assess the relevant legal issues differently than the courts currently considering the constitutionality of S.B. 1070.

I. BACKGROUND

The foreign born population of the United States has grown rapidly from the 1980s onward. A significant component of this population, an estimated 28% in 2009,[11] resides in the United States without legal authorization, either as a result of fraudulent or surreptitious entry or of overstaying nonimmigrant visas that had allowed their temporary presence in the country. In 1986, approximately 3 million unauthorized aliens resided in the United States. By 2006, the estimated number of unauthorized aliens had more than tripled.[12]

As the population of unauthorized aliens grew, several impacted states sued the federal government to recover the costs of benefits and services they were required to provide unauthorized aliens because of the alleged failure of the federal government to enforce immigration law adequately. These lawsuits failed.[13] Meanwhile, many jurisdictions throughout the country have sought to deter the presence of unauthorized aliens and reduce attendant costs through a variety of enforcement measures of their own.[14]

As a legal matter, states have inherent "police powers" to promote and regulate safety, health, welfare, and economic activity within their respective jurisdictions. The exercise of state police powers may be limited by the rights owed to individuals under the Constitution. Moreover, these powers can be affected by assertions and delegations of federal authority, which may change over time. When they do, state powers can be concomitantly restricted or expanded. Beginning in the 1970s, federal legislation on aliens more frequently regulated the incidents of daily life of noncitizens, lawful and unlawful. Prime examples include rules on noncitizen access to public benefits and programs, and sanctions against employers who hire unauthorized workers. To some degree, new federal restrictions crowded out concurrent state regulation. At the same time, however, the push by Congress to regulate the stay of aliens in the United States more comprehensively also included, particularly in two statutes enacted in 1996,[15] increased authority for the states to mirror federal benefit restrictions and cooperate with immigration enforcement generally.

Laws like Arizona's S.B. 1070, even as modified by H.B. 2162, appear to test the legal limits of a trend toward greater state involvement. Nevertheless, not all jurisdictions have reacted similarly in responding to the influx of unauthorized aliens and the perception of growing state and local authority to react to it. At the one end of the spectrum, some jurisdictions (occasionally referred to as "sanctuary cities") have been unwilling to assist the federal government in enforcing measures that distinguish between legal and nonlegal residents of the community, and, in some cases, have actively opposed providing assistance to federal enforcement efforts.[16] Moving toward the middle of the spectrum, some states and localities communicate with federal immigration enforcement officers under limited circumstances (e.g., after arresting an unauthorized alien for a criminal offense), but for various reasons do not take a more active role in deterring illegal immigration.

At the other end of the spectrum are jurisdictions, like Arizona, that have actively sought to deter the presence of unlawfully present aliens within their territory. Some of these jurisdictions have assisted federal authorities in apprehending and detaining unauthorized aliens, including under written agreements with federal immigration authorities made under § 287(g) of the Immigration and Nationality Act (INA).[17] More controversially, some states and localities have considered, and in a few cases enacted, measures intended to deter the presence of aliens who are in the United States without legal authorization, including by limiting access to housing, employment, or municipal services.[18] In May 2011, the Supreme Court ruled in the case of *Chamber of Commerce v. Whiting* that federal law did not preempt a state statute requiring employers to use the federal government's E-Verify system to determine the work eligibility of employees, and which authorized the suspension or revocation of the business licenses of entities that knowingly employed unauthorized aliens.[19] It seems likely that this ruling will inform deliberations by some states or localities as to whether to adopt similar measures.[20]

II. Major Provisions of S.B. 1070, as Modified

Section 1 of S.B. 1070 declares that the provisions of the legislation are "intended to work together to discourage and deter the unlawful entry and presence of aliens and economic activity by persons unlawfully present in the United States."[21] It further declares the intent to establish a state-wide policy of "attrition through enforcement." [22] "Attrition through enforcement" has been described by some observers as an approach to deter unlawful migration and encourage the compelled or voluntary exit of unlawfully present aliens through the "steady, across-the-board enforcement of our immigration laws."[23] This approach is most often associated with more vigorous and efficient implementation of employer sanctions, improved recordkeeping and more secure documents, and other measures to make current law more effective. It can also imply better cooperation between the states and federal immigration authorities, and the adoption of state and local laws that discourage the presence of unauthorized aliens.[24]

These objectives are reflected in the major provisions of S.B. 1070, which can arguably be characterized as falling into two categories: (1) those provisions that seek to bolster direct enforcement of federal immigration law, including through the identification and apprehension of aliens who are unlawfully present in the United States, by state and local law enforcement; and (2) those provisions that criminalize conduct which may facilitate the presence of unauthorized aliens within Arizona. Sections 2 and 6 of S.B. 1070 can be characterized as falling within the former category, while Sections 3-5 fall within the latter.

Section 2 of S.B. 1070 directs state and local law enforcement officers and agencies, whenever making a lawful stop, detention, or arrest pursuant to the enforcement of state or local laws, to make a reasonable attempt whenever practicable to determine the person's immigration status, if there is reasonable suspicion to believe the person is an alien who is unlawfully present in the country.[25] A person is presumed not to be an unlawfully present alien if he can provide specified documentation, such as an Arizona driver's license.[26] An attempt to determine status need not be made if it would hinder or obstruct an investigation.[27] The immigration status of a person who is arrested must be determined before the person is released.[28] In implementing these provisions, law enforcement officials "may not consider race, color, or national origin" except to the extent permitted by the U.S. or Arizona Constitution.[29] Section 2 further mandates that the U.S. Immigration and Customs Enforcement (ICE) or Customs and Border Protection (CBP) be notified when an unlawfully present alien who has been convicted of a crime is released from prison or is assessed a monetary penalty.[30] Additionally, S.B. 1070 authorizes state and local law enforcement officials to transport unlawfully present aliens in their custody to a federal facility.[31]

Section 2 also prohibits restrictions upon state or local officials or agencies sending, receiving, exchanging, or maintaining information relating to the immigration status of an individual for the purpose of determining eligibility for public services or benefits, verifying domicile or residence, or determining whether a person is in compliance with federal alien registration laws.[32] It further provides that any legal resident of Arizona may bring suit to challenge any state or local policy that restricts the enforcement of federal immigration laws to less than the full extent permitted by federal law.[33]

Section 3 criminalizes some activities currently proscribed by federal immigration laws. If a person violates 8 U.S.C. §§ 1304(e) or 1306(a),[34] he will also be guilty of the state crime of "willful failure to complete or carry an alien registration document."[35] Modifications by H.B. 2162 eliminated the penalty structure under S.B. 1070 for alien registration violations, which would have made these offenses felonies in certain circumstances, and substituted a provision making all violations misdemeanors.[36] This section does not apply with respect to aliens who maintain authorization from the federal government to remain in the United States.[37]

Sections 4 and 5 of S.B. 1070 address activities relating to the transport and harboring of unlawfully present aliens. Section 4 modifies a preexisting Arizona statute addressing alien smuggling, but this amendment does not alter the earlier statute's substantive scope.[38] More significantly, Section 5 adds a new criminal statute prohibiting alien smuggling-related activities, when such activities are committed by a person who is also in violation of another criminal offense. Specifically, Section 5 imposes criminal penalties upon the transport of an alien within the state in furtherance of the alien's illegal presence in the United States, when done with knowledge or in reckless disregard of the alien's unauthorized status.[39] Harboring an alien or encouraging an alien to come to or reside in Arizona with knowledge or in reckless disregard of the fact that the alien's presence is in violation of the law is also prohibited.[40] Further, vehicles used in committing an offense under the new smuggling statute are subject to mandatory immobilization or impoundment.[41]

Section 5 also makes it an Arizona crime for an unlawfully present alien to apply for or solicit work in the state, or work as an employee or an independent contractor in the state.[42] Separately, it is unlawful for an occupant of a motor vehicle that is stopped on a roadway to pick up and hire, or attempt to hire, passengers for work at a different location, if the motor vehicle blocks or impedes the normal movement of traffic.[43] Section 5 also makes it unlawful for a person to enter the motor vehicle in such circumstances, in order to be hired by the vehicle's occupant.[44]

Section 6 further authorizes officers to make an arrest without a warrant if they have probable cause to believe the person to be arrested has committed any "public offense" that makes the person removable from the United States.[45] Arizona law elsewhere defines a "public offense" as any "conduct for which a sentence to a term of imprisonment or of a fine is provided by any law of the state in which it occurred," and, if the act occurred outside Arizona, would have been punishable under Arizona law if it had occurred in the state.[46]

III. Overview of Preemption

The central issue that has been raised in litigation challenging S.B. 1070 concerns whether its major provisions are preempted by federal law. The doctrine of preemption derives from the Supremacy Clause of the Constitution, which establishes that federal law, treaties, and the Constitution itself are "the supreme Law of the Land."[47] Thus, one essential aspect of the federal structure of government is that states can be precluded from taking actions that are otherwise within their authority if federal law is thereby thwarted. "States cannot, inconsistently with the purpose of Congress, conflict or interfere with, curtail or complement, the federal law, or enforce additional or auxiliary regulations."[48] An act of Congress may preempt state or local action in a given area in any one of three ways: (1) the statute expressly states preemptive intent (express preemption); (2) a court concludes that Congress intended to occupy the regulatory field,[49] thereby implicitly precluding state or local action in that area (field preemption); or (3) state or local action directly conflicts with or otherwise frustrates the purpose of the federal scheme (conflict preemption).[50] The delineation between these categories, particularly between field and conflict preemption, is not rigid.[51]

The power to set rules for which aliens may enter and remain in the United States is undoubtedly federal, and the breadth and detail of regulation Congress has established in the INA[52] precludes substantive state regulation concerning which noncitizens may enter or remain. Nevertheless, the Supreme Court has never held that "every state enactment which in any way deals with aliens is a regulation of immigration and thus *per se* pre-empted by this constitutional power, whether latent or exercised."[53] In the 1976 case of *De Canas v. Bica*, the Court held that state regulation of matters within their jurisdictions that were only tangentially related to immigration would, "absent congressional action[,] ... not be an invalid state incursion on federal power."[54] The Court further indicated that field preemption claims against state action that did not conflict with federal law could only be justified when the "complete ouster of state power ... was the clear and manifest purpose of Congress."[55] Still, the *De Canas* Court recognized that, even in situations where federal immigration law "contemplates some room for state legislation," a state measure might nonetheless be unenforceable on conflict preemption grounds if it "stands as an obstacle to the accomplishment and execution of the full purposes and objectives of Congress in enacting the INA."[56]

A separate but somewhat related legal issue concerns the authority of states and localities to directly enforce provisions of the INA, including by investigating and making arrests for criminal and civil violations of federal immigration law. As a general matter, it appears well established that states have at least implicit authority to make arrests for violations of federal law, unless the nature or purpose of the federal regulatory scheme precludes state action.[57] Historically, the authority for state and local law enforcement officials to enforce immigration law has been construed to be generally limited to certain criminal provisions of the INA.[58] By contrast, the enforcement of the civil provisions, including the apprehension and removal of deportable aliens, has been viewed as a federal responsibility, with states and localities preempted from playing more than an incidental supporting role, except to the extent specifically authorized by federal law.[59]

For the first several decades following the INA's enactment, the prevailing assumption appears to have been that the INA's deportation provisions constituted a pervasive regulatory scheme under which state and local enforcement was preempted.[60] Then in the 1980s and 1990s, some jurisdictions that were heavily impacted by immigration grew more insistent in characterizing federal enforcement of federal immigration law as inadequate. In part to address these concerns, Congress included authority in the Illegal Immigration Reform and Immigrant Responsibility Act of 1996 (IIRIRA) for the Attorney General (now the Secretary of Homeland Security) to enter into cooperative agreements with states and localities under which trained state and local law enforcement officers can, under federal supervision and subject to federal direction, perform certain functions relative to the investigation, apprehension, or detention of unlawful aliens to the extent permitted by state or local law.[61] The enacted version of this measure was significantly narrower than some of those considered (a House-passed version, for example, would have authorized agreements permitting states to carry out all deportation functions, including prosecution, adjudication, and physical removal[62]), but all of the proposals that were seriously considered seem to have reflected a perception that, absent a cooperative arrangement with federal authorities, states and localities would play at most a secondary and supportive role in the enforcement of the civil provisions of the INA.

But a restrictive view of a state and local role in the enforcement of immigration law may be changing. In 2002, the Office of Legal Counsel (OLC) within the DOJ issued a memorandum which concluded that "federal law did not preempt state police from arresting aliens on the basis of civil deportability," and it withdrew the advice of a 1996 OLC opinion which had suggested otherwise.[63] Additionally, a series of cases decided by the Tenth Circuit variously drew no distinction between the criminal and civil provisions of the INA in relation to state and local enforcement authority, or alluded to the "implicit authority" or the "general investigatory authority" of the states to engage in civil immigration enforcement activities.[64] More recently in litigation concerning S.B. 1070, however, a majority of the reviewing Ninth Circuit panel rejected the argument that states have implicit or inherent authority to enforce the civil provisions of the INA.[65]

State Enforcement of Immigration Law Under Section 2

Much of the attention surrounding S.B. 1070 has centered on Section 2 of the enactment. As discussed previously, Section 2 requires state and local law enforcement officials to facilitate the detection of unauthorized aliens in their daily enforcement activities, presumably so that these aliens may be transferred to federal custody for removal. This requirement was challenged in the DOJ's suit against Arizona, and its implementation was preliminarily enjoined by the district court because the court found that the government was likely to prevail in its argument that the requirement is preempted by federal law. In a 2-1 ruling, the reviewing Ninth Circuit panel affirmed. Other aspects of Section 2 were neither challenged by the DOJ nor enjoined by the district court, including the provision concerning the sharing of immigration-related information by state and local authorities, as well as the provision authorizing Arizona residents to bring suit challenging state or local policies which limit the enforcement of federal immigration law.

Sharing of Immigration Status Information between Government Entities

Federal law contemplates some level of cooperation between state and federal agencies in the enforcement of immigration laws. In 1996, Congress passed measures intended, at least in part, to deter states and localities from limiting information-sharing with the federal government on immigration matters. Pursuant to IIRIRA § 642 and § 434 of the Personal Responsibility and Work Opportunity Reconciliation Act of 1996 (PRWORA), states and localities may not limit their governmental entities or officers from maintaining records regarding a person's immigration status, or bar the exchange of such information with any federal, state, or local entity. In addition to imposing obligations upon states and localities to refrain from restricting their agencies and officers from communicating with federal authorities regarding immigration matters, IIRIRA § 642 also imposed an obligation upon federal immigration authorities to respond to immigration-related inquiries from states and localities. Specifically, IIRIRA § 642(c) requires federal immigration authorities

> to respond to an inquiry by a Federal, State, or local government agency, seeking to verify or ascertain the citizenship or immigration status of any individual within the jurisdiction of the agency for any purpose authorized by law, by providing the requested verification or status information.[66]

Aspects of S.B. 1070 have clearly been informed by these measures. Generally, provisions of S.B. 1070 that concern determinations of persons' immigration status require verification with the federal government pursuant to the mechanism established by IIRIRA § 642(c). Other provisions of S.B. 1070 resemble those provisions of PRWORA and IIRIRA that prohibit state and local agencies from restricting the sharing of information related to immigration status with other federal, state, and local entities. Section 2 of S.B. 1070 bars any restriction (other than those imposed by federal law) upon state or local officers and agencies sending, receiving, maintaining, or exchanging information on immigration with other federal, state, and local government entities, when such activity is done for the purpose of determining eligibility for public services or benefits, verifying a person's claim of domicile or residence, or determining whether a person is complying with federal alien registration laws. On their face, these provisions might reasonably be viewed as consonant with provisions of PRWORA and IIRIRA concerning the sharing of immigration-related information by federal, state, and local entities. On the other hand, it is possible that these provisions could be interpreted more broadly to, for example, permit the fostering of inquiries into immigration status by state and local employees beyond those inquiries currently undertaken incident to those employees' official duties.

Detection of Unauthorized Aliens By State and Local Law Enforcement under Section 2

Those provisions of S.B. 1070 which contemplate state and local law enforcement actively participating in the detection of unauthorized aliens raise more significant preemption issues. Especially prior to its modification by H.B. 2162, Section 2 of S.B. 1070 arguably appeared to authorize intensive, daily involvement in immigration law enforcement by state and local officers beyond established precedents. As originally enacted, a component of Section

2 (generally referred to as "Section 2(B)" in the opinions of the district and appellate courts) provided that whenever a law enforcement officer had "lawful contact" with a person and reasonable suspicion existed that the person was an unlawfully present alien, the officer was required, where practicable, to determine the person's immigration status. Case law in the Tenth Circuit has supported the authority of police to inquire into immigration status in certain circumstances incidental to otherwise authorized enforcement of criminal law, violations of state traffic laws, and similar offenses.[67] Inquiring into status pursuant to "lawful contact" perhaps could have been read as sufficiently circumscribed to fit within this line of cases (though its reception by the Ninth Circuit, where Arizona rests, appeared less certain at the time when S.B. 1070 was enacted[68]). However, "lawful contact" also appeared susceptible to an interpretation that covered any manner of casual interaction between the police and the public that was "lawful." H.B. 2162 modified this provision to limit immigration status inquiries to situations where a law enforcement agency or officer made a "lawful stop, detention, or arrest" for a violation of state or local law.[69] In addition, S.B. 1070, as modified, also establishes that persons arrested by state or local law enforcement shall have their immigration status verified with federal authorities prior to their release.[70] Federal immigration authorities also shall be notified when an unauthorized alien is released from prison or has been assessed a monetary penalty, and local law enforcement officials may transport unauthorized aliens in their custody to a federal facility.[71]

Many of the above-described activities are the kind often contemplated in cooperative agreements between the Department of Homeland Security (DHS) and state or local law enforcement authorities. In 1996, Congress authorized the Attorney General (now the Secretary of Homeland Security) to enter into formal agreements with state or local entities that permit those entities to play a direct role in the enforcement of federal immigration law. Agreements entered pursuant to INA § 287(g) (commonly referred to as "287(g) agreements") enable specially trained state or local officers to perform specific functions relative to the investigation, apprehension, or detention of aliens, during a predetermined timeframe and under federal supervision. For example, the DHS has entered 287(g) agreements with several jurisdictions to allow correctional officers and other jail personnel to question persons who are being detained for crimes about their immigration status and begin paperwork for transferring suspected removable aliens to federal custody upon their release. Some other agreements authorize a limited number of highly trained personnel to more broadly engage in field enforcement under direct supervision of federal immigration agents.[72] State or local officers performing functions pursuant to 287(g) agreements are not considered federal employees, except for purposes relating to certain tort claims and compensation matters, but are considered to be acting under color of federal law for purposes of liability and immunity from suit in any civil actions brought under federal or state law.[73] There are several 287(g) agreements in place between federal immigration authorities and Arizona state, city, and county law enforcement agencies, permitting designated officers to perform specified functions under federal supervision.[74]

Section 2(B) of S.B. 1070 does not purport to be based on a delegation of federal immigration enforcement authority under INA § 287(g). Instead, its legal foundation appears premised on the belief that states generally possess inherent power to enforce federal laws, and that federal immigration law does not preempt the kind of enforcement activities contemplated by S.B. 1070.[75] This position appears to be based on similar legal reasoning as that found in the 2002 OLC opinion and the Tenth Circuit cases mentioned above.[76] To the extent that the performance of immigration enforcement functions by Arizona officials is not done pursuant to a 287(g) agreement, arguments may be raised that states and localities are preempted from engaging in such functions. It should be noted, however, that INA § 287(g)(10) plainly states that a written 287(g) agreement is not required for state or local entities to "cooperate ... in the identification, apprehension, detention, or removal of aliens not lawfully present in the United States."[77] An issue which may arise in litigation concerning state efforts to enforce federal immigration law is whether the "cooperation" contemplated under INA § 287(g)(10) requires states and localities to consult and coordinate their immigration enforcement efforts with federal authorities, or whether "cooperation" may also be interpreted to permit states and localities to independently enact measures that are consistent with, and arguably further, federal policies related to the detection and removal of unauthorized aliens.

The DOJ challenged the provision of Section 2(B) requiring state law enforcement to investigate the immigration status of stopped persons who are suspected of being unlawfully present aliens, claiming that this provision was preempted. The DOJ argument focused on the "mandatory" nature of this scheme. According to the DOJ, this scheme would result in a "dramatic increase" in the number of requests for immigration status verification received by federal immigration enforcement authorities,[78] "diverting resources and attention from the dangerous aliens who the federal government targets as its top enforcement priority."[79] The DOJ also claimed that Section

2(B) would impose impermissible burdens upon lawfully present aliens and U.S. citizens who are stopped or detained by Arizona law enforcement and cannot readily prove their citizenship or legal immigration status; a "form of treatment which Congress has plainly guarded against in crafting a balanced, federally-directed immigration enforcement scheme."[80] The district court held that the government would likely succeed on this challenge, and a three-judge Ninth Circuit panel affirmed in a 2-1 decision.

While the district court focused primarily upon the potential burdens that S.B. 1070 would impose on lawful immigrants and federal resources,[81] the majority of the circuit panel found that Section 2(B) was likely preempted for different reasons. Writing for the panel majority, Judge Richard A. Paez stated that Section 2(B) conflicted with the federal immigration enforcement scheme, which the majority characterized as permitting "state officers to systematically aid in immigration enforcement *only* under the close supervision" of federal immigration authorities.[82] In reaching this conclusion, the panel majority focused primarily upon the meaning of INA § 287(g).[83] A majority of the reviewing Ninth Circuit panel found that the provisions of INA § 287(g) authorizing the Secretary of DHS to enter into written agreements enabling state and local officers to perform specific immigration enforcement functions under federal direction to be indicative of congressional intent for state involvement in immigration enforcement to generally occur under federal supervision.[84] The majority further found that INA § 287(g)(10), which refers to state and local "cooperation" in immigration enforcement in the absence of a 287(g) agreement, as encompassing only assistance on "an incidental and as needed basis" when requested by the Secretary or otherwise necessary.[85]

The majority also rejected Arizona's argument that "Congress has expressed a clear intent to *encourage* the assistance from state and local law enforcement officers" when it required, via enactment of IIRIRA § 642(c),[86] that DHS respond to inquiries from state and local governments regarding the immigration status of individuals. While the Ninth Circuit panel agreed that IIRIRA § 642(c) "demonstrates that Congress contemplated state assistance in the identification of undocumented immigrants," the majority opinion concluded that such assistance must occur within the boundaries established by INA § 287(g), rather than "in a manner dictated by a state that furthers a state immigration policy."[87]

A majority of the circuit panel also held that Section 2(B) was likely preempted because its verification requirements would "interfere[] with Congress' delegation of discretion to the Executive branch in enforcing the INA."[88] The court reached this conclusion, in part, through application of the

Supreme Court's decisions in *Crosby v. National Foreign Trade Council* and *Buckman Co. v. Plaintiffs' Legal Committee.*[89] In *Crosby*, the Court found that a statute prohibiting state agencies from buying goods or services from companies that do business with Myanmar (Burma) was preempted by a federal statute that "Congress clearly intended ... to provide the President with flexible and effective authority" in dealing with Myanmar,[90] while in *Buckman*, the Court similarly found that tort claims under state law that were based on alleged fraud perpetuated against the Food and Drug Administration were preempted, because such claims would interfere with the "flexibility [which] is a critical component of the [federal] statutory and regulatory framework."[91] The circuit panel majority described the INA as giving the President similar flexibility in the area of immigration enforcement, and found that Section 2(B) represented an attempt by Arizona "to hijack a discretionary role that Congress delegated to the Executive."[92]

The panel majority further found that the government was likely to prevail in its preemption challenge to Section 2(B) because of the measure's "deleterious effect" on foreign relations, as well as "the threat of 50 states layering their own immigration enforcement rules on top of the INA."[93] In finding that Section 2(B) was very likely preempted on foreign policy grounds, the majority opinion emphasized the Supreme Court's statement in *American Insurance Association v. Garamendi* that "even . . . the *likelihood* that state legislation will produce something more than *incidental* effect in conflict with express foreign policy of the National Government would require preemption of the state law."[94] It found such an effect here, given that a number of foreign leaders and international organizations have criticized S.B. 1070, and Mexico had taken "affirmative steps" to protest it, including postponing review of a U.S.-Mexico agreement on emergency management cooperation.[95] The majority also found that the possibility of similar enactments by other states weighed in favor of preemption given that "each additional state statute incrementally diminishes the agency's control over enforcement of the federal statute and thus further detracts from the integrated scheme of regulation created by Congress."[96]

In addition to joining the majority opinion, Judge John T. Noonan wrote a separate concurrence to emphasize his view that Section 2(B) and other provisions of S.B. 1070 were inconsistent with federal foreign policy. He further characterized the regulation of immigration as a subset of foreign policy, and argued that the "foreign policy of the United States preempts the field entered by Arizona."[97]

In a partial dissent from the majority's ruling, including its conclusion that Section 2(B) of the Arizona statute was preempted, Judge Carlos T. Bea disputed the majority's finding that Section 2(B) impermissibly burdened federal immigration enforcement priorities. According to the dissent, through the enactment of INA § 287(g)(10) and IIRIRA § 642(c), "Congress has clearly expressed its intention that state officials *should* assist federal officials in checking the immigration status of aliens and in the 'identification, apprehension, detention, or removal of aliens not lawfully present in the United States.'"[98] Additionally, the dissent argued that the verification requirements established by Section 2(B) did not encroach on "federal flexibility," because the mandatory language of IIRIRA § 642(c) made clear that Congress did not intend for the executive branch to have any flexibility in determining whether to provide states with properly requested immigration status information.[99] The dissent also disputed the majority's conclusion that Section 2(B) was likely preempted on foreign policy grounds. According to the dissent, preemption is warranted only when a state or local measure conflict with "*established* foreign relations goals," and no goal had been identified that was in conflict with Section 2(B).[100] The dissent also disagreed with the majority's conclusion that state measures like Section 2(B) threatened to disrupt the immigration enforcement scheme established by Congress. The dissent viewed the adoption of such measures as being entirely consistent with the immigration enforcement framework established by federal law, which purportedly reflected Congress's desire for states to play an active role in the identification of unlawfully present aliens.[101]

The Ninth Circuit's analysis of Section 2(B) did not address every issue raised by the district court. Notably, the appellate court did not directly opine on the lower court's determination that Section 2(B) was likely preempted because of the burdens it would impose upon lawfully present aliens.[102] In reaching this conclusion, the district court relied heavily on the Supreme Court's ruling in the 1941 case of *Hines v. Davidowitz*.[103] In *Hines*, the Supreme Court struck down a Pennsylvania law that generally required adult aliens to register with the state once a year. According to the *Hines* Court, this requirement "necessarily place[d] lawfully present aliens (and even U.S. citizens) in continual jeopardy of having to demonstrate their lawful status to nonfederal officials," despite Congress's manifest intent to regulate immigration "in such a way as to protect the personal liberties of law-abiding aliens through one uniform national ... system[] and to leave them free from the possibility of inquisitorial practices and police surveillance."[104] The district court concluded that, like the state law struck down in *Hines*, the Arizona law's mandatory immigration status verification requirement would place an impermissible burden upon lawfully present aliens.[105]

It should be noted, however, that Ninth Circuit panel and the district court focused upon the "mandatory" nature of the immigration verification regime established by Section 2(B) in finding that the government is likely to succeed in its challenge. Thus, the courts' rulings would not necessarily bar Arizona law enforcement from attempting to verify the immigration status of apprehended persons on a more limited, case-by-case basis. In fact, the panel majority's opinion apparently contemplates such attempts at verification in limited circumstances.[106] The DOJ also seemed to suggest in its argument before the district court that it did not view discretionary attempts by state or local law enforcement to verify the immigration status of individuals as raising the same preemption concerns as Arizona's "mandatory" requirements relating to status verification.[107]

It is also unclear to what extent the reviewing courts' respective analysis of the burdens imposed by Section 2(B) upon the federal government and lawfully present aliens is dependent upon the government's current immigration enforcement priorities and allocation of resources, and whether any future changes in federal enforcement priorities would alter such analysis.[108]

Authorization of Private Suits in Response to State or Local Limitations on Enforcement of Immigration Law

Issues might also be raised with respect to the provision of S.B. 1070 authorizing any legal resident of Arizona to file suit to challenge any policy of a state or local government entity that "limits or restricts the enforcement of federal immigration laws to less than the full extent permitted by federal law."[109] This authority might be seen as helping to ensure that state and local agencies comply with all applicable federal immigration statutes, and that these entities do not impede the federal government's ability to carry out its immigration enforcement activities (e.g., by restricting their employees from sharing immigration information with federal authorities).[110] Alternatively, it might plausibly be interpreted more expansively to allow suits challenging whether Arizona officials are actively enforcing federal immigration law to the fullest extent possible. If the latter interpretation is adopted, the extent to which states or localities may permissibly enforce federal immigration law could become an issue in future litigation.

The district court that considered the DOJ's challenge to S.B. 1070 did not view the federal government as having directly challenged this provision,[111] and it did not enjoin it from taking effect.[112] It did, however, note that this provision could encourage Arizona law enforcement to more rigorously enforce other provisions of S.B. 1070 that raised preemption issues.[113]

Warrantless Arrests of Persons Who Have Committed a Criminal Offense Making Them Deportable

The district court also preliminarily enjoined the enforcement of Section 6 of S.B. 1070, pending a final ruling on the merits of the DOJ's claims. This holding was affirmed by the reviewing Ninth Circuit panel in a 2-1 decision. As discussed earlier, Section 6 authorizes Arizona law enforcement to make warrantless arrests of aliens when there is probable cause to believe that they have committed "public offenses" which make them removable under the INA. Arizona law defines "public offense" as conduct punishable under a state's law by fine or imprisonment, provided, in cases where the offense occurs outside Arizona, that the activity would have been punishable under Arizona law if it had occurred in the state.[114] The implications of this provision may depend on how broadly it is interpreted and applied. On one hand, if Section 6 is interpreted in a limited fashion, so as to permit the arrest of persons to face criminal proceedings in Arizona or another state having criminal jurisdiction, it would not facially appear to raise significant preemption issues.[115] On the other hand, more serious preemption issues might be raised if Section 6 is interpreted to permit the arrest of aliens who have already been convicted of a criminal offense and completed their sentences, so that such persons may be transferred to federal custody for removal. The latter interpretation was adopted by both the reviewing district court and Ninth Circuit panel.[116]

When assessing the district court's determination that Section 6 was likely preempted, the circuit panel identified the central legal question as being "whether federal law likely preempts Arizona from allowing its officers to effect warrantless arrests based on probable cause of removability."[117] A majority of the reviewing panel found that Section 6 was likely preempted, because it "interferes with the carefully calibrated scheme of immigration enforcement that Congress has adopted...."[118] The majority noted that Congress had expressly authorized state and local police to make arrests for civil immigration violations in more limited circumstances than permitted under the Arizona statute. Specifically, pursuant to § 439 of the Antiterrorism and Effective Death Penalty Act of 1996 (AEDPA, P.L. 104-132),[119] Congress had expressly authorized state and local police to arrest unlawfully present aliens who had previously been convicted of a felony so that they could be transferred to the custody of federal immigration authorities, provided that certain other requirements were fulfilled. The panel majority viewed Section 6 to be inconsistent with congressional intent because it permits state and local police to arrest aliens for civil deportation violations in a broader set of circumstances than had been authorized under AEDPA § 439 (e.g., in situations where an alien had committed a misdemeanor offense that made him removable). The majority also found it significant that Section 6 gives state and local officers broader authority to make warrantless arrests than federal law provides to federal immigration officers.[120]

In finding that the government is likely to prevail in its challenge to Section 6, the panel majority plainly held that states do not possess the inherent authority to enforce the civil removability provisions of the INA without express federal authorization[121] – a conclusion which had been suggested, but not definitively decided, in a prior ruling by the Ninth Circuit in the case of *Gonzales v. City of Peoria* (in that same opinion, the court held that state and local officers were *not* preempted from arresting persons for criminal violations of federal immigration law).[122] In support of this holding, the circuit panel noted that a similar decision had been reached by the U.S. Court of Appeals for the Sixth Circuit.[123] The majority also discussed and rejected the reasoning of a series of decisions by the U.S. Court of Appeals for the Tenth Circuit, which have been understood to support the position that state and local authorities possess the inherent authority to enforce both the civil and criminal provisions of the INA.[124]

The panel majority's conclusion that state and local officers generally cannot arrest persons for civil immigration violations was partially based upon its characterization of various provisions of federal immigration law. In particular, the majority interpreted AEDPA § 439 as reflecting Congress's view that state and local officers generally lack authority to enforce the civil provisions of the INA, absent authorization from the federal government. The majority also found that INA § 287(g)(10) "neither grants, nor assumes the preexistence of, inherent state authority to enforce civil immigration laws in the absence of federal supervision."[125] If INA § 287(g)(10) were understood to confer or recognize such authority, the majority claimed, it would render AEDPA § 439 and the remainder of INA § 287(g) "superfluous, and we do not believe that Congress spends its time passing unnecessary laws."[126]

The majority concluded that it was:

> not persuaded that Arizona has the inherent authority to enforce the civil provisions of federal immigration law. Therefore, Arizona must be federally-authorized to conduct such enforcement. Congress has created a comprehensive and carefully calibrated scheme—and has authorized the Executive to promulgate extensive regulations—for adjudicating and enforcing civil removability. S.B. 1070 Section 6 exceeds the scope of federal authorization for Arizona's state and local officers to enforce the civil provisions of federal immigration law. Section 6 interferes with the federal government's prerogative to make removability determinations and set priorities with regard to the enforcement of civil immigration laws. Accordingly, Section 6 stands as an obstacle to the full purposes and objectives of Congress.[127]

Additionally, the panel majority found that Section 6 posed a similarly detrimental effect upon foreign affairs as Section 2(B), and could "lead to 50 different state immigration schemes piling on top of the federal scheme."[128]

In his dissent from the majority's ruling that Section 6 was likely preempted, Judge Bea criticized the panel for holding that states and localities are generally preempted from enforcing the civil provisions of the INA. He characterized most jurisprudence as supporting the proposition that state and local officers are generally not preempted from making arrests for violations of federal law, including arrests for immigration violations.[129] The dissent also construed INA § 287(g)(10) as reflecting congressional recognition that state police may assist in the enforcement of both the civil and criminal provisions of the INA , even in the absence of a 287(g) agreement. The dissent further claimed that AEDPA § 439 was not intended to define the parameters of state authority to arrest aliens for civil immigration violations.[130]

Although the Ninth Circuit panel upheld the lower court's preliminary injunction against Section 6, its preemption analysis was much different. Whereas the appellate court's analysis focused directly on the issue of whether state and local officers were preempted from enforcing the civil provisions of the INA in the absence of express federal authorization, the lower court's analysis focused primarily on the perceived burdens that Section 6 would impose upon lawfully present aliens who might be mistakenly arrested by Arizona law enforcement, given the "substantial complexity [involved] in determining whether a particular public offense makes an alien removable from the United States." [131] The district court viewed Section 6 as requiring state and local officers to make two determinations when arresting persons for offenses in other states: (1) whether the conduct would have been a crime if committed in Arizona,[132] and (2) whether the conduct constituted a deportable offense under federal immigration law. The court characterized the latter determination, in particular, as a "task of considerable complexity that falls under the exclusive authority of the federal government."[133] It further noted that, although some provisions of S.B. 1070 require that DHS be contacted in order to verify immigration status, Section 6 contains no such mandate.[134] Moreover, the court did not believe that DHS officers would necessarily be able to provide Arizona authorities with information as to whether a particular offense made an alien deportable.[135] Rather, the court characterized administrative immigration judges and the federal appellate courts as having the ultimate responsibility for determining whether an alien has committed a deportable offense.[136]

Criminalization of Immigration-Related Conduct

As a general matter, preemption issues may potentially be raised whenever states criminalize immigration-related conduct. State measures addressing issues that have traditionally been subject to state regulation and upon which federal law remains silent seem least susceptible to legal challenge. More serious preemption concerns may be raised when states criminalize matters already regulated by federal immigration law. Of this latter category, the most serious preemption arguments likely exist where state law attempts to reach past traditional police powers to regulate matters closely related to the entry and removal of aliens from the United States, and the conditions of their lawful presence within the country. State laws addressing such matters appear most susceptible to preemption challenges, as federal law is arguably intended to wholly occupy this field.

Provisions of S.B. 1070 criminalizing immigration-related conduct have been subject to legal challenge. Some, but not all, of S.B. 1070's criminal provisions have been enjoined by the district court from taking effect, pending a final ruling on the merits of the federal government's challenge. The Ninth Circuit unanimously affirmed the district court's injunction of the Arizona provisions relating to alien registration and the solicitation or performance of work by unauthorized aliens.

Criminalizing the Hiring of Persons Picked up along Roadways

Section 5 of S.B. 1070 makes it a misdemeanor offense under Arizona law for an occupant of a motor vehicle stopped on the roadway to attempt to hire or hire and pick up passengers for work at a different location, if the motor vehicle blocks or impedes the normal movement of traffic. The law also imposes a misdemeanor penalty upon those persons who enter a stopped motor vehicle to be hired and transported to work at a different location, if the vehicle blocks or impedes the normal traffic flow. Although these provisions cover conduct that often facilitates the employment of unauthorized aliens, the provisions criminalize conduct without regard to the participants' citizenship or immigration status.[137] This provision was not challenged in the DOJ's lawsuit against Arizona, and it has not been enjoined from taking effect. Challenges have been brought against this provision by a few private parties,[138] but the reviewing court has yet to rule on the merits of their claims.[139]

It is well established that not every state law which tangentially touches upon immigration matters is preempted.[140] Further, courts have stated that when a state acts pursuant to its historic police powers, there is a presumption against preemption of the state law, unless federal law evidences a "clear and manifest purpose" to supersede state action.[141] The regulation of the hiring of persons along busy roadways appears well within a state's traditional powers, and federal law is silent on this matter. Accordingly, it does not appear that this provision facially poses a serious preemption issue, though it is possible that preemption issues could be raised in its application (e.g., if the law was only applied when law enforcement suspected that the prospective employee was an unauthorized alien).

Occasionally, local laws barring solicitation of employment along public streets have been stricken by the courts as violating the First Amendment.142 The underlying legal theory is that streets are important public forums where the government can impose only narrowly tailored restrictions on speech to serve significant government interests. The requirement in S.B. 1070 that premises a violation on the blocking or impeding of normal traffic may make the provision less vulnerable to First Amendment attack, but the state might nevertheless eventually bear the burden of showing that there are alternative public places for soliciting employment and that other activity that can impede traffic (e.g., solicitation of charitable contributions) is similarly regulated. This argument was not raised by the federal government in its challenge to S.B. 1070, but the district court indicated its view in dicta that a recent Ninth Circuit decision in the case of Comite de Jornaleros v. City of Redondo Beach "forecloses a challenge to [this provision of S.B. 1070] on First Amendment grounds."143 Following the district court's decision, however, the Ninth Circuit agreed to an en banc rehearing of Redondo Beach.144 The en banc court's ruling will likely determine the viability of any First Amendment challenge to S.B. 1070's restriction on roadside hiring.

Criminalizing Alien Smuggling Activities

Under INA § 274, the federal government has criminalized various activities relating to the transportation of unauthorized aliens into or within the United States, as well as the harboring of such aliens in the country, or encouraging or inducing such aliens to come to or reside in the United States.[145] For criminal liability to attach, the offender must generally act with knowledge or in reckless disregard of the alien's unlawful status. Provisions of S.B. 1070 imposing criminal penalties upon alien smuggling activities and amending a previously-enacted Arizona alien smuggling statute have been challenged on the ground that they are preempted by INA § 274, but these challenges have thus far proven unsuccessful.

Even prior to the enactment of S.B. 1070, Arizona law imposed criminal penalties for certain activities that are likely also subject to criminal penalty under INA § 274. Arizona's "human smuggling" statute, which was enacted in 2005, generally makes it a felony under state law for any person, for profit or commercial purpose, to transport or procure transportation for an unauthorized alien, when the offender knows or has reason to know the person's unauthorized status.[146] Section 4 of S.B. 1070 makes a minor amendment to this statute that does not affect its substantive scope. More significantly, Section 5 adds a separate criminal offense under state law for any person, "who is in violation of a criminal offense," to transport or harbor unauthorized aliens, or encourage or induce such aliens to come to or reside in the state, when such activities are done in knowing or reckless disregard of the alien's unauthorized status.[147] The purpose of the phrase "who is in violation of a criminal offense" is unclear. The offenses described in Section 5 of S.B. 1070 would almost always constitute criminal offenses under INA § 274, meaning that any offense under Section 5 would presumably be committed by a person "who [was also] in violation of a criminal offense" under the federal alien smuggling statute. On the other hand, the phrase "who is in violation of a criminal offense" could be interpreted in a more limited manner to only permit persons to be prosecuted under the new Arizona law for smuggling-related activities when they were also engaged in criminal conduct not described under the state statute.

In sum, Arizona has established criminal penalties under state law, pursuant to the 2005 "human smuggling" statute and the new offense created under Section 5 of S.B. 1070, for conduct similar to that which is prohibited under the federal alien smuggling statute.[148] Because Arizona's alien smuggling laws operate in an area where the federal government exercises authority via INA § 274 and other immigration statutes, arguments have been raised that these laws are preempted. Federal law does not expressly preempt state or local measures criminalizing activities related to alien smuggling (though a provision of the federal alien smuggling statute impliedly authorizes states and localities to make arrests for violations of the statute[149]). As a result, preemption challenges against the smuggling provisions of S.B. 1070 (or Arizona's preexisting "human smuggling" statute) have either been based upon arguments that federal alien smuggling restrictions occupy the regulatory field and preclude enforcement of similar state laws, or upon arguments that the Arizona smuggling statute directly conflicts with or otherwise frustrates the purposes of federal immigration law and policy, including by purportedly attempting to regulate the unlawful entry of aliens into the country.[150]

The historic police power of states generally permits them to define and punish criminal activities occurring within their territory.[151] Thus far, Arizona's criminalization of smuggling activities occurring within its jurisdiction—both under S.B. 1070 and under the "human smuggling" statute passed in 2005—has been held by reviewing courts to fall within the scope of its traditional police powers,[152] and a presumption may exist that Congress's imposition of criminal penalties upon alien smuggling was not intended to preclude Arizona or other states from enacting and imposing measures consistent with federal law.[153] On the other hand, courts have recognized that a presumption against preemption *does not* exist in cases where a state "regulates in an area where there has been a history of significant federal presence."[154] Given that federal regulation of alien smuggling has been both long-standing and pervasive in scope,[155] it could be argued that there is no presumption against preemption of Arizona's alien smuggling laws.[156]

Even assuming that Arizona's laws concerning alien smuggling are not entitled to a presumption against preemption given the degree of federal activity in this area, the measures might nonetheless be deemed valid if they are consistent with pertinent federal laws and objectives.[157] Thus far, state and federal courts that have considered challenges to S.B. 1070 and Arizona's 2005 human smuggling statute have rejected field preemption arguments against the statute's enforcement.[158]

Although the federal government requested that S.B. 1070's anti-smuggling provisions be enjoined from taking effect, the district court denied this request. In doing so, it rejected the federal government's arguments that the new smuggling offense established by S.B. 1070 was barred by the Dormant Commerce Clause,[159] and that it was an impermissible attempt by Arizona to regulate immigration. With respect to the latter argument, the reviewing court wrote that the new alien smuggling offense established by S.B. 1070

> does not attempt to regulate who should or should not be admitted into the United States, and it does not regulate the conditions under which legal entrants may remain in the United States. Therefore, the Court concludes that the United States is not likely to succeed on its claim that [the new alien smuggling offense established by S.B. 1070] is an impermissible regulation of immigration.[160]

The federal government did not appeal the district court's decision.

While Arizona's 2005 "human smuggling" statute has not been directly challenged by the federal government in litigation concerning S.B. 1070, the statute has been considered by state and federal courts. In 2009, the U.S. District Court for Arizona upheld the statute against a field preemption challenge in the case of *We Are America/Somos America, Coalition of Arizona v. Maricopa County Board of Supervisors*. The plaintiffs in the case, which included six Mexican nationals who had been charged with conspiracy to violate the Arizona statute, argued that the statute was unenforceable on field preemption grounds, as it impermissibly duplicated federal immigration law in object and effect.[161] In declining to exercise jurisdiction to consider claims raised by the Mexican nationals pending completion of the state criminal proceedings against them, the district court found that the plaintiffs could not demonstrate that the Arizona statute was unenforceable on field preemption grounds. The district court noted that the plaintiffs did not argue that the Arizona statute was in disharmony with the INA, but only that it was duplicative. The court rejected the plaintiffs' field preemption challenge, finding that plaintiffs had failed to demonstrate, "either based upon the language or the legislative history of the INA, that 'Congress intended to preclude harmonious state regulation touching on the smuggling of illegal aliens.'"[162] The district court's ruling was subsequently appealed to the Ninth Circuit, where the appellate court affirmed the lower court's ruling in part, including its determination not to exercise jurisdiction to review the Mexican nationals' claims pending completion of state proceedings. With respect to the plaintiffs' field preemption claim, the appellate court simply stated that "Arizona has an important interest in enforcing its criminal statutes, and it's not 'readily apparent' that federal law preempts" either the Arizona statute or its enforcement of the law.[163] The circuit court also stated that the nationals had an adequate opportunity to litigate their constitutional claims in the state court proceedings.[164]

It is possible that Arizona's criminalization of alien smuggling might nonetheless be subject to preemption challenges on other grounds which have not been directly opined upon by federal courts which have reviewed either S.B. 1070 or the earlier smuggling statute. For example, even state laws that are duplicative of federal law may be subject to challenge on preemption grounds if they "stand[ ] as an obstacle to the accomplishment and execution of the full purposes and objectives of Congress."[165] It could be argued, for example, that when Congress established criminal penalties for alien smuggling, it did so under the expectation that offenders would not also be subject to additional criminal penalties under state law. Potential tension may arise between federal and state policies if the federal government declined to prosecute alien smuggling conduct that was subsequently prosecuted by Arizona. Such tension might be particularly significant when the federal government declines to prosecute a non-citizen for an alien smuggling offense, with the intention of permitting the alien's continued presence in the United States, only for the alien to be convicted of the offense in state court. Not only might a state conviction make the alien deportable, but it might also disqualify him from being eligible for many legal forms of relief from deportation (e.g., asylum or temporary protected status).[166] These considerations might merit particular consideration if Arizona opts to prosecute unlawfully present aliens under the statute on the grounds that they conspired with others to smuggle *themselves* into the United States (an interpretation that has been applied with respect to the 2005 Arizona smuggling statute).[167]

Although this argument already has been raised in at least one of the legal challenges to Arizona's "human smuggling" statute,[168] thus far the reviewing courts have concluded that the punishment of alien smuggling activities is consistent with federal objectives to deter that activity.[169] Nonetheless, it is uncertain whether other courts would reach similar conclusions,[170] as the degree to which states may impose additional criminal sanctions upon activities already regulated by the INA remains an unsettled issue.

Criminalizing Violations of Federal Alien Registration Requirements

Section 3 of S.B. 1070 establishes criminal penalties under Arizona law for violations of federal requirements concerning alien registration. The INA generally prohibits a visa from being issued to any alien seeking admission to the United States until he has registered with immigration authorities.[171] Moreover, any unregistered alien present in the United States who is over the age of 14 must apply for alien registration with immigration authorities within 30 days of entry (aliens under 14 must apply for registration within 30 days of reaching their fourteenth birthday).[172] Registration requirements are enforced in part by INA § 266(a), which makes it a misdemeanor offense, subject to imprisonment for up to six months and/or a fine, for an alien to willfully fail or refuse to file a registration form required under federal immigration law.[173] Moreover, INA § 264(e) requires all registered aliens who are at least 18 years of age to carry with them and have in their personal possession "any certificate of alien registration or alien registration receipt card issued" to them.[174] Failure to comply with this requirement constitutes a misdemeanor, and is subject to imprisonment for not more than 30 days and/or a fine.[175] It should be noted that although an alien without legal authorization to be in the country is deportable under the INA, unlawful presence is not a crime under either federal or Arizona law.[176] Indeed, an alien who is unlawfully present in the United States has not necessarily engaged in conduct that would make him criminally liable under alien registration laws.[177]

Pursuant to S.B. 1070, a person is subject to criminal penalty under Arizona state law if he is determined to be guilty of a violation of INA § 264(e) (failure to carry registration documents) or INA § 266(a) (willful failure to complete a registration document). In enforcing the statute, an alien's immigration status may be determined through verification with immigration authorities. Initially, S.B. 1070 made a first-time offense a misdemeanor subject to fine and imprisonment for up to six months, and subsequent offenses were felonies. If aggravating factors existed, offenses would have been subject to more significant felony penalties.[178] H.B. 2162 amended this provision to make all offenses misdemeanors, with available penalties being lesser than or equal to those imposed directly under federal law.[179]

Arizona's criminalization of violations of the federal alien registration requirements was challenged on preemption grounds by the DOJ, and the district court preliminarily enjoined its enforcement after finding that the federal government is likely to prevail on the merits of its argument. The Ninth Circuit panel unanimously affirmed this decision because those sections of the

INA establishing federal registration requirements constitute a "comprehensive scheme" and "include no mention of state participation."[180] It found this omission significant given that other provisions of the INA explicitly provide for state and local involvement.[181] The court also expressly rejected Arizona's assertion that those provisions of federal law authorizing states to limit certain immigrants' eligibility for benefits and impose certain sanctions on employers of unauthorized immigrants reflect Congress's "invitation" to states to "reinforce federal alien classifications."[182] According to the court, the authorities that Arizona relied upon in making this claim are separate from the registration provisions, and "[a]n authority from one section does not—without more—carry over to other sections."[183]

Like the district court, the Ninth Circuit relied upon the Supreme Court's ruling in *Hines v. Davidowitz* in finding that Arizona's alien registration provisions are likely preempted. In *Hines*, the Court found that a Pennsylvania statute requiring aliens to register with the state was preempted by the Federal Alien Registration Act of 1940.[184] Although federal law did not expressly preempt state laws concerning alien registration, the *Hines* Court held that the federal law was intended to preempt states from imposing their own alien registration requirements. Examining the legislative history of the federal law, the Supreme Court concluded that Congress had intended to establish "a single integrated and all-embracing system" for the registration of aliens. This system precluded the enforcement of state laws that "inconsistently with the purpose of Congress, conflict or interfere with, curtail or complement, the federal law, or enforce additional or auxiliary regulations" related to alien registry.[185] According to the Ninth Circuit panel, Arizona's imposition of penalties for federal alien registration violations is similarly preempted because the INA constitutes a "complete scheme of regulation" that cannot be supplemented by state or local enactments.[186] Additionally, the panel opinion characterized S.B. 1070's alien registration requirements as likely being preempted because they had the "potential to lead to 50 different state immigration schemes piling on top of the federal one," and at least two of the three panel members also believed the measure to likely be preempted on account of the "detrimental effect" it could have on foreign affairs.[187]

It should be noted that even if states are preempted from establishing "additional or auxiliary regulations" related to alien registry, including through the enactment of state laws punishing alien registration violations, this does not necessarily mean that they are preempted from enforcing federal alien registration requirements by arresting criminal offenders with the expectation of transferring them to federal law enforcement custody. As previously discussed, it seems well recognized (including in the Ninth Circuit) that states have implied authority to make arrests for many criminal violations of the INA, so long as those constitutional requirements concerning the ability to stop, detain, or arrest persons are satisfied and such arrests are permissible under state law.[188] Arguably, this authority extends to making arrests for criminal violations of federal alien registration requirements.[189] This issue has not been definitively resolved, however, and it is possible that there may be limitations upon a state's ability to arrest persons for suspected criminal violations of federal alien registration requirements.[190] In upholding the lower court's preliminary injunction of Arizona's alien registration requirement, the circuit panel claimed that "[n]othing in the text of the INA's registration provisions indicates that Congress intended for states to participate in the enforcement or punishment of federal immigration registration rules"[191] – a statement that arguably raises some uncertainty as to whether state and local police are preempted from making arrests for federal alien registration violations.[192]

Criminalizing the Solicitation or Performance of Work by Unauthorized Aliens

Prior to the enactment of the Immigration Reform and Control Act of 1986 (IRCA, P.L. 99-603), federal immigration law did not comprehensively address the employment of unlawfully present aliens, and regulation of such matters was thought to primarily be an issue governed by state law. States were understood to have "broad authority" to regulate employment relationships within their territory to protect workers and state fiscal interests.[193] In *De Canas v. Bica*, decided a decade prior to the passage of IRCA, the Supreme Court recognized that states were largely free to imple-ment measures restricting the employment of unauthorized aliens within their territory, at least so long as such restrictions were focused "directly upon ... essentially local problems and [were] tailored to combat effectively the perceived evils."[194] The Court recognized that a state might have legitimate reasons for restricting the employment of unauthorized aliens, particularly in times of high unemployment, in order to protect the fiscal and economic interests of both the state and its lawfully resident labor force.[195]

With the enactment of IRCA, Congress amended the INA to establish a scheme to combat the employment of unauthorized aliens, and this system is now "central to the policy of immigration law."[196] The INA now generally prohibits the hiring, referring, recruiting for a fee, or continued employment of aliens lacking authorization to work in the United States.[197] Violators may be subject to cease and desist orders, civil monetary penalties, and (in the case of serial offenders) criminal fines and/or imprisonment. In establishing this system, Congress also expressly preempted any state or local measure "imposing civil or criminal sanctions (other than through licensing and similar laws) upon those who employ, or recruit or refer for a fee for employment, unauthorized aliens."[198]

In recent years, some states and localities concerned with the employment of unauthorized aliens within their jurisdictions have attempted to supplement federal law with enforcement measures of their own, including by denying or revoking business licenses of entities who have hired unauthorized aliens. Many of these measures have been subject to legal challenge, with courts reaching conflicting rulings as to their permissibility.[199] In 2007, Arizona enacted the Legal Arizona Workers Act, which authorized state courts to suspend or revoke the business licenses of entities found by state officials to have knowingly or intentionally hired aliens who were not authorized under federal law to work in the United States.[200] Arizona also required employers within the state to confirm the employment eligibility of workers via the E-Verify program, a generally voluntary program operated by the Department of Homeland Security and the Social Security Administration that enables employers to verify an employee's work eligibility. In May 2011, the Supreme Court held in the case of *Chamber of Commerce v. Whiting* that the Arizona Workers Act was not preempted by the INA and other federal measures (the United States had filed an amicus brief in the case, arguing that the Arizona measure was preempted) and did not otherwise conflict with federal law.[201]

Section 5 of S.B. 1070 establishes new measures to deter the employment of unauthorized aliens within Arizona. Whereas most recent state activity in this area, including the Arizona Workers Act upheld by the Supreme Court in *Whiting*, have targeted employers of unlawfully present aliens, S.B. 1070 directly sanctions unauthorized alien employees. Specifically, S.B. 1070 makes it a misdemeanor offense for an unlawfully present alien, lacking authorization to work in the United States, "to knowingly apply for work, solicit work in a public place or perform work as an employee or independent contractor in this state."[202] The approach taken by S.B. 1070 to deter the employment of unauthorized aliens is markedly different from that established under IRCA, potentially raising preemption concerns.

On its face, Arizona's imposition of criminal penalties upon unlawfully present aliens who seek employment in the state does not appear to be expressly preempted by the INA. The regime established by the INA to deter the employment of unauthorized aliens primarily imposes sanctions upon *employers*, rather than alien employees (though aliens may be subject to penalty if they use fraudulent documents to circumvent work eligibility requirements[203]). While the INA, as amended by IRCA, contains a provision expressly preempting states and localities from imposing criminal or civil penalties upon *employers* of unauthorized aliens, this provision does not expressly preempt state sanctions against unauthorized alien *employees*.

An examination of the legislative history behind the enactment of IRCA suggests its focus upon employers was intentional. Although there appears to have been some consideration given to the possibility of imposing criminal sanctions upon unauthorized aliens who sought employment in the United States, Congress did not pursue this option. Describing the legislative history and purposes of IRCA in 1990, the Ninth Circuit stated that in establishing a federal regime to deter the employment of unauthorized aliens, "Congress quite clearly was willing to deter illegal immigration by making jobs less available to illegal aliens but not by incarcerating or fining aliens who succeeded in obtaining work."[204] Although the INA was amended in 1990 to establish civil penalties for immigration-related document fraud, including the presentation of fraudulent documents to demonstrate work eligibility,[205] and other criminal statutes may apply to those aliens who seek employment through the use of fraudulent documents or false statements,[206] the federal regime does not impose any penalties against aliens solely on account of working or seeking employment in the United States.

In its suit challenging S.B. 1070, the DOJ claimed that the provision of the Arizona statute imposing criminal penalties upon unlawfully present aliens who work or seek employment in the state had been impliedly preempted. The reviewing district court issued a preliminary injunction barring the provision's enforcement pending a final ruling in the case, having concluded that the government was likely to succeed on the merits of its claim.[207] The Ninth Circuit panel unanimously affirmed, finding that these provisions "conflict[] with what we have [previously' found was Congress' IRCA intent."[208] The court found that the relevant provisions of IRCA constitute a "complex scheme" to discourage the employment of unauthorized immigrants, "primarily by penalizing employers who negligently and knowingly hire them."[209] It also found that penalizing unauthorized workers conflicts with Congress's intent not to criminalize work and provision of affirmative protections for unauthorized workers.[210] While noting that congressional "inaction" (i.e., failure to impose penalties upon unauthorized workers) is not necessarily indicative of preemption, the court found that "Congress' inaction in not criminalizing work, joined with its action of making it illegal to hire unauthorized workers, justifies a preemptive inference that Congress intended to prohibit states from criminalizing work."[211] The court also rejected Arizona's argument that its imposition of penalties against aliens seeking unlawful employment furthers Congress's policy of "prohibiting illegal aliens from seeking employment in the United States."[212] Noting that the Supreme Court has recognized that "conflict[s] in technique can be fully as disruptive to the system Congress erected as conflict in overt policy,"[213] the Ninth Circuit found that the provisions of S.B. 1070 criminalizing the seeking of employment by unauthorized aliens constitute a "substantial departure" from the approach Congress has taken to this problem:

> By criminalizing work, S.B. 1070 Section 5(C) constitutes a substantial departure from the approach Congress has chosen to battle this particular problem. Therefore, Arizona's assertion that this provision "furthers [a] strong federal policy" does not advance its argument against preemption. Sharing a goal with the United States does not permit Arizona to "pull[] levers of influence that the federal Act does not reach." By pulling the lever of criminalizing work—which Congress specifically chose not to pull in the INA—Section 5(C) "stands as an obstacle to the accomplishment and execution of the full purposes and objectives of Congress."[214]

The majority of the circuit panel also held that, like the other provisions of S.B. 1070 it considered, Arizona's criminalization of work by unlawfully present aliens was likely preempted because of its "detrimental effect on foreign affairs" and the possibility that it could "lead to 50 different state immigration schemes piling on top of the federal scheme."[215]

IV. Racial Profiling Issues

In the 1968 case of *Terry v. Ohio*, the Supreme Court held that the Fourth Amendment permits a law enforcement officer to stop and briefly detain a person when the officer reasonably suspects that the person has committed a crime.[216] Reasonable suspicion may not be based on a mere hunch, but instead upon "specific reasonable inferences which [the officer] is entitled to draw from the facts in light of his experience."[217] Section 2 of S.B. 1070, as amended by H.B. 2162, generally requires that in the context of a lawful stop, detention or arrest by state and local law enforcement pursuant to the enforcement of a state or local law, law enforcement must determine the person's immigration status, if practicable, when "reasonable suspicion exists that the person is an alien ... who is unlawfully present in the United States."[218] Some have expressed concern that this provision may lead to the harassment of certain racial and ethnic groups by Arizona law enforcement. The Arizona statute does not expressly prohibit law enforcement from relying, at least in part, upon an individual's racial or ethnic background when assessing whether to pursue an inquiry into the person's immigration status; instead, as amended by H.B. 2162, it provides that law enforcement may not consider the race, color, or national origin of an individual when determining whether there is reasonable suspicion to believe the person is an unlawfully present alien, "except to the extent permitted by the United States or Arizona Constitution."[219]

Although the issue was not raised in the DOJ's lawsuit challenging S.B. 1070, some have expressed concern that enforcement of S.B. 1070 would lead to constitutionally impermissible "racial profiling."[220] Partially to address such concerns, Arizona Governor Jan Brewer issued an executive order on the same day she signed the bill into law, which requires state law enforcement officers to undergo training concerning the implementation of S.B. 1070. Among other things, such training is intended to "provide clear guidance to law enforcement officials regarding what constitutes reasonable suspicion, and shall make clear that an individual's race, color or national origin alone cannot be grounds for reasonable suspicion to believe any law has been violated."[221]

Whether or not it is constitutionally permissible for race, ethnicity, or national origin to be considered as a factor by Arizona authorities when determining whether to inquire into a person's immigration status may depend upon a number of considerations. On several occasions, courts have decided cases involving law enforcement authorities stopping persons for suspected immigration violations on account of those persons' suspected Mexican ancestry. Supreme Court jurisprudence holds that race or ethnicity cannot be the sole factor giving rise to a law enforcement stop for suspected immigration violations, but that at least in cases near the U.S.- Mexican border, stops may be partially based on race.[222] Nevertheless, the Court has suggested that a different conclusion might be reached if stops based partially on Mexican ancestry occur in places farther removed from the U.S.-Mexican border.[223]

In 2000, the Ninth Circuit, sitting *en banc*, ruled that the Border Patrol could not take into account Hispanic origin when making stops in Southern California, concluding that in areas "in which the majority—or even a substantial part—of the population is Hispanic," as was the case in Southern

California, the probability that any given Hispanic person "is an alien, let alone an illegal alien, is not high enough to make Hispanic appearance a relevant factor in the reasonable suspicion calculus."[224] This ruling would seem to preclude Arizona law enforcement from using Hispanic origin as a factor in the "reasonable suspicion" test in areas with similar demographics as Southern California.

In sum, court jurisprudence indicates that Arizona law enforcement may not stop persons for suspected immigration-related violations solely on account of such persons' race or ethnicity, but that at least in certain circumstances, suspicion may partially be based on such considerations. Additional considerations, including population demographics, may also affect the weight to which suspicions based on race or ethnicity may be permissibly given.

CONCLUSION

In recent decades, Congress has increasingly focused federal immigration policy on the daily incidents of alien residency. Concomitantly, Congress has enlarged the opportunities for states to become involved in enforcing immigration law. S.B. 1070 is in the vanguard of testing the legal limits of these increased opportunities, though H.B. 2162 modified some of its more legally ambitious efforts. Although a federal district court has issued a preliminary injunction barring implementation of some provisions of S.B. 1070, the ultimate legal fate of these provisions (as well as those which were not enjoined by the district court) remains to be decided. At least some other states and localities that see themselves as heavily impacted by unauthorized immigration likely will join Arizona on any new ground that S.B. 1070 establishes. And this potential for diverse and possibly fragmented immigration enforcement doubtless will be among the many issues considered by the courts as legal challenges to S.B. 1070 proceed.

End Notes

[1] The text of S.B. 1070, as amended by H.B. 2162, can be viewed at http://www.azleg.gov/alispdfs/council/SB1070-HB2162.PDF.

[2] Under the Arizona Constitution, acts approved by the legislature do not become operative until 90 days after the close of the legislative session during which they were passed. ARIZ. CONST. art. 4, § 1(3).

[3] United States v. Arizona, No. CV-10-1413, Complaint (D. Ariz. filed July 6, 2010), available at http://www.justice.gov/opa/documents/az-complaint.pdf [hereinafter "Arizona Complaint"]; Plaintiff's Motion for a Preliminary Injunction and Memorandum of Law in Support Thereof (D. Ariz. filed July 6, 2010) [hereinafter "Plaintiff's PI Motion"], available at http://www.justice.gov/usao/az/press_releases/2010/Arizona%20PI%20Brief%20(2).pdf. Besides the federal government, several other entities also brought suit challenging S.B. 1070. See, e.g., Friendly House v. Whiting, No. CV 10-1061, Complaint (D. Ariz., filed May 17, 2010), available at http://www.aclu.org/files/assets/az_sb1070_complaint_20100517.pdf.

[4] See United States v. Arizona, 703 F. Supp. 2d 980, 987 (D. Ariz. 2010) [hereinafter "Arizona I"].

[5] See Arizona I, 703 F. Supp. 2d at 987 (listing those sections of S.B. 1070 that the federal government did not seek to preliminarily enjoin); id. at 1000, 1003-1004 (finding the United States is not likely to succeed on its claim that sections of S.B. 1070 relating to alien smuggling are preempted by federal law).

[6] Arizona sought expedited review of its appeal by the Ninth Circuit, but this motion was denied. See Circuit Court Denies Motion to Expedite Appeal in AZ SB 1070 Case, AILA InfoNet, Aug. 2, 2010, available at http://www.aila.org/content/default.aspx?docid=32544.

[7] 2011 U.S. App. LEXIS 7413 (9th Cir. Apr. 11, 2011) [hereinafter "Arizona II"]. One judge dissented in part, and would have reversed the district court's finding that the federal government was likely to prevail on the merits of its challenge to those provisions of S.B. 1070 pertaining to immigration status determinations and warrantless arrests. See id. at *81-*147. A district court decision granting a preliminary injunction is reviewed for abuse of discretion and may be reversed if based on an erroneous legal standard or clearly erroneous findings of fact. Id. at *4. Conclusions on issues of law, including the construction of federal statutes and whether they preempt state or local measures, are reviewed de novo. Id.

[8] See Ginger Rough and Michael Kiefe, Gov. Jan Brewer wants Supreme Court to Overturn SB 1070 Ruling, ARIZ. REP., May 9, 2011.

[9] A motion for a preliminary injunction is granted when, inter alia, the plaintiff has shown likelihood of success on the merits and would suffer irreparable harm if the injunction is not granted. See, e.g., Winter v. NRDC, Inc., 555 U.S. 7, 129 S. Ct. 365, 374 (2008). However, a likelihood of irreparable harm can generally be easily shown where "an alleged constitutional infringement" is involved. Monterey Mech. Co. v. Wilson, 125 F.3d 702, 715 (9th Cir. 1997). See also Morales v. Trans World Airlines, Inc., 504 U.S. 374, 381 (1992) (stating that a federal court may enjoin "state officers who threaten and are about to commence proceedings, either of a civil or criminal nature, to enforce against parties affected an unconstitutional act, violating the Federal Constitution") (internal citations omitted); Chamber of Commerce of the United States v. Edmondson, 594 F.3d 742, 771 (10th Cir. 2010) (suggesting that irreparable injury is an inherent result of the enforcement of a state law that is preempted on its face). On April 5, 2011, the district court granted the Arizona State Legislature permission to intervene in DOJ's challenge to S.B. 1070. See AZ State Legislature Will Intervene in Defense of SB 1070 against Obama Justice Department, JD J., Apr. 6, 2011, available at http://www.jdjournal.com/2011/04/06/az-state-legislature-will-intervene-in-defense-of-sb-1070-against-obama-justicedepartment.

[10] Although Arizona will apparently seek Supreme Court review of the circuit panel's decision, it is possible that it may reconsider, or that it will seek *en banc* review if the Court declines to grant certiorari to review the panel's ruling.

[11] Jeffrey S. Passel & D'Vera Cohn, Pew Hispanic Center, *U.S. Unauthorized Immigration Flows Are Down Sharply Since Mid-Decade*, at iv (Sept. 1, 2010). Recent estimates suggest that both the migration and overall population of unauthorized aliens residing in the United States have decreased to mid-decade levels. *See id.* at 3.

[12] *See* CRS Report RL33874, *Unauthorized Aliens Residing in the United States: Estimates Since 1986*, by Ruth Ellen Wasem.

[13] *E.g.*, Texas v. United States, 106 F.3d 661 (5th Cir. 1997); Chiles v. United States, 874 F. Supp. 1334 (S.D. Fla. 1994).

[14] According to one commentator, a total of 1,562 bills on illegal immigration were introduced in the 50 state legislatures in 2007, 240 of which were enacted into law. Kris W. Kobach, *Reinforcing the Rule of Law: What States Can and Should Do to Reduce Illegal Immigration*, 22 GEO. IMM. L.R. 459, 459 (2008).

[15] Illegal Immigration Reform and Immigrant Responsibility Act (IIRIRA), P.L. 104-208, Division C; Personal Responsibility and Work Opportunity Reconciliation Act of 1996 (PRWORA), P.L. 104-193.

[16] The federal government has taken steps to eliminate sanctuary policies. Pursuant to PRWORA § 434 and IIRIRA § 642, states and localities may not limit their governmental entities or officers from maintaining records regarding a person's immigration status, or bar the exchange of such information with any federal, state, or local entity. For further discussion, see CRS Report RS22773, *"Sanctuary Cities": Legal Issues*, by Michael John Garcia.

[17] 8 U.S.C. § 1101, *et seq.* INA § 287(g) authorizes the Secretary of Homeland Security to enter a written agreement with a State, or any political subdivision of a State, pursuant to which an officer or employee of the State or subdivision, who is determined … to be qualified to perform a function of an immigration officer in relation to the investigation, apprehension, or detention of aliens in the United States (including the transportation of such aliens across State lines to detention centers), may carry out such function at the expense of the State or political subdivision and to the extent consistent with State and local law. 8 U.S.C. § 1357(g)(1). INA § 287(g)(10) further provides that this section does not require the existence of such an agreement in order for a state or local entity to "cooperate with … [federal immigration authorities] in the identification, apprehension, detention, or removal of aliens not lawfully present in the United States." 8 U.S.C. § 1357(g)(10).

[18] *See generally* CRS Report RL34345, *State and Local Restrictions on Employing, Renting Property to, or Providing Services for Unauthorized Aliens: Legal Issues and Recent Judicial Developments*, by Kate M. Manuel, Jody Feder and Alison M. Smith.

[19] Chamber of Commerce of the United States v. Whiting, 2011 U.S. LEXIS 4018 (U.S. May 26, 2011).

[20] It is unclear how courts will apply the *Whiting* decision when reviewing other state and local immigration measures. *Whiting* focused primarily upon questions of statutory interpretation pertaining to state restrictions upon employing unauthorized aliens, but the majority seemed skeptical of arguments that state enactments in this area disrupted the balance between deterring unauthorized immigration, protecting employers from burdensome requirements, and preventing discrimination established under federal law and policy. It remains to be seen whether courts will find the majority's treatment of balancing with respect to employer sanctions relevant to other immigration matters.

[21] S.B. 1070, § 1.

[22] *Id.*

[23] CRS Report R41207, *Unauthorized Aliens in the United States*, by Andorra Bruno, at 12 (quoting Mark Krikorian, *Attrition by Enforcement is the Best Course of Action*, SPARTANBURG (S.C.) HERALD-JOURNAL (Sept. 30, 2007)).

[24] *Id.* at 12-13.

[25] S.B. 1070, § 2, as amended by H.B. 2162, § 3. Before being modified by H.B. 2162, S.B. 1070 also called for law enforcement to inquire into the immigration status of any person with whom they had "lawful contact," upon reasonable suspicion that the person was an unlawfully present alien. This language appeared to encompass a far wider range of interactions than the modified provision. *See* S.B. 1070, § 2 (as originally enacted).

[26] S.B. 1070, § 2.

[27] *Id.*

[28] *Id.* There is some ambiguity as to how this provision is to be construed in light of the provision requiring immigration status determinations during lawful stops, detentions, or arrests. On one hand, these provisions could be read separately, meaning that *all* arrested persons would need to have their immigration status verified prior to release. On the other hand, reading these provisions in conjunction might support an interpretation of more limited scope. Under this more narrow interpretation, Arizona law enforcement officers are generally required to inquire into the immigration status of persons who are stopped, detained, or arrested whenever they have reasonable suspicion to believe such persons are unlawfully present aliens. However, persons who were stopped or detained may be released from custody pending verification of their immigration status with federal authorities, while those who have been arrested may not be released until their status has been verified. In reviewing S.B. 1070, both the district court and a majority of the appellate court panel adopted the former interpretation. See Arizona I, 703 F. Supp. 2d at 994; Arizona II, 2011 U.S. App. LEXIS 7413, at *11-*15.

[29] S.B. 1070, § 2, as amended by H.B. 2162, § 3. Prior to amendment by H.B. 2162, the act provided that race, color, or national origin could not be the "sole factor" for determining reasonable suspicion, except to the extent authorized by the U.S. or Arizona Constitution.

[30] Id.

[31] Id.

[32] Id.

[33] Id., § 2, as amended by H.B. 2162, § 3. Prior to being modified by H.B. 2162, S.B. 1070 had authorized residents to bring suits to challenge state and local practices, as well.

[34] 8 U.S.C. § 1304(e) mandates that every alien over the age of 18 carry any certificate of alien registration or alien registration receipt card issued to him, and makes failure to comply a misdemeanor offense. 8 U.S.C. § 1306(a) makes it a misdemeanor offense for an alien who is required to apply for registration and be fingerprinted to willfully fail or refuse to do so.

[35] S.B. 1070, § 3.

[36] Id., as amended by H.B. 2162, § 4.

[37] Id.

[38] Specifically, S.B. 1070 provides that in the enforcement of the earlier smuggling statute, ARIZ. REV. STAT. § 13-2319, a law enforcement officer is authorized to stop any person operating a motor vehicle if the officer has reasonable suspicion that the person violated a civil traffic law. S.B. 1070, § 4.

[39] S.B. 1070, § 5.

[40] *Id.*

[41] *Id.*

[42] *Id.*

[43] *Id.*

[44] *Id.*

[45] *Id.*, § 6. *See generally* CRS Report RL32480, *Immigration Consequences of Criminal Activity*, by Michael John Garcia (discussing criminal activity making an alien removable). There is also potential ambiguity as to the meaning of this provision. *See infra* footnote 115 and accompanying text.

[46] ARIZ. REV. STAT. § 13-105(26) (2009).

[47] U.S. CONST. art. VI, cl. 2.

[48] Hines v. Davidowitz, 312 U.S. 52, 66-67 (1941) (internal citations omitted).

[49] Congressional intent to "occupy the field" to the exclusion of state law can be inferred when "[1] the pervasiveness of the federal regulation precludes supplementation by the States, [2] where the federal interest in the field is sufficiently dominant, or [3] where the object sought to be obtained by the federal law and the character of obligations imposed by it ... reveal the same purpose." Schneidewind v. ANR Pipeline Co., 485 U.S. 293, 300 (1988) (internal quotations omitted).

[50] *See, e.g.,* Crosby v. Nat'l Foreign Trade Council, 530 U.S. 363, 373 (2000); English v. Gen. Elec. Co., 496 U.S. 72, 78-79 (1990); Silkwood v. Kerr-McGee Corp., 464 U.S. 238, 248-49 (1984); Pac. Gas & Elec. Co. v. State Energy Res. Conservation & Dev. Comm'n, 461 U.S. 190, 203-04 (1983).

[51] *See English*, 462 U.S. at 79 n.5 ("By referring to these three categories, we should not be taken to mean that they are rigidly distinct. Indeed, field pre-emption may be understood as a species of conflict pre-emption: A state law that falls within a pre-empted field conflicts with Congress' intent (either express or plainly implied) to exclude state regulation."); *Crosby*, 530 U.S. at 373 n.6.

[52] 8 U.S.C. § 1101, et seq.

[53] De Canas v. Bica, 424 U.S. 351, 355 (1976). Indeed, during the nineteenth century, when federal regulation of immigration was far more limited in scope, state legislation limiting the rights and privileges of certain categories of aliens was common. *See* Gerald L. Neuman, *The Lost Century of American Immigration Law (1776-1875)*, 93 COLUM. L. REV. 1833 (1993). Many of these restrictions would now be preempted by federal immigration law.

[54] *De Canas*, 424 U.S. at 356.

[55] *Id.* at 357.

[56] *Id.* at 363 (internal quotations omitted). *See also Crosby*, 530 U.S. at 373 (2000) (quoting *Hines*, 312 U.S. at 67). *De Canas* concerned a California statute that imposed sanctions on employers who hired unlawful aliens if that employment adversely affected lawful workers. When Congress added federal employer sanctions to the INA in 1986, it expressly preempted state or local laws that sanctioned employers (other than through licensing or similar laws) for hiring unauthorized workers. *See* INA § 274a(h)(2), 8 U.S.C. § 1324a(h)(2).

[57] *See, e.g.,* Florida Lime & Avocado Growers, Inc. v. Paul, 373 U.S. 132, 142 (1963) ("The principle to be derived from our decisions is that federal regulation of a field of commerce should not be deemed preemptive of state regulatory power in the absence of persuasive reasons—either that the nature of the regulated subject matter permits no other conclusion, or that the Congress has unmistakably so ordained."); Gonzales v. City of Peoria, 722 F.2d 468, 473 (9th Cir. 1983) ("The general rule is that local police are not precluded from enforcing federal statutes."), *overruled on other grounds*, Hodgers-Durgin v. de la Vina, 199 F.3d 1037 (9th Cir. 1999).

[58] *Gonzalez*, 722 F.2d at 474-75 (9th Cir. 1983). *See also* Dept. of Justice, Office of Legal Counsel, *Assistance by State and Local Police in Apprehending Illegal Aliens*, 20 Op. O.L.C. 26, 1996 WL 33101191 at *4-6 (Feb. 5, 1996) [hereinafter "1996 OLC Opinion"]; Jeff Lewis, et al., *Authority of State and Local Officers to Arrest Aliens Suspected of Civil Infractions of Federal Immigration Law*, 7 BENDER'S IMMIGRATION BULLETIN No. 15, at 944 (Aug. 1, 2002).

[59] For further discussion, see CRS Report R41423, *Authority of State and Local Police to Enforce Federal Immigration Law*, by Michael John Garcia and Kate M. Manuel.

[60] *Gonzalez*, 722 F.2d at 474-75. *See also* 1996 OLC Opinion, *supra* footnote 58, 1996 WL 33101191, at *13-*16; Lewis, *supra* footnote 58, at 944.

[61] IIRIRA, P.L. 104-208, Div. C, § 133, adding INA § 287(g), 8 U.S.C. § 1357(g).

[62] H.R. 2202, § 133 (104th Cong., 2nd Sess.) (House-passed version).

[63] Dept. of Justice, Office of Legal Counsel, *Non-preemption of the Authority of State and Local Law Enforcement Officials to Arrest Aliens for Immigration Violations*, at 8 (Apr. 3, 2002) [hereinafter "2002 OLC Opinion"]. Initially, the DOJ did not make the 2002 OLC opinion publicly available. Several immigration and public interest groups sought disclosure under the Freedom of Information Act. *See* Nat'l Council of La Raza v. Dep't of Justice, 411 F.3d 350 (2nd Cir. 2005). As a result of this litigation, the DOJ was required to release a redacted version of the opinion, which can be viewed at http://www.aclu.org/FilesPDFs/ACF27DA.pdf or http://www.fairus.org/site/DocServer/OLC_Opinion_2002.pdf?docID=1041. *See also* 1996 OLC Opinion, *supra* footnote 58, 1996 WL 33101191, at *16 ("[W]e conclude that state and local police lack recognized legal authority to stop and detain an alien solely on suspicion of civil deportability").

[64] United States v. Santana-Garcia, 264 F.3d 1188 (10th Cir. 2001); United States v. Vasquez-Alvarez, 176 F. 3d 1294 (10th Cir. 1999); United States v. Salinas-Calderon, 728 F.2d 1298 (10th Cir. 1984). *See generally* CRS Report R41423, *Authority of State and Local Police to Enforce Federal Immigration Law*, by Michael John Garcia and Kate M. Manuel.

[65] *Arizona II*, 2011 U.S. App. LEXIS 7413, at *58 ("Arizona suggests ... that it has the inherent authority to enforce federal *civil* removability without federal authorization, and therefore that the United States will not ultimately prevail on the merits. We do not agree.").

[66] 8 U.S.C. § 1373(c).

[67] The Tenth Circuit has upheld inquiries and arrests by state law enforcement officers related to suspected immigration law violations, without appearing to distinguish between violations which are civil or criminal in nature. *See, e.g., Santana-Garcia*, 264 F.3d at 1194 (state law enforcement officers have "implicit authority" within their respective jurisdictions to investigate and make arrests for violations of immigration law, even without express authorization from the state); *Vasquez-Alvarez,* 176 F.3d at 1295 (INA provision authorizing state officials to arrest and detain unlawfully present aliens who had previously been deported on criminal grounds, but only upon confirmation of aliens' illegal status with federal authorities, "does not limit or displace the preexisting general authority of state or local police officers to investigate and make arrests for violations of federal law, including immigration law"); *Salinas-Calderon*, 728 F.2d at 1301 n. 2 ("A state trooper has general investigatory authority to inquire into possible immigration violations"). For additional discussion of these opinions, see CRS Report R41423, *Authority of State and Local Police to Enforce Federal Immigration Law*, by Michael John Garcia and Kate M. Manuel. *See also* Kris W. Kobach, *The Quintessential Force Multiplier: The Inherent Authority of Local Police to Make Immigration Arrests*, 69 ALB. L. REV. 179 (2005) (discussing decisions by

the 10th Circuit and other federal courts which arguably support the authority of states and localities to make arrests for civil violations of federal immigration law).

68 *See, e.g., Gonzalez*, 722 F.2d at 476 ("[A]n intent to preclude local enforcement may be inferred where the system of federal regulation is so pervasive that no opportunity for state activity remains. We assume that the civil provisions of the [INA] regulating authorized entry, length of stay, residence status, and deportation, constitute such a pervasive regulatory scheme, as would be consistent with the exclusive federal power over immigration.").

69 H.B. 2162, § 3. Arizona law contains a few criminal offenses in which unauthorized immigration status is an element of the offense (e.g., smuggling unauthorized aliens, failing to comply with federal requirements for alien registration). Accordingly, an Arizona law enforcement officer's suspicion that a person is an unauthorized alien might be a relevant factor when assessing whether there is reasonable suspicion to stop the person for a suspected violation of state law. However, neither federal nor state law makes it a criminal offense for an alien to be unlawfully present in the United States. The fact that an officer has reasonable suspicion to believe that an alien is unlawfully present might not alone provide sufficient grounds to reasonably suspect that he has committed a criminal offense. *See infra* text accompanying footnote 177 (describing other requirements besides unauthorized status that are necessary for an alien to be criminally liable under federal alien registration law).

70 S.B. 1070, § 2.

71 *Id.*

72 *See* CRS Report R41423, *Authority of State and Local Police to Enforce Federal Immigration Law*, by Michael John Garcia and Kate M. Manuel.

73 INA § 287(g)(7)-(8), 8 U.S.C. § 1357(g)(7)-(8).

74 *See* U.S. Immigration and Customs Enforcement, Office of State and Local Coordination, *Delegation of Immigration Authority Section 287(g) Immigration and Nationality Act*, *available at* http://www.ice.gov/pi/news/factsheets/section287_g.htm#top (discussing 287(g) program and providing links to copies of agreements in force).

75 United States v. Arizona, No. CV-10-1413, Defendant's Response to Motion for Preliminary Injunction (D. Ariz. filed July 20, 2010) [hereinafter "Arizona Response"], at 14, 18 (approvingly citing the DOJ's 2002 OLC Opinion, which recognized state authority to enforce civil provisions of the INA, and arguing that immigration verification requirements contained in Section 2 of S.B. 1070 codified the state's "existing authority"), *available at* http://azgovernor.gov/dms/upload/PR_072010_USvAZDefendantsResponsePlaintiffMotion PI.pdf. *See also Arizona II*, 2011 U.S. App. LEXIS 7413, at *58 (noting Arizona's argument that it has inherent authority to enforce federal immigration statutes without express federal authorization).

76 *See supra* text accompanying footnote 67; 2002 OLC Opinion, *supra* footnote 63 , at 2-4.

77 INA § 287(g)(10), 8 U.S.C. § 1357(g)(10). However, state and local authorities engaging in immigration enforcement functions under INA § 287(g)(10) would not appear to possess the same rights and immunities as state and local authorities acting pursuant to a 287(g) agreement. *See* INA § 287(g)(7)-(8), 8 U.S.C. § 1357(g)(7)-(8) (providing that state and local authorities acting under a 287(g) agreement shall be treated as federal employees for purposes of compensation by the federal government for injuries occurring during the performance of their duties, and also stating that such persons shall be considered to be acting under color of federal law in any civil suit arising from their immigration enforcement activities).

[78] *Plaintiff's PI Motion*, *supra* footnote 3, at 51.

[79] *Arizona Complaint*, *supra* footnote 3, at 17.

[80] *Id.* at 18.

[81] *See Arizona I*, 703 F. Supp. 2d at 995-98.

[82] Arizona II, 2011 U.S. App. LEXIS 7413, at *21-*22 (emphasis in original).

[83] *Id.*, at *15-*22.

[84] *Id.* at *16-*17.

[85] *Id.* at *19. *Id.* at *18. The majority was concerned that reading INA § 287(g)(10) without reference to subsections (g)(1)-(9) would "nullify" these provisions. Specifically, the majority pointed to use of the word "removal" in subsection (g)(10)(B) as indicating that "cooperation" is generally limited to assistance under a 287(g) agreement because states and localities cannot remove aliens, only the federal government can. *Id.* at *18-*20. Apparently taking the view that the federal government must authorize state and local enforcement of federal immigration law, the majority found that INA § 287(g)(10) does not "operate as a broad alternative grant of authority" for state and local officers to enforce federal law absent a 287(g) agreement, or permit them to "adopt laws dictating how and when state and local officers *must* communicate with the Attorney General regarding the immigration status of an individual." *Id.* at *18, *20. The majority did not address the argument that states and localities have inherent authority to enforce federal immigration law in its discussion of Section 2(B), although it did in its discussion of Section 6. *See infra* footnotes 114 to 136 and accompanying text.

[86] *Arizona II*, 2011 U.S. App. LEXIS 7413, at *22-*23 (emphasis in original).

[87] *Id.* at *23.

[88] *Arizona II*, 2011 U.S. App. LEXIS 7413, at *26. The district court had also found that Section 2(B) imposed an impermissible burden upon the federal government, but its analysis focused upon the provision's effect upon federal resources. The lower court concluded that Section 2(B) would result in a large number of immigration status requests being received by federal authorities. *Arizona I*, 703 F. Supp. 2d at 995. The court characterized this increase in number as likely to impermissibly tax federal resources and "redirect federal agencies away from the priorities they have established." *Id.* at 996. The court noted, for example, that a large number of persons are "technically 'arrested' but never booked into jail or perhaps even transported to a law enforcement facility." *Id.* at 995. The court also suggested, but did not address, the possibility that the period of detention for at least some arrestees awaiting verification of their immigration status could be lengthened to such a degree as to violate the Fourth Amendment. *Id.* at 995 n.6.

[89] *See id.* at *27.

[90] 530 U.S. 363, 374 (2000).

[91] 531 U.S. 341, 349 (2001).

[92] *Arizona II*, 2011 U.S. App. LEXIS 7413, at *28.

[93] *Id.* at *24. The district court had similarly expressed concern that Section 2(B) could potentially interfere with the federal government's responsibility "to maintain international relationships, for the protection of American citizens abroad as well as to ensure uniform national foreign policy." 703 F. Supp. 2d at 997 (citing Hines v. Davidowitz, 312 U.S. 52, 62-63 (1941), and also quoting Zadvaydas v. Davis, 533 U.S. 678, 700 (2001) ("We recognize ... the Nation's need to 'speak with one voice' in immigration matters.")).

[94] *Arizona II*, 2011 U.S. App. LEXIS 7413, at *29 (quoting with added emphasis Am. Ins. Ass'n v. Garamendi, 539 U.S. 396, 420 (2003)).

[95] *Arizona II*, 2011 U.S. App. LEXIS 7413, at *30-*31.

[96] *Id.* at *34 (quoting Wis. Dep't of Indus., Labor & Human Relations v. Gould, Inc., 475 U.S. 282, 288 (1986) (internal punctuation omitted)).

[97] *Arizona II*, 2011 U.S. App. LEXIS 7413, at *75-*77 (Noonan, J., concurring).

[98] *Arizona II*, 2011 U.S. App. LEXIS 7413, at *86-*87 (Bea, J., dissent) (quoting INA § 287(g)(10)(B)).

[99] *Id.* at *115-*116 (Bea, J., dissent).

[100] *Id.* at *118-*119 (Bea, J., dissent).

[101] *Id.* at *120-*121 (Bea, J., dissent).

[102] *Arizona I*, 703 F. Supp. 2d at 997-98. When discussing these provisions, the district court also noted, but did not address, the possibility that they could result in impermissible racial profiling. *Id.* at 997 n.11.

[103] 312 U.S. 52 (1941).

[104] *Id.* at 74.

[105] Although the status verification requirements of Section 2(B) are directed towards persons suspected of being unlawfully present aliens, the district court stated that lawfully present aliens are also likely to be affected: Legal residents will certainly be swept up by this requirement, particularly when the impacts of the provisions pressuring law enforcement agencies to enforce immigration laws are considered. Certain categories of people with transitional status and foreign visitors from countries that are part of the Visa Waiver Program will not have readily available documentation of their authorization to remain in the United States, thus potentially subjecting them to arrest or detention, in addition to the burden of "the possibility of inquisitorial practices and police surveillance." *Arizona I*, 703 F. Supp. 2d at 997 (internal citations omitted).

[106] *Arizona II*, 2011 U.S. App. LEXIS 7413, at *19-*20 (noting that state and local authorities can communicate immigration status information obtained or needed in the performance of "regular state duties," so long as these duties do not entail the systematic enforcement of federal immigration law absent a 287(g) agreement).

[107] *Plaintiff's PI Motion*, *supra* footnote 3, at 25 ("Before passage of S.B. 1070, Arizona police had the same discretion to decide whether to verify immigration status during the course of a lawful stop as any other state or federal law enforcement officer.").

[108] *But see Arizona II*, 2011 U.S. App. LEXIS 7413, at *113-*114 (Bea, J., dissent) ("The internal policies of ICE do not and cannot change this result. The power to preempt lies with Congress, not with the Executive ... Otherwise, evolving changes in federal 'priorities and strategies' from year to year and from administration to administration would have the power to preempt state law, despite there being no new Congressional action.").

[109] S.B. 1070, § 2, as amended by H.B. 2162, § 3.

[110] Indeed, H.B. 2162 amended the original language of S.B. 1070 to specify that a person could bring suit against those government entities that were in violation of PRWORA and IIRIRA provisions which bar states and localities from implementing policies which restrict communication with federal authorities regarding immigration matters. H.B. 2162, § 3.

[111] *Arizona I*, 703 F. Supp. 2d at 986. In its complaint, the DOJ had suggested that this provision of S.B. 1070, acting in conjunction with the separate provision requiring law enforcement to investigate the immigration status of stopped, detained, or arrested persons suspected of being unlawfully present, would eliminate officer discretion to decline to apply S.B. 1070's provisions. *Arizona Complaint*, *supra* footnote 3, at 16-17.

[112] *Arizona I*, 703 F. Supp. 2d at 986. As originally enacted, S.B. 1070 also allowed suits challenging *practices* that limit or restrict the enforcement of federal immigration law. However, this language was deleted by H.B. 2162.

[113] *See Arizona I*, 703 F. Supp. 2d at 997.

[114] ARIZ. REV. STAT. § 13-105.

[115] Indeed, in Arizona law enforcement training materials, Section 6 is characterized as "not appear[ing] to change Arizona law." *Arizona I*, 703 F. Supp. 2d at 1004 (quoting Arizona Peace Officer Standards and Training Board, *Implementation of the 2010 Ariz. Immigration Laws - Statutory Provisions for Peace Officers*. at 11 (Jun. 2010), *available at* http://agency.azpost.gov/supporting_docs/ArizonaImmigrationStatutesOutline.pdf. Under Arizona law, state and local law enforcement were generally permitted to make warrantless arrests for public offenses when probable cause exists (and, in the case of misdemeanors, the underlying conduct was committed in the officer's presence). *Id. See also* ARIZ. REV. STAT. § 13-105(26) (defining "public offense" and "offense" synonymously), § 13-3883 (authorizing warrantless arrests for felony, misdemeanor, and traffic offenses when certain criteria are met). Even under a narrow interpretation of Section 6, it is possible that legal arguments might be raised against the provision, including its authorization of warrantless arrests of misdemeanor offenses. There may be little precedent for warrantless arrests for out-of-state misdemeanors (or for in-state misdemeanors not committed in an officer's presence) with an apparent expectation that the arrestee will be detained and deported.

[116] *Arizona II*, 2011 U.S. App. LEXIS 7413, at *55

[117] *Id.*

[118] *Id.* at *58. The dissent, however, disagreed with the majority's conclusion that AEDPA § 432 represents the "full extent" of the arrest power that Congress intended state and local officers to exercise, as well as the view that state and local officers' authority to make warrantless arrests cannot exceed that of federal officers. *Id.* at *137-*140 (Bea, J., dissent).

[119] 8 U.S.C. § 1252c.

[120] *Id.* at *57. According to the majority, this conflicts with the INA because "we are not aware of any INA provision indicating that Congress intended state and local law enforcement officers to enjoy greater authority to effectuate a warrantless arrest than federal immigration officers." *Id.*

[121] *Id.* at *58.

[122] In *Gonzales*, the Ninth Circuit had "*assume[d]* that the civil provisions of the [INA] regulating authorized entry, length of stay, residence status, and deportation, constitute such a pervasive regulatory scheme, as would be consistent with exclusive federal power over immigration." 772 F.2d 468, 475 (9th Cir. 1983) (emphasis added) (holding that federal law does not preempt state and local enforcement of the criminal provisions of the INA), *overruled on other grounds by* Hodgers-Durgin v. de la Vine, 199 F.3d 1037 (9th Cir. 1999).

[123] *Arizona II*, 2011 U.S. App. LEXIS 7413, at *60 (citing United States v. Urrieta, 520 F.3d 569 (6th Cir. 2008)).

[124] *Arizona II*, 2011 U.S. App. LEXIS 7413, at *63-67* (recognizing conflict with and expressing criticism of United States v. Vasquez-Alvarez, 176 F.3d 1294 (10th Cir. 1999)). For further discussion regarding the conflicting circuit views concerning the authority of state and local officers to enforce federal immigration law, see CRS Report R41423, *Authority of State and Local Police to Enforce Federal Immigration Law*, by Michael John Garcia and Kate M. Manuel.

[125] *Arizona II*, 2011 U.S. App. LEXIS 7413, at *67.

[126] *Id.*

[127] *Id.* at *69-*70.

[128] *Id.*

[129] *See Arizona II*, 2011 U.S. App. LEXIS 7413, at *127-*128, *132-*134 (Bea, J., dissent) (citing and discussing, *inter alia*, United States v. Di Re, 332 U.S. 581 (1948) (involving arrest by state officers of person for knowingly possessing counterfeit gasoline ration coupons, in violation of federal law); Muehler v. Mena, 544 U.S. 93 (2005) (holding that that local police officers' questioning of an individual regarding her immigration status while they searched the premises of a house she occupied for dangerous weapons did not violate the Fourth Amendment).

[130] *See Arizona II*, 2011 U.S. App. LEXIS 7413, at *136-*146 (Bea, J., dissent).

[131] *Arizona I*, 703 F. Supp. 2d at 1006.

[132] *Id.* at 1005.

[133] *Id.*

[134] *Id.* at 1006.

[135] *Id.* at 1006 n. 21.

[136] *Id.* at 1005-1006.

[137] S.B. 1070, § 5 also makes it a misdemeanor for an unlawfully present alien to knowingly apply for work, solicit work in a public place, or perform work as an employee or independent contractor in Arizona. This provision is discussed elsewhere in this report.

[138] *See, e.g., Friendly House, supra footnote 3*, at 36-39;

[139] *See* Friendly House v. Whiting, No. CV 10-1061, Order (D. Ariz., May 10, 2011) (denying without prejudice petitioner's motion for preliminary injunction of S.B. 1070's restriction on roadside hiring, and declining to consider merits of petitioner's argument pending *en banc* decision by the Ninth Circuit in another case involving roadside hiring, as this decision which would likely impact the district court's analysis of S.B. 1070).

[140] *De Canas*, 424 U.S. at 355. *See also* League of United Latin Am. Citizens v. Wilson, 908 F. Supp. 755 (C.D. Cal. 1995) (striking down portions of state measure that sought to deter unauthorized migration through various state enforcement activities, but upholding portion criminalizing the making or use of false documents to conceal the "true citizenship or resident status" of a person, because state had a legitimate interest in "criminalizing conduct that is dishonest and deceptive").

[141] Ray v. Atlantic Richfield Co., 435 U.S. 151, 157 (1978) (quoting Rice v. Santa Fe Elevator Corp., 331 U.S. 218, 230, (1947)). *But see* United States v. Locke, 529 U.S. 89, 108 (2000) ("an 'assumption' of nonpre-emption is not triggered when the State regulates in an area where there has been a history of significant federal presence").

[142] *E.g.*, Comite de Jornaleros v. City of Redondo Beach, 475 F. Supp. 2d 952 (C.D. Cal. 2006), *reversed by* 607 F.3d 1178 (9th Cir. 2010), *en banc* rehearing agreed to, 623 F.3d 1054 (9th Cir. 2010).

[143] *Arizona I*, 703 F. Supp. 2d at 1000 n.16. A month prior to the district court's ruling, the Ninth Circuit Court of Appeals had found that a provision of a city municipal code that prohibited the act of standing on a street or highway and soliciting employment, business, or contributions from occupants of vehicles constituted a valid time, place, or manner restriction upon speech, in part, because it did not "single out particular ideas for differential treatment." *City of Redondo Beach*, 607 F.3d at 1187. *See also* ACORN v. City of Phoenix, 798 F.2d 1260, 1273 (9th Cir. 1986) (upholding a municipal ordinance which provided that "[n]o person shall stand on a street or highway and solicit, or attempt to solicit, employment, business or contributions from the occupants of any vehicle").

[144] 623 F.3d 1054 (9th Cir. 2010).

[145] 8 U.S.C. § 1324. *See also* CRS Report RL34501, *Alien Smuggling: Recent Legislative Developments*, by Michael John Garcia.

[146] ARIZ. REV. STAT. § 13-2319 (2009). Although the federal alien smuggling statute also criminalizes the transport of unauthorized aliens, for liability to attach transport must be done in furtherance of an alien's unlawful presence, whereas the Arizona statute requires that the transport be done with knowledge or in reckless disregard of the alien's unlawful status and for profit or a commercial purpose. The new smuggling offense added by S.B. 1070 more closely mirrors the language of the federal statute concerning when criminal liability for alien transport attaches. Arizona is not the only state that criminalizes alien smuggling activities. *See, e.g.*, 21 OKL. ST. ANN. § 446 (2009). 147 S.B. 1070, § 5.

[148] It should be noted that although smuggling offenses under Arizona law closely resemble offenses under the federal alien smuggling statute, the substantive scope of these offenses is not wholly identical. Notable as well, Arizona state and federal district courts have interpreted the state's preexisting human smuggling statute to cover persons who conspire to smuggle *themselves* into the United States. *See* State v. Barragan-Sierra, 196 P.3d 879 (Ariz. Ct. App. 2008). *See also* We Are America/Somos America, Coalition of Arizona v. Maricopa County Bd. of Sup'rs, 594 F.Supp. 2d 1104 (D. Ariz. 2009) (rejecting field preemption challenge raised with respect to persons charged under Arizona law with conspiring to smuggle themselves), *affirmed in part and reversed in part*, 386 Fed. Appx. 726 (9th Cir. 2010).

[149] INA § 274(c), 8 U.S.C. § 1324(c) ("No officer or person shall have authority to make any arrest for a violation of any provision of this section except officers and employees of the Service designated by the Attorney General, either individually or as a member of a class, and all other officers whose duty it is to enforce criminal laws.").

[150] *See, e.g., Plaintiff's PI Motion, supra* footnote 3, at 39-41, 44-45 (arguing that smuggling provisions of S.B. 1070 constituted an impermissible regulation of immigration); State v. Flores, 188 P.3d 706 (Ariz. Ct. App. 2008) (discussing and rejecting preemption arguments raised by criminal defendants prosecuted under the 2005 smuggling statute enacted by Arizona).

[151] See, e.g., Abbate v. United States, 359 U.S. 187, 195 (1959) ("States under our federal system have the principal responsibility for defining and prosecuting crimes.").

[152] See, e.g., Flores, 188 P.3d at 711-712 (finding that "Arizona's human smuggling law furthers the legitimate state interest of attempting to curb 'the culture of lawlessness' that has arisen around this activity by a classic exercise of its police power"); Barragan-Sierra, 196 P.3d at 890 (holding that Arizona's human smuggling statute was a valid exercise of its police powers). Cf. Plyler v. Doe, 457 U.S. 202, 225 (1982) (recognizing that "States have some authority to act with respect to illegal aliens, at least where such action mirrors federal objectives and furthers a legitimate state goal").

[153] See De Canas, 424 U.S. at 357 ("[W]e will not presume that Congress, in enacting the INA, intended to oust state authority to regulate ... [employment of unauthorized aliens] in a manner consistent with pertinent federal laws. Only a demonstration that complete ouster of state power including state power to promulgate laws not in conflict with federal laws was 'the clear and manifest purpose of Congress' would justify that conclusion.").

[154] Locke, 529 U.S. at 108.

[155] Statutory proscriptions against the illegal importation of aliens into the United States can be found as far back as 1875. Act of March 3, 1875, §§ 2-4, 18 Stat. 477. The modern alien smuggling statute predates the INA, and courts have interpreted it as broadly covering many forms of assistance provided to unauthorized aliens. See generally CRS Report RL34501, Alien Smuggling: Recent Legislative Developments, by Michael John Garcia.

[156] See Maricopa County Bd. of Sup'rs, 594 F. Supp. 2d at 1111 (appearing to find that a presumption against preemption did not exist with respect to Arizona's "human smuggling" statute, but nonetheless concluding that the statute was not preempted by federal law).

[157] See De Canas, 424 U.S. at 357.

[158] Arizona I, 703 F.Supp.2d at 1004; Maricopa County Bd. of Sup'rs, 594 F. Supp. 2d at 1114; Barragan-Sierra, 196 P.3d at 890-91; Flores, 188 P.3d at 711-12.

[159] Arizona I, 703 F. Supp. 2d at 1003-1004. The court found that the government was unlikely to prevail on its argument that the challenged provision violates the Dormant Commerce Clause because, even assuming the provision has a substantial effect on interstate commerce, it does not discriminate between in-state and out-of-state economic interests. Id. at 1004. The "Dormant Commerce Clause" is the name given to the judicial doctrine which recognizes the Commerce Clause of the U.S. Constitution as having a "'negative' aspect that denies the States the power unjustifiably to discriminate against or burden the interstate flow of articles of commerce." Or. Waste Sys., Inc. v. Dep't of Envtl. Quality, 511 U.S. 93, 98 (1994). "The dormant *Commerce Clause* is implicated if state laws regulate an activity that 'has a substantial effect' on interstate commerce such that Congress could regulate the activity." Nat'l Ass'n of Optometrists & Opticians Lenscrafters, Inc. v. Brown, 567 F.3d 521, 525 (9th Cir. 2009) (emphasis in original). 160 *Arizona I*, 703 F. Supp. 2d at 1003. The government apparently abandoned its challenge to the provisions of S.B. 1070 which amended Arizona's 2005 "human smuggling" statute for purposes of its motion for a preliminary injunction. Section 4 of S.B. 1070 amends the earlier Arizona law to add that, "[n]otwithstanding any other law, in the enforcement of this section[,] a peace officer may lawfully stop any person who is operating a motor vehicle if the officer has reasonable suspicion to believe the person is in violation of any civil traffic law." In its motion requesting a preliminary injunction, the federal government sought to enjoin enforcement of Section 4, but not the underlying Arizona statute that it amended. However, its arguments before the district court focused upon the underlying Arizona statute, not Section 4, prompting the court to deny the government's motion for a preliminary injunction as to this provision. *See id.* at 1000 ("Nothing about the section standing alone warrants an injunction.").

[161] *Maricopa County Bd. of Sup'rs*, 594 F. Supp. 2d at 1111.

[162] *Id.* at 1112 (quoting *Barragan-Sierra*, 196 P.3d at 890).

[163] We Are America/Somos America, Coalition of Arizona v. Maricopa County Bd. of Sup'rs, 386 Fed. Appx. 726 (9th Cir. 2010).

[164] *Id.*

[165] *Crosby*, 530 U.S. at 373 (2000) (quoting *Hines*, 312 U.S. at 67).

[166] For example, the INA defines certain offenses as "aggravated felonies," whether committed in violation of federal or state law, including any offense *described* in the federal alien smuggling statute. *See* INA § 101(a)(43), 8 U.S.C. § 1101(a)(43). Conviction for an "aggravated felony" is a ground for deportation and also makes an alien ineligible for most forms of relief from deportation. A conviction for an offense under Arizona's "human smuggling" statute would generally appear to fall under this definition. Although the new alien smuggling statute created by S.B. 1070 only imposes a misdemeanor penalty for a first-time offense, courts have recognized that certain misdemeanors fall under the INA's definition of "aggravated felony." *See, e.g.*, Biskupski v. Attorney General of U.S., 503 F.3d 274 (3rd Cir. 2007) (holding that misdemeanor offense of federal alien smuggling statute constituted an "aggravated felony" under the INA); United States v. Gonzalez-Tamariz, 310 F.3d 1168 (9th Cir.2002) (state misdemeanor battery conviction constituted

"aggravated felony"). Misdemeanor offenses may sometimes have immigration consequences, even if they do not fall under the definition of "aggravated felony" used by the INA. *See generally* CRS Report RL32480, *Immigration Consequences of Criminal Activity*, by Michael John Garcia.

[167] *See Flores*, 188 P.3d at 707-709 (reviewing case of alien who was initially charged with having conspired to have himself smuggled into the United States in violation of Arizona's human smuggling statute, and who subsequently pled guilty to soliciting the commission of a human smuggling offense).

[168] *See* We Are America/Somos America, Coalition of Arizona v. Maricopa County Bd. of Sup'rs, No. CIV 06-2816, 2007 WL 2775134 , *6-7 (D. Ariz., Sept. 21, 2007) (court order in the *Maricopa County Bd. of Sup'rs* litigation recognizing that Arizona's human smuggling statute was consistent with federal immigration policy, and noting that federal government has discretion to mitigate some of the immigration consequences of a state conviction by exercising waiver authority over application of certain INA provisions).

[169] *See id.*; *Barragan-Sierra*, 196 P.3d at 890; *Flores*, 188 P.3d at 711.

[170] For example, a few state and federal courts have considered preemption challenges to local ordinances that bar the harboring or renting of property to unauthorized aliens. These courts have generally either concluded that the ordinances are preempted by federal immigration laws, or have enjoined enforcement of the ordinances pending trial on account of the preemption concerns they raise. *See, e.g.,* Lozano v. City of Hazleton, 620 F.3d 170 (3rd Cir. 2010) (finding that local prohibition on renting or leasing dwelling units to unauthorized aliens constituted an impermissible regulation of immigration that was preempted by federal law); Garrett v. City of Escondido, Order Granting Plaintiffs' Application For Temporary Restraining Order, 465 F. Supp. 2d 1043 (S.D. Cal. 2006) (granting temporary restraining order against local ordinance imposing civil and criminal penalties upon persons renting property to unauthorized aliens, in part because serious field preemption concerns existed because of the federal alien smuggling statute). *See also* State of New Hampshire v. Barros-Batistele, No. 05-CR-1474, 1475 (N.H. Dist. Ct. August 12, 2005), *available at* http://www.courts.state.nh.us/district/orders/criminal_trespass_decision.pdf (lower state court ruling dismissing on field preemption grounds trespassing charges against an alien on account of his suspected unlawful entry in the United States, as the regime of "offenses, sanctions and penalties" established by the INA left no room for supplemental action by the states).

[171] 8 U.S.C. § 1301. This requirement may be waived in the case of nonimmigrants entering the United States under INA §101(a)(15)(A) (ambassadors and diplomats) or INA §101(a)(15)(G) (representatives to, and officials and employees of, international organizations). INA § 221(b), 8 U.S.C. § 1201(b).

[172] 8 U.S.C. § 1302. For additional discussion regarding alien registration, see CRS Report RL31570, *Immigration: Alien Registration*, by Andorra Bruno.

[173] 8 U.S.C. § 1306(a).

[174] 8 U.S.C. § 1304(e). Accordingly, an alien who was not issued a registration certificate or card would not be in violation of this section. United States v. Mendez-Lopez, 528 F. Supp. 972 (N.D. Ok. 1981) (alien who unlawfully entered the United States and had not registered with immigration authorities was not subject to criminal penalties under INA § 264(e), because the provision attaches liability only to those persons who fail to carry an "issued" document).

[175] 8 U.S.C. § 1304(e).

[176] The only situation where unlawful presence is itself a crime is when an alien is found in the country after having been formally removed or after voluntarily departing the country while a removal order was outstanding. INA § 276, 8 U.S.C. § 1326.

[177] For example, a registered alien who overstayed his visa would not have committed a criminal offense (presuming he carried his registration with him at all times and notified immigration authorities of any change in his address), even though he was unlawfully present. Further, although all nonregistered aliens who are present in the country are required to register with the federal government, criminal liability generally only attaches if the alien *willfully* fails to apply for registration within 30 days of entry. Accordingly, an unauthorized alien present in the country less than 30 days, or who has been in the United States longer than 30 days but is unaware of alien registration requirements, would not be criminally liable. *See* I.N.S. v. Lopez-Mendoza, 468 U.S. 1032, 1056-57 (1984) (Brennan, J., dissenting) (describing some of the situations where an unauthorized alien would not have committed a criminal violation of alien registration laws). *See also* Bryan v. United States, 524 U.S. 184, 191 (1998) ("As a general matter, when used in the criminal context, a 'willful' act is one undertaken with a 'bad purpose.' In other words, in order to establish a 'willful' violation of a statute, the Government must prove that the defendant acted with knowledge that his conduct was unlawful.") (internal quotations omitted).

[178] S.B. 1070, § 3.

[179] H.B. 2162, § 4.

[180] *Arizona II*, 2011 U.S. App. LEXIS 7413, at *37.

[181] *Id.* ("By contrast, Congress provided very specific directions for state participation in [INA § 287], demonstrating that it knew how to ask for help where it wanted help; it did not do so in the registration scheme.").

[182] *Id.* at *38.

[183] *Id.*

[184] The requirements of the 1940 Act were largely incorporated into the INA. Although criminal penalties concerning failure to register were imposed by the 1940 Act, criminal penalties concerning failure to carry registration documents were added by the INA in 1952.

[185] *Hines*, 312 U.S. at 66-67.

[186] *Arizona II*, 2011 U.S. App. LEXIS 7413, at *38-*39. In the district court litigation, Arizona had argued that *Hines* only precluded states from adopting registration requirements that were substantively different from those established by federal law, and not the imposition of separate state penalties for violations of the federal registration requirements. *Arizona Response*, *supra* footnote 75, at 22. However, the district court rejected this argument because it viewed S.B. 1070 as impermissibly altering the penalties for alien registration violations that had been established by Congress. *Arizona I*, 703 F. Supp. 2d at 999. Although the court did not specify how S.B. 1070 alters the penalties for federal alien registration violations, it might have been alluding to the fact that enforcement of Arizona's alien registration law could result in the state imposing additional criminal sanctions for federal alien registration violations, separate and apart from those already imposed under federal law. Alternatively, the court might have been concerned that, as the DOJ argued, S.B. 1070 diverges from federal law by imposing the same penalty for all violations of federal registration requirements, while federal law provides for different penalties for each alien registration violation. *See Plaintiff's PI Motion*, *supra* footnote 3, at 36, n.33 ("Unlike S.B. 1070, Congress carefully calibrated and imposed different penalties for each specific alien registration violation."). The Constitution's protections against double jeopardy do not preclude prosecutions for the same acts or omissions by separate sovereigns. *See* Bartkus v.

People of State of Ill., 359 U.S. 121 (1959); United States v. Lanza, 260 U.S. 377 (1922); State v. Berry, 650 P.2d 1246 (Ariz. Ct. App. 1982) (finding that double jeopardy clauses of the Constitutions of the United States and Arizona did not bar successive prosecutions under federal and Arizona law for same conduct). At one time, Arizona barred state convictions for acts or omissions which had previously been tried by either the federal government or another state, but this statutory prohibition appears to have been eliminated. ARIZ. REV. STAT. § 13-112 (1980). Other restrictions upon dual state and federal prosecutions for alien registration violations might nonetheless still apply.

[187] *Arizona II*, 2011 U.S. App. LEXIS 7413, at *42. In his partial dissent from the majority, Judge Bea noted that he concurred with the most of the majority's reasoning regarding S.B. 1070's alien registration requirements, except for the portion which he characterized as "allow[ing] complaining foreign countries to preempt a state law." *Id.* at *86 (Bea, J., dissent).

[188] *See supra* "III. Overview of Preemption."

[189] *See* 1996 OLC Opinion, *supra* footnote 58, 1996 WL 33101191, at *3 ("absent knowledge of an established federal policy of not prosecuting such offenses, state police may, in our opinion, legally detain alien suspects for disposition by federal agents when there is reasonable suspicion that the suspects have violated or are violating the two commonplace misdemeanor provisions of the INA, 8 U.S.C. § 1304(e) (lack of alien registration documents) or § 1325 (illegal entry), or other criminal provisions of the INA"); U.S. Attorney's Criminal Resource Manual, § 1918, *Arrest of Illegal Aliens by State and Local Officers* (discussing state and local law enforcement officers' ability to make arrests for criminal offenses of the INA, including for criminal violations of the INA's alien registration requirements), *available at* http://www.justice.gov/usao/eousa/foia_reading_room/usam/title9/crm01918.htm.

[190] *See* 1996 OLC Opinion, *supra* footnote 58, 1996 WL 33101191, at *11 (interpreting Ninth Circuit's ruling in Mountain High Knitting, Inc. v. Reno, 51 F.3d 216 (9th Cir. 1995), as suggesting that state authority to arrest an alien for a criminal violation of federal registration requirements may be legally suspect if there is reason to believe that the federal government will not prosecute the offender for the violation).

[191] *Arizona II*, 2011 U.S. App. LEXIS 7413, at *42

[192] Indeed, although Judge Bea argued in partial dissent from the majority that state and local police were generally not preempted from assisting in the enforcement of federal immigration law, he nonetheless appeared to take the view that states were preempted from directly enforcing the INA's alien registration requirements. *See id.* at *122 (Bea, J., dissent) (claiming that Arizona's alien registration law "impermissibly infringes on the federal government's uniform, integrated, and comprehensive system of registration which leaves no room for its enforcement by the state.").

[193] *De Canas*, 424 U.S at 356.

[194] *Id.* at 357.

[195] The *De Canas* Court described some of the reasons why a state might legitimately act to restrict the employment of unauthorized aliens: Employment of illegal aliens in times of high unemployment deprives citizens and legally admitted aliens of jobs; acceptance by illegal aliens of jobs on substandard terms as to wages and working conditions can seriously depress wage scales and working conditions of citizens and legally admitted aliens; and employment of illegal aliens under such conditions can diminish the effectiveness of labor unions. *Id.*

[196] Hoffman Plastic Compounds, Inc. v. N.L.R.B, 535 U.S. 137, 147 (2002) (internal quotations omitted).

[197] INA § 274A; 8 U.S.C. § 1324a.

[198] INA § 274A(h)(2); 8 U.S.C. § 1324a.

[199] For further discussion, see CRS Report RL34345, *State and Local Restrictions on Employing, Renting Property to, or Providing Services for Unauthorized Aliens: Legal Issues and Recent Judicial Developments*, by Kate M. Manuel, Jody Feder, and Alison M. Smith.

[200] Ariz. H.B. 2745 (2008). Further information regarding the act, as amended, is available at http://www.azag.gov/LegalAZWorkersAct/.

[201] Chamber of Commerce v. Whiting, 2011 U.S. LEXIS 4018 (U.S., May 26, 2011).

[202] S.B. 1070, § 5. Section 5 of S.B. 1070 also makes minor modifications to the Legal Arizona Workers Act, though these amendments do not seem to immediately raise any significant issues. It also imposes penalties upon the roadside hiring of laborers. The legal implications of these penalties are discussed *supra*, at "Criminalizing the Hiring of Persons Picked Up Along Roadways."

[203] *See* INA § 274C, 8 U.S.C. § 1324c (establishing civil penalties for immigration-related document fraud); INA § 274a(b)(2), 8 U.S.C. § 1324a(b)(2) (providing that false attestations of employment eligibility are subject to penalty of perjury).

[204] National Center for Immigrants' Rights, Inc. v. I.N.S., 913 F.2d 1350 (9th Cir. 1990) *rev'd on other grounds*, 502 U.S. 183 (1991) ("While Congress initially discussed the merits of fining, detaining or adopting criminal sanctions against the *employee*, it ultimately rejected all such proposals.... Instead, it deliberately adopted sanctions with respect to the employer only .... Although some continued to argue for restraints against the employee, the approach of controlling employment through *employer* not *employee* sanctions was adjudged by Congress to provide the only realistic and appropriate solution."). *See also, e.g.,* House Jud. Comm., H.REPT. 99-682 (1986)(I), at 48 ("Employment is the magnet that attracts aliens here illegally or, in the case of nonimmigrants, leads them to accept employment in violation of their status. Employers will be deterred by the penalties in this legislation from hiring unauthorized aliens and this, in turn, will deter aliens from entering illegally or violating their status in search of employment.... Now, as in the past, the Committee remains convinced that legislation containing employer sanctions is the most humane, credible and effective way to respond to the large-scale influx of undocumented aliens.").

[205] INA § 274C, 8 U.S.C. § 1324c.

[206] For discussion of some of the potentially applicable laws, see CRS Report RL32657, *Immigration-Related Document Fraud: Overview of Civil, Criminal, and Immigration Consequences*, by Michael John Garcia.

[207] *Arizona I*, 703 F. Supp. 2d at 1000-02.

[208] *Arizona II*, 2011 U.S. App. LEXIS, at *45-*46.

[209] *Id.* at *46.

[210] *Id.* at *48-*50.

[211] *Id.* at *51.

[212] *Id.* at *51

[213] *Arizona II*, 2011 U.S. App. LEXIS, at *51-*52 (quoting *Gould*, 475 U.S. at 286).

[214] *Arizona II*, 2011 U.S. App. LEXIS, at *53 (internal citations omitted) (quoting *Crosby*, 530 U.S. at 379-80 ("[A] common end hardly neutralizes conflicting means."). In a separate opinion, Judge Bea noted that he concurred with much of the majority's analysis regarding provision, as well as its conclusion that it was likely preempted, but dissented from the portion he characterized as permitting "complaining foreign countries to preempt a state law" *Id.* at *86 (Bea, J., dissent).

[215] *Arizona II*, 2011 U.S. App. LEXIS, at *53

[216] 392 U.S. 1 (1968).

[217] *Id.* at 27.

[218] The act does not require a determination to be made when "the determination may hinder or obstruct an investigation." Further, a person is presumed not to be an unlawfully present alien if he can provide specified documentation. S.B. 1070, § 2.

[219] H.B. 2162, § 3. Prior to amendment, S.B. 1070 provided that race, color, or national origin could not be the "sole factor" considered in determining whether there was reasonable suspicion to believe a person was an unauthorized alien, except to the extent permitted by the U.S. or Arizona Constitutions. S.B. 1070, § 2.

[220] *See, e.g., Friendly House, supra* footnote 3, at 47-51.

[221] Arizona State Executive Order 2010-09, Establishing Law Enforcement Training for Immigration Laws, Apr. 23, 2010, *available at* http://www.azgovernor.gov/dms/ upload/ EO_201009.pdf.

[222] *Compare* United States v. Brignoni-Ponce, 422 U.S. 873 (1975) (ruling unconstitutional a roving stop of a vehicle by the Border Patrol near the U.S.-Mexican border, when the stop was based solely on the vehicle occupant's apparent Mexican ancestry) *with* United States v. Martinez-Fuerte, 428 U.S. 543 (1976) (permitting the stopping of persons at fixed inspection checkpoints near the Mexican border when such stops were partially based on race).

[223] *Martinez-Fuerte*, 428 U.S. at 563, n.17.

[224] United States v. Montero-Camargo, 208 F.3d 1122, 1132 (9th Cir. 2000).

INDEX

D

E

F

G

H

I

J

L

M

N

O

P

Q

R

S